Nineties to Now

Nineties to Now

The Evolution of American Popular Culture

MATTHEW MCKEEVER

McFarland & Company, Inc., Publishers
Jefferson, North Carolina

This book has undergone peer review.

ISBN (print) 978-1-4766-8206-8
ISBN (ebook) 978-1-4766-4392-2

LIBRARY OF CONGRESS AND BRITISH LIBRARY
CATALOGUING DATA ARE AVAILABLE

Library of Congress Control Number 2021042591

© 2021 Matthew McKeever. All rights reserved

No part of this book may be reproduced or transmitted in any form or by any means, electronic or mechanical, including photocopying or recording, or by any information storage and retrieval system, without permission in writing from the publisher.

Front cover image © 2021 elenabsl/Shutterstock

Printed in the United States of America

*McFarland & Company, Inc., Publishers
Box 611, Jefferson, North Carolina 28640
www.mcfarlandpub.com*

To John
and to Liz

Acknowledgments

I owe a great debt to an anonymous reader for McFarland, who marked up the manuscript with detailed, helpful, challenging, and encouraging comments. In the unlikely event that they look at this book alongside their marked-up draft, they will see I have made many changes, big and small, in response to their comments. Similarly, I thank reader two, all of whose changes I implemented.

Next, both Datri Bean and Caitlín Nic Íomhair read big chunks of a near-final version and provided helpful written comments; discussions with them about the structure of the book were very helpful. It's a cliché to point out that any errors remaining are the author's, but it's true, especially in this case.

John McKeever helped with copyediting of draft two and Ravi Thakral helped with the final draft, and I thank them too. Finally, I am grateful to Dré Person and the whole team at McFarland for being a pleasure to work with throughout and helping see this book through the process.

Personally, I thank my mother, Liz McKeever, while living with whom I wrote the first and last drafts, and the rest of my family—Caitlín and John and Mikey. I wrote the second draft and made some breakthroughs while traveling round Europe with Datri, who also tolerated with good grace my frequent complaining about having to write, so I thank her too.

Table of Contents

Acknowledgments — vi
Preface — 1
Introduction — 5

1. Generation X and Nostalgia — 11
2. Explainer: The Economics of 1946–1974 — 19
3. Lynch and Tarantino — 31
4. Explainer: Postmodernism — 46
5. *Seinfeld* — 59
6. Explainer: Branding — 68
7. _____, Race, Gender and Representation — 74

Interlude: The 90s in Ten Events — 91

8. *The Simpsons* — 97
9. Explainer: The Media and Recent American History — 114
10. David Foster Wallace as Religious Poet — 123
11. Explainer: Psychiatry — 132
12. And Then … 9/11, the Financial Crisis, the iPhone, Trump — 139
13. Pop Culture Today — 158

Chapter Notes — 187
Bibliography — 191
Index — 195

Preface

As the close past recedes further from view it becomes clearer: distance brings focus. It does so for at least two reasons: new scholarship teaches us things about the period we didn't know even a decade earlier, and new art, either by continuing or by breaking with the style of the historical period, signals similarities and discontinuities between then and now.

This clearer view of the past brings with it a clearer view of the present. If we want to understand what's distinctive about today, we need to look back to see what the difference is between today and yesterday. An era—perhaps anything—can only be understood for what it is when compared with what it is not.

And we surely do want to understand what's distinctive about now. With the presidency of Trump, with Europe fraying, with lives lived to a large extent online, with mental illness rates skyrocketing, with young people one of the first generations for a long time worse off than their parents, the question asks itself: Why this? How did we get here?

It's doubtful anybody could answer this question definitively and to everyone's satisfaction. Nevertheless, I want to present *one* story of the close past and how it became the present. I will do so by looking in detail at selected works of U.S. art of the 1990s, and their ideological and historical background, and attempting to give a unique analysis of them. And then I'll use that analysis to try to gain a clearer view of the present, of what is unique about life as we move into the third decade of the 21st century. With the 30th anniversary of 1990 and the 20th of 2000 just passed, we have reached the time where we are distanced enough to look with outsiders' ideas but close enough to still feel at home—it is a fitting time for such a study.

I'm not the first to have realized this, and this book follows roughly in the tradition of at least two different sorts of books. There are more or less popular works of what we could call roughly the social history of

Preface

decades, which attempt to paint a portrait of an era to help us understand the time in which it was written (for the 1990s, the relevant book is Telly Davidson's 2016 *Culture War*; we will discuss books for other eras in passing). And there are more scholarly works which focus on philosophical or intellectual and artistic features of a period (some relevant books here are, respectively, James Livingstone's 2016 *The World Turned Inside Out: American Thought and Culture at the End of the 20th Century* and Colin Harrison's 2010 *American Culture in the 90s*).

The present book falls, I think, somewhere in between these two genres in many respects, but is distinguished in at least one important way. A central theme of this book concerns the *evolution of culture*. Other books can tell you what is special about the art or thought of the period (I think the second class of books mentioned does so). And other books can draw comparisons between today and the past. I want to do both these things, as well as explain how it is that cultural difference arises. If a feature is present in 1990s culture and absent in 2010s culture, can we explain the disappearance? If a feature is present in 1990s culture and *also* present in 2010s culture, can we explain the continuity? This book attempts to provide general answers to these questions. It attempts to explain, for example, why contemporary literary fiction, or the contemporary sitcom, is considerably more straight than its 90s ancestors. *The Simpsons* is zany and postmodern, playing with form and style; the virtue of *Brooklyn Nine-Nine* is simply that it's funny. The same applies to David Foster Wallace's postmodern novels and Sally Rooney's wildly popular comedies of manners. What explains these stylistic differences? Bill Hicks's comedy is replete with absurd scatological political humor; so is the popular podcast *Chapo Trap House*. What explains this continuity? That is to say, what explains the differences and similarities between seminal works of 90s pop culture and seminal works of the culture of the 2010s?

In the first part of the book, I look at 90s culture, alternating chapters on a given work of art with chapters explaining relevant social, intellectual, and political background. I then briefly survey the epochal first decade of the new millennium before looking in detail at life today. On a completely different topic, I will throughout write "90s" instead of the slightly more correct "'90s" (or "nineties") in the same way we write "phone" instead of "'phone." I will also use "90s" adjectivally as in "90s culture." This is purely for aesthetic reasons—too many apostrophes dotting the page strikes me as unpleasant. I also will

Preface

mostly throughout use "internet" to mean something like world wide web, or even what others might call "web 2.0." Again, this is purely stylistic.

As a perusal of the table of contents indicates, this book is quite exclusionary. There are many extremely popular works of pop culture which I don't discuss. There is no *Jurassic Park* or *Friends* here, for example. More concerningly, the vast majority of the voices considered here are those of straight white men. That, you might think, is simply no good in 2021.

I agree, as will become clear later. The reason I discuss the artists I discuss is because I think I have a story to tell about them and contemporary art and culture, in a way that I don't think I have such a story to tell for the above works, or for *And the Band Played On*, or for, say, Toni Morrison's *Beloved*, or even for *Sex and the City*. That's not to say there isn't such a story—just that I don't know what it is.

Of course, part of the reason for that, for my ignorance here, is the culture I was brought up on. For me as a teenager in a smallish town in Northern Ireland in the 90s, *The Simpsons* and *Pulp Fiction* were hard to miss, *Beloved* easy to miss. As a young adult, I was more drawn to the postmodern zaniness of David Foster Wallace or the surrealism of Lynch than stories of racism and homophobia and the institutions that further them.

Maybe this is a bad feature of the society in which I grew up, or even a bad reflection on my character. But it is also true that there is value to attending to the works I discuss. I hope that I will succeed in showing that there is, and that even though what follows is just one slanted perspective, from a particular place in space and time and society, it is a useful perspective that will further our understanding of life today and life in the recent past.

But more importantly, even if this book is overly populated with white males, a central concern of it is nevertheless precisely why this is so—why, when telling the story of the 90s, does it seem just about acceptable to only focus on one such demographic? That is to say, why is *Seinfeld* all white? Why do *The Simpsons* and the work of Lynch hearken back to the 50s, an era before the Civil Rights Act? Where are the powerful women in 1990s culture?

That is to say, one of the central concerns of this book is the *absence* of these other voices, and a central part of the theory developed below is that this absence is itself a key feature of 90s culture that calls out for explanation, and I will suggest an answer. So, at the risk of being

Preface

needlessly paradoxical, the absence of such voices in fact is a big presence in this book.

One more thing about the range and ambitions of this book. Readers of earlier drafts of this book felt that in addition to excluding material that perhaps ought to have been included, I included too much information not strictly relevant to my argument. In Chapter 2, for example, I go quite deep into the weeds of 20th-century economic history to present material far removed from 90s pop culture; in a later chapter, I recount events like Watergate and the Iraq War. But this is intentional. One of the aims of the book is to function as a sort of *vade mecum*, a mini-encyclopedia of important facts about the social world of the 90s (and later) that aren't collected elsewhere in a single volume. This risks superficiality, but I hope that the references I provide will help those who want to learn more, and I encourage those who find these discussions to be old news to simply skip them.

The optimistic author hopes that most of their readers will be younger than they are, and so do I, and so I write for one for whom this book might be the first glimpse into this recent past, with the belief that that past can only be understood when viewed through as many lenses as possible, and in the hope that I've managed to provide some of those lenses.

Introduction

What is it like to live today? To be the first era to rely on the internet for work, socializing, dating, money, entertainment, and more? To have no long-term prospects of jobs, to be priced out of the housing market, harangued by ironic kekking Nazis, presided over by Trump and part of an economy that, for many of us, hasn't done much for 40 years except increase inequality?

The Germans have a nice word for what I'm looking for—Zeitgeist, or spirit of the age. What is the spirit of our age? What does living in such a world do to us; how does what it does to us get reflected in the art we produce, the way we communicate, the lives we lead? What is particular and *new* about our experience?

These are the big questions I hope to answer or at least to ask properly in this book. I hope to do so by what might seem initially like a somewhat roundabout way: by considering, in detail, what it *was* like to live yesterday, and in particular to live in the last pre-internet culture, the era of Generation X (and some older millennials, including your author), the 1990s. The thought underlying this is twofold. We can only understand the present if we understand the past, because only then can we see what's *unique* to the present. To put it in a simple and perhaps simplistic way: what's unique to the present is what we get when we subtract from the sum total of present things those which were already there in the past. As we'll see, income inequality, precarity, irony—these all are features of the 1990s social-cultural-political-economic scene. Indeed, I will argue that much of what we take as definitive of our age was already around then and will present a history of these big concepts—how income inequality arose from neoliberal economics starting in the early 70s, how precarity arose with the branding revolution of the late 80s, how irony and detachment arose as a result of political scandal and the omnipresence of the media. We'll come to see that some of the things we think of as definitive of our age aren't, in fact, so.

Introduction

This can be helpful. If we see how, for example, the great creators—and there are, undoubtedly, a range of great artists in the 1990s—responded to these situations, we can maybe correct for blind spots in our own understanding of them. Moreover, we can then trace the *development* of the thing in question, of irony, for example, and thus not only say what, but ask why. We can try to trace the development of irony from works like *Seinfeld* and *The Simpsons* through the so-called "new sincerity" in the work of people like David Foster Wallace and up to the present day. The hope is we can understand *why* some young people support Donald Trump, or why memes are a popular way for well-educated people to communicate political opinions today.

The 1990s are the perfect period to study for this. It presents to us a neoliberal society in many ways similar to ours but separated by the era-defining disruptions of the early noughties: 9/11, the mainstreaming of the internet, and the financial crisis of 2008. This period is thus simultaneously close and far. Its closeness allows a vantage point for understanding our present, and its distance provides a reference for how things have changed.

Generation X also has another advantage thanks to their place in time. To see this, recall some basic points of history, to be considered in more detail later: in the 50s and 60s, America was perhaps the greatest powerful economy the world has ever seen, it was, at least when squinted at, something to be proud of, and it was more economically equal than it's ever been before or since. From 1974, things politically and economically collapsed: it was the year of Watergate (see Chapter 9) and an oil crisis that caused wages to fall. This collapse spurred conservative economic theory by seemingly falsifying a key feature of the opposing economic view (stagflation—see Chapter 2), which in turn paved the way for Reaganomics, and the massive inequality that has been our lot for the past 30–40 years. Things didn't improve: we went from the folksy, quick-witted, and cruel Reagan to Clinton, who claimed to feel people's pain but who made the poor poorer, freed the banks from regulation, and who was never far from career-ruining sex scandals.

By contrast, if 1974 marked a sociopolitical nadir, around 1970 marked what might be thought of as a moral acme, or at least a local maximum. Around these years—give or take—occurred the Stonewall riots, *Roe v. Wade*, the submission of the Equal Rights Amendment for ratification, the enshrining of the right even for minors to use contraception, while a few years before, the Civil Rights Act and the Voting Rights Act were passed (see Chapter 7 for detailed discussion).

Introduction

The key point is this. In many ways, an adult of the 1990s lived in a world like ours—economically and politically bad, with things being more hopeful for formerly marginalized groups. But unlike for the average young adult of today, for them there was something entirely different on the edge of past time. They could remember, or almost remember, or at least had definitely been reared by, people who lived through a time before things changed so dramatically. They were thus well placed to analyze neoliberal society, because they had something to compare it to, and this gap, and the nostalgia it generates is, I suggest, one main cause of the cynicism or disaffectedness or ironic distance people tend to associate with the 90s, a fact only compounded by the political and economic developments of the Clintonian third-way Democrats, which seemed, at least initially, to further show the supremacy of neoliberalism (the seemingly anti–Keynesian recovery from the crisis of the early 90s) but also its inherent cruelty and unfairness (the welfare reforms of 1996, the banking deregulation of 1999, all of which will be discussed in a later chapter).

It's different for the young adults of today. For most of us, the pre–1974 era of prosperity and equality (prosperity and equality provided one were white and male and straight and middle-class, which must always be borne in mind) belongs to history. All young people know is neoliberalism, and so they have nothing to compare our current state with: the past is more of the same, and we have never not lived in a world where inequality predominates, where things are patently *unfair*. This is a disadvantage: having no different past in view, the distinctness of the present becomes obscure. Generation X had this advantage; and I hope by attending to its culture, we can come to possess it too.

There's a related point. The 90s were an era of relative stability. Someone looking back to 1983 from 2000 would see, certainly, a different world in many respects, but there would also be a clear sense of continuity. By contrast, if you consider the last 20 or so years, there have been so many big events that it can be hard to incorporate them into a coherent picture. One might think that we're in an era that can only be explained by pointing to the exogenous shocks to our political, economic, and cultural system that the noughties brought. And this leads, in a way similar to that just mentioned, to adopting an ahistorical viewpoint. But again, this is to miss out some important things. When faced with the prevalence of precarious employment, we might try to say it's just an aftereffect of the crash; by pulling back a bit, though, we can see that it isn't.

Introduction

Because of all this, I think the artists of the 90s perceive more clearly than we do the weirdnesses of neoliberal society, and I intend to show how they do so in the course of the book, and hopefully thereby make those weirdnesses fresh to us.

Let me take an example, to be discussed at much more length later. A brand is a strange thing. It's the driving force of our economy, but it is, almost literally, a distinction without a difference. Set a Nike shoe and a generic one, or Coca-Cola and a generic soda next to each other; there's very little difference between the two products: bits of material or combinations of chemicals, one of which has a tick on it or comes in a red can, and the other of which doesn't.

We are somewhat numb to this presence of brands, in a way that the 90s from the book *Generation X* at the start of the decade to *The Simpsons* (floruit c. 1995) to *Fight Club* at its end were not. Trying to tell someone of my generation about the wickedness of brands is likely to receive a sarcastic "yeah yeah, Tyler Durden" or "how profound, Melanie Klein." It's cliché to get worked up about them.

But that's a mistake on our part. Branding is weird, and we should not be blind to it. Moreover, recognizing this weirdness, we can look again at features of our own existence to understand them better. As we will see, branding has a sort of inverse—if as a company it's really the brand which is selling the product, the stuff that goes into making it—the fabric, the factories, and, crucially, the workers—become less important. This leads to companies attempting to dephysicalize themselves—to get rid of the physical trappings, both the marginal and fixed costs that make business expensive. And so we see outsourcing, casualization, temp work, and so on. But we also see things like Uber and Airbnb, cornerstones of many young people's daily lives today. Just as Nike is a shoe company that doesn't spend so much time and attention on its shoes, so Uber is a transportation company that doesn't own vehicles or have employees, and Airbnb an accommodation company that doesn't own property or pay hoteliers. We live in an age in which what we'll later call the logic of the brand has further developed, but the key point is this isn't new—it's something that was already around in the 1990s and the object of a lot of attention.

Thinking about 90s work then can get us to focus on the ubiquity of brands, and once we're thus focused we can see what brands are now, how they've developed, and how others look at them, and thus can make this piece of our social reality a bit clearer.

I will do this for a range of different phenomena. One of the most

Introduction

baffling features of contemporary society is the widespread use of a very confusing irony, exhibited by Pepe-wielding Donald Trump followers on Reddit, or again by leftists on Twitter who use scatological humor to respond to the latest right-wing enormity. What's the root of this insincere, distanced, mocking attitude? I will attempt to answer this by looking at the great comedies of the 90s, such as *The Simpsons* and *Seinfeld*.

Or, think again about the widely recognized epidemic of mental illness and, especially in the U.S., drug addiction. This is a central concern of, to my mind, the most interesting popular writer of the decade, David Foster Wallace. His work can be seen, I'll claim, as an attempt to make sense of such illness, to give it a meaning beyond the neurobiological picture, now widely accepted by most all of us, that it's a question of neurochemical imbalances correctible by drugs. And I'll claim it retains its force to do so because the concept of mental illness, as I'll show, hadn't become completely mainstream by then—it was the decade of Prozac, but it hadn't yet become received wisdom. We, however, are in danger of being blinded by the received wisdom (which, as we'll see, is based on very bad science), and I'll ask what that does to our conceptions of ourselves to think that way, to have always a few clicks away a Wikipedia or the DSM to pathologize ourselves with. Similarly, I'll look at claims that the internet has had a specially pernicious effect on the mental health of young people and make the point (not original to me, but presented from a different angle here) that, when historicized correctly, this claim loses some of its appeal.

So that's the plan—look at some works of art and their ideological context, both for their own sake but also the better to understand our own times. To this end, the book consists mostly of alternating chapters, the first of which analyses a work of art, and the second of which describes various important ideas, in economics, politics, philosophy, business, neurochemistry, and so on.

Having discussed the art and ideological background of the 90s in depth in the first roughly two-thirds of the book, I will then move forward in time to the Big Events of the first decade of the new millennium which might seem to define and mark off our era as distinctively new, and see how they affect the big ideas we introduced. And then I'll look at how art has changed, and what picture of life today we get from contemporary pop culture.

Before getting down to that, though, I want to reiterate an important point from the preface. Although this book is mostly concerned, at least in its discussion of 90s culture, with white male culture, that it

Introduction

not from some chauvinist prejudice. It seems hard to deny that, if one is asked to list the top comedies of the decade, *Seinfeld* and *The Simpsons*, both almost entirely white male affairs, will quickly come to mind. But at the same time, if asked to list the top comedies of recent times, people will mention things like *Brooklyn Nine-Nine* or *Fleabag*. In these newer shows, white male dominance is much less pronounced. At the same time, as we'll see, the historical underpinnings that made life better for woman and people of color began to happen around the 70s, with things like *Roe v. Wade* and the (earlier) Civil Rights Act. So a question arises: in light of the history, why was 90s culture still so dominated by white male voices, and what has caused things to change (if indeed they have)? In order to answer that, I think one needs to investigate those white-dominated shows themselves, and so for that reason—in addition to their inherent quality—I think that the following study has value even for one who deplores the comparative absence of diversity in the works discussed. If the reader remains unconvinced by this promissory note, I suggest skimming forward to Chapter 7 first, where the argument of this paragraph is made at much greater length.

1

Generation X and Nostalgia

On February 28, 1991, the Gulf War ended. This was a war waged by the United States when Iraq's ruler Saddam Hussein invaded Kuwait, and the first war to be broadcast round the clock on TV. Watching rolling news channels, viewers could hear news anchors praise the technical prowess of the rockets as they watched them destroy foreign cities, and do so (those same viewers might think) in order to protect American oil interests or, even more cynically, to increase America's faith and confidence in the concept of war itself which had been bruised post–Vietnam.[1]

Into such a world—depressing, media saturated, and politically alienated—was released Canadian writer Douglas Coupland's *Generation X* (March 1991). If you haven't heard of the book, you've probably heard of the term: Generation X are those born after the boomers but before the millennials, so roughly from the mid–60s to early 80s (for more on the idea of generations, see Strauss and Howe *Generations*, 1991, which, incidentally, gave us the term "millennials"). Coupland's book was intending to give a voice to the children of the boomers born after the war, and I think that studying it will give us a better sense of Generation X's millennial followers.

With that said, let's turn to the book which gave the generation its name. It was popular: by 1995, it had sold nearly 400,000 copies,[2] which, it is fair to say, is pretty good for non-genre fiction.

Coupland was lauded as a voice for a generation and his novel holds up, 26 years on, as an account of the life of one who grew up in the 1980s and facing the 90s. In particular it holds up because it presents the lives of people less desensitized than we are to some of the weird features of what some call "postindustrial" or "neoliberal" capitalism, to be discussed a bit more in the next chapter, from whose viewpoint we can learn things important for our lives.

Nineties to Now

There isn't that much of a plot. It's about three friends, Andy (who narrates), Dag, and Claire, who live in Palm Springs, a town where rich people "come to buy back their youth" (*Generation X*, p. 12) where the protagonist's dogs, on the second page, get their snouts in a bag of fat removed by liposuction, where "gray hair gobble[s] up the jewels and perfumes" (p. 11) at one of the protagonists' work, and where there is "no weather ... also no middle class" (p. 12). There is just the affluent and those whom they serve in a society clearly warped by financial inequality.

They have come here to work jobs that are beneath them, what Coupland calls, in one of the book's many coinages, "McJobs," that is a "low-pay, low-prestige, low-dignity, low-benefit, no-future job in the service sector" (p. 6) which were, indeed, when he was writing, a central prop of the economy, escaping work in soul-destroying office jobs among yuppies of the sort that would be satirized in Mike Judge's still highly watchable *Office Space* of 1999.

Out here, in the desert which in a microcosm is what the whole U.S. was and still is becoming—an artificial (deserts aren't meant for humans, fat isn't meant to be sloughed off by machines), unequal world—they spend their lives telling stories, some real and some surreal, about their lives or loosely allegorized versions thereof. From the very beginning—the whole book is very readable, but if you want to quickly get at its pith, the first chapter is representative—there's a sense of disappointment, a sense that they are missing out. His friends' smiles

> are the same as the smiles worn by people who have been good-naturedly fleeced, but fleeced nonetheless, in public and on a New York sidewalk by card-sharks, and who are unable because of social convention to show their anger, who don't want to look like poor sports [p. 8].

These are people belonging to a generation who feel *shortchanged*. And this is the first thing I want to focus on. To feel shortchanged or cheated is to feel that you have less than you deserve. The protagonists of *Generation X* feel that way for two reasons: the presence in their lives of the older generation, and memory.

The former is revealed in their work and in particular by the presence of their luckily successful bosses. The following, from when Dag storms out of his job, could be spoken today:

> Do you really think we *enjoy* hearing about your brand-new million-dollar home when we can barely afford to eat Kraft Dinner sandwiches in our grimy little show boxes and we're pushing *thirty*? A home you won in a genetic

1. Generation X and Nostalgia

lottery, I might add, sheerly by dint of your having been born at the right time in history? You'd last about ten minutes if you were my age.... I have to endure pinheads like you rusting about me for the rest of my life, always grabbing the best piece of cake first and then putting a barbed-wire fence around the rest [p. 26].

But if this is a reaction most young people today can immediately recognize, the protagonists' *reaction* to this state of affairs is markedly and importantly different to ours. While we look to the future and the hope that someone can wrestle politics away from its domination by money and the moneyed, or perhaps to universal basic income or "fully automated luxury communism,"[3] they look to the past. Because the adults of the era have an advantage or a disadvantage over the young adults of today: they can see, beyond in the past, something different. That is, they are *nostalgic*. Millennials aren't nostalgic (they have nothing to be nostalgic for) and that's a major difference between the art of the 90s and that of today, for good and for bad, as we'll see repeatedly.

Let's consider some examples of nostalgia in the book. Ostensibly a frame narrative, it consists mostly of the stories the protagonists tell to each other before or after working shifts at their McJobs. There's the story about Texlahoma, for example, the planet stuck perennially in 1974. Andy tells it on a picnic in a ghost town of which you get the impression that in "1958, Buddy Hackett, Joey Bishop, and a bunch of Vegas entertainers all banded together to make a bundle on this place" (p. 17), but it failed and now all it has are some windmills which "power detox air conditioners and cellulite vacuums of the region's burgeoning cosmetic surgery industry" (pp. 117–18). That is, they tell a story about being stuck in 1974, the year when things started getting bad, about a town that got stuck around 1958, when they would have been good.

Moreover, the novel ends as they cross the border, looking to make a new life in Mexico, "a newer, less-monied world, where a different food chain carves its host landscape in alien ways I can scarcely comprehend ... [once across the border] automobile models will mysteriously end around the decidedly Texlahoman year of 1974" (pp. 199–200).

So 1974—that's twice it's occurred. Coupland tells us explicitly what's important about that year: it's "the year after the oil shock and the year from which real wages in the U.S. never ever grew again." We will say a bit more about the economic background in the next chapter, and in general 1974 will function as something like a hinge year in my narrative—it's the last time before things got messed up not only economically but also politically (Watergate), but also when things seemed full of progress morally for marginalized groups.

That, then, is the first dominant theme I want to pick up—nostalgia, and a closely aligned sense of being cheated, of being swindled out of something which one deserves. The Generation X-ers look back to a time, a time of capitalism triumphant for all, when there were chances for most, and a car, a house, and so on came along with a steady job.

(A brief digression: if nostalgia was a central feature of 90s culture—and undoubtedly it was—it isn't a *uniquely* defining feature of it. As David Sirota, in a book that covers similar ground for the 80s as this does for the 90s [*Back to Our Future*, Ballantine, 2011], points out, nostalgia was already a cultural force in the 1980s. For example, 1985's top-grossing movie, the still fondly remembered *Back to the Future*, tells the story of a boy who goes back in time to 1955; *Happy Days*, which ended in 1984, presented life in the 50s and 60s. Retromania can even be seen in the choice of Reagan as president, who was still acting into the 50s and who seemed to represent the golden age of America before things got ugly in the 1970s. In general, I think this is arguable: cultures are always to some extent nostalgic. But this doesn't affect my point, because I will be concerned not just about the surface fact but what about this particular 1990s nostalgia for this particular [pre–1974] period has to tell us.)

It's worth taking a step back, or rather a step forward, at this point, and asking ourselves whether the nostalgic vision of the book is something we should seek. Should we pine for an era of fairer capitalism, or seek something new? As we think, in 2021, post–Trump (I'm thinking wishfully here) et al. of what our vision of the future should be, should it be that—should we look to re-create the 50s and 60s, albeit one in which the social inequalities then rampant were resolved? That seems what a lot of us are de facto doing, in supporting people like Bernie Sanders whose overall goals, as has been pointed out, aren't exactly radical: a decent safety net and some provision for social care.[4] Should that be our goal?

Maybe not. Perhaps we have an advantage over Generation X in not being lured by the promise of a fair capitalism on the edge of memory, and perhaps we can or should use that fact to think about alternative ways to live (indeed, that is precisely what the books like Bastani's [an influential figure in UK leftist media] mentioned in the previous endnote attempt to do). I'll later consider to what extent, if any, we see such

1. Generation X and Nostalgia

possibilities realized in the art of our era, and to what extent they rely on nostalgia.

The second theme from *Generation X* I want to focus on is consumerism, and in particular being offended by consumerism. This is one aspect which, I think, marks a crucial difference between us and them. They remain alive to the ridiculousness of capitalism in a way that we can sometimes fail to. We'll see, in the explainer in Chapter 6, why this is so: they were living through a time in which the rise of megabrands and billion-dollar advertising budgets was new, or at least had recently become gaudier and more central to all aspects of life, but for now let's just look at the text.

Here are some examples of what I mean. There are a lot of passages like the following, where the narrator is about to storm of out his job:

> God, Margaret. You really have to wonder why we even bother to get *up* in the morning. I mean, really: *Why work*? Simply to buy *more stuff*? What makes us *de*serve the ice cream and running shoes and wool Italian suits we have? I see all of us trying so hard to acquire so much stuff but I can't help but feel that we didn't merit it [p. 28, all italics in original].

Or like

> You mean to tell me we can drive all the way here from L.A. and see maybe ten thousand square miles of shopping malls, and you don't have maybe the *weentsiest* inkling that something, somewhere, has gone *very very* cuckoo? [p. 69].

Or like

> Otis got to thinking: Hey! these aren't houses at all—*these are malls in disguise* ... Otis developed the shopping mall correlation: kitchens became the Food Fair; living rooms the Fun center; the bathroom the Water Park. Otis said to himself, "God, what goes through the *minds* of people who live in these things—are they shopping?" [p. 80].

For a reader living today, it can be quite hard to *feel* this sentiment. But it wasn't for a previous generation, a generation whose movies blended in a hallucinatory style extreme consumption and extreme violence (*American Psycho* [2000], based on Bret Easton Ellis's same-named 1991 novel; *Fight Club* [1991], based on the 1996 Chuck Palahniuk novel); whose popular nonfiction lifted the lid on the fake world of fast food, a world where the aroma of a grilled hamburger or sautéed onions was made in a laboratory by chemists (*Fast Food Nation*, Eric Schlosser, 2001, p. 129).

For the typical millennial, this is old hat. But let's at least try to see these cultural productions with less jaded eyes in case it can help us understand ourselves. I again run the risk of sounding trite, but consider the following. In the 1980s and early 90s, gadgets and shoes made money. What makes money now? Well, to a large extent, ads. But what gets people to look at ads? Well, to a large extent, *we* do.

It sounds already trite, but there is a good case to be made for the claim that we, literally, are products on social media. We are what is given, in the sense that without our activity, the ads which make companies money (allegedly) wouldn't get sold. And given that, we might think about whether this being made into products affects us. While we maybe don't need these works of art to provoke such reflections, I do think it's troublesome that our popular art today to a large extent seems to ignore such questions.

The third thing I want to talk about is the *mood* of *Generation X*. I've already said something: it's disappointment. But it's more than that. It's a very melancholy book infused with a sense of "inevitable 'what-am-I-going-to-do-with-my-life?' semiclinical depression" (p. 82). Or again it's a sort of numbness (it's interesting to note that the book contains almost no sex, suggestive of the low libido of one on antidepressants, or perhaps because as a male writer coming after Mailer and Roth and Updike [albeit one both Canadian and gay, and writing about straight people], it just felt done to absolute death, and seldom well). As we progress through the generation, the mood gradually changes, and from elegiac sadness turns to cynicism, depression, and anger.

But it's important to realize that this is a much *less* cynical book than one might imagine. It has no problem whatsoever expressing non-ironically the genuine feeling the characters have for one another. The characters love each other, they are there for each other, and in their friendship life gets its meaning. And it could be that that—the warmth of feeling that suffuses the novel—is related to the fact that they've *seen* something beyond. This again ties in with the nostalgia. The most sentiment-full section of the book is perhaps when they discuss "some small moment from your life that *proves you're really alive*" (p. 105); they all give moments from their childhood. A time (1974, incidentally) when Dag is filling up his father's gas tank and accidentally spills it everywhere and is scared he's going to get into trouble but doesn't and his father says, "Hey, Sport. Isn't the smell of gasoline great? Close your eyes and inhale. So *clean*. It smells like the *future*," and Dag does so and closes his eyes and sees "the big orange light of the sun coming through my eyelids" (pp. 107–8) and feels happy; for another it's a spontaneous

1. Generation X and Nostalgia

family breakfast where she is "so close to tears, listening to everyone make jokes and feeding the dog bits of egg [and] feeling homesick for the event while it was happening" (p. 108). We might note that "nostalgia" is roughly Greek for homesickness.

As we will see, this sort of sentiment goes somewhat against the grain of what we think of as echt-90s, in particular things like *Seinfeld*, the films of Tarantino, and *The Simpsons*, in which referential playfulness and emotional coldness predominate.

It's this that gives the book its heart and causes it to have aged quite well. Not only is there a mordant awareness of the disappointment of modern life, but there is a sensibility still alive enough to register that disappointment, to really feel it, as opposed to just sardonically noting it. This is, I think, a distinct point in our phenomenology of the Zeitgeist. As we progress, the awareness, a deep consciousness of the messes of society, won't go, but the vision of beyond will gradually, with some notable exceptions, dissipate.

For now, though, I want to focus on the awareness. Because I think with it we have something truly distinctive of the modern era: the advent of a generation with an extremely high level of intellectual development but with an extremely low level of socioeconomic development. People with a lot of learning in their brain but with little money in their bank account. The people of *Generation X* read Camus and have copies of the *Frankfurter Allgemeine Zeitung* on their tables. They understand the extent to which they exploit and are exploited and the complex interconnectedness of modern life, and they are able to pronounce wittily on it:

> I work from 8 to 5 in front of a sperm-dissolving VDT performing abstract tasks that indirectly enslave the Third World [p. 22].

What's noteworthy here, I think, is the exhibition of intelligence enough to realize what one is doing, and a sense of complicity (à la the contemporary social media slogan, "There is no ethical consumption under late capitalism"). We can maybe make the case that the irony and distanced-ness and cynicism which one thinks of as so typically a late 20th-century phenomenon is precisely this combination of being highly intelligent and yet being trapped in a way of life you know is bad which you have no capacity to change and yet which also you know—you can remember, you can see it in your neighbors—doesn't have to be this way. It is, finally, a resignation that marks out the Generation X attitude from that of earlier cynicisms and ironies, a resignation which, arguably, you see in Kurt Cobain's armless dancing in the video for "Smells Like Teen Spirit."

Indeed, I'm somewhat tempted to say that this is one of the defining features of our lives: we are fully aware of the badness of the system *and* we don't benefit from it. You might think this is a somewhat unique historical perspective to adopt. At all times, there have been winners and losers, exploiters and the exploited. The winners enjoyed the privilege of education to see, if they wished, the extent to which their victory was bought with the suffering of others. But, as winners, they typically had no concern for it. The losers didn't have the education to realize to quite what extent they were being screwed, how unfair the whole thing was (I could be wrong about this). But Generation X combined educational richness with economic poverty, and that, perhaps, is the source of the very distinct anomie of the 1990s. At least, it's a hypothesis worth considering, and we can and I will suggest there's a distinct narrative that shows a correlation between one's intellectual awareness of the nature of modern life and one's disgusted or disappointed or merely numb reaction toward it.

So, then, to conclude: *Generation X* gives us a picture of the start of the 90s, a view of the world melancholic about some unattainable past, resigned to socioeconomic exile but nevertheless not despairing, or not too much despairing, because of the love that binds friends and family. In the next chapter, we'll have a look at how that unattainable past became unattainable, by tracing the development of economic thought from the 50s and 60s on.

2

Explainer: The Economics of 1946–1974

In this chapter I want to try and give a sense of the economic climate of the 90s by considering some of the economic history that led up to it. One of the theses of this book is that this climate is reflected in various ways in the works we are examining, and in particular the triumph of a free market politico-economic ideology determined, to some extent, the cynicism and disaffection typical of the 90s Zeitgeist.

In more detail, I'll claim that the authors of the 90s were (a) aware that the prevailing capitalist system wasn't working for most people but (b) unable to see an alternative. This provoked various responses, from nostalgia to cynicism to anger, as we'll see. Making the case for (a) and (b) will require a decent bit of sometimes economic theory and history, which I propose to begin reviewing, but I can actually make the two central points very quickly, by pointing to two important facts crucial to understanding the era.

Firstly, as to (a), we've already seen Coupland note 1974 as a key year, and it is generally recognized as the year when economic inequality started kicking in. In the post-war years, 1946–74, the productivity of the economy rose sharply, but so did wages. By contrast, from then on, while productivity has continued to rise, average wages haven't, and instead we've seen the ballooning of salaries of the top people and the rise of a rich managerial class while the average salary has stagnated.

This fact is very important to my analysis: even if the authors don't explicitly address this fact, I want to claim it's something in the air, that people recognize this inequality is bad. In some, it's explicit and is manifested, for example, in the nostalgia we see in Coupland and later Lynch. In others, it manifests in other ways. For example, at the later end of the nineties, a work like *Fight Club* has swapped melancholic nostalgia for anger; I claim that this is a consequence of moving further away from the crucial pre–1974 period when things were better.

Nineties to Now

As to point (b), this will require a bit more work, but I will want to claim that the seeming success, at least according to popular opinion, of a cluster of ideas relating to free markets, combined with the fall of the Berlin Wall, caused people to think there was no alternative to small-state capitalism, that greed, indeed, was good, and in particular that selfish self-interest was the best way to be; that the rising tide lifts all boats, and even *if* one fails to see the advantages of growth, under other systems things would be even worse (and anyway one is already implicated by virtue of the sweatshop Walkman [iPhone] in your hand so to criticize would be hypocritical).

Let me now spell some of that out in more detail. In a couple of sentences, the economic development of the U.S. since the Second World War would go as so. The post-war years saw a massive development of the economy, as productivity rose dramatically, unemployment fell, and wages rose. In the 50s, the life of the typical person became something we would recognize as desirable: filled with consumer goods such as technology (television and white goods, for example), houses with adequate plumbing and heating and air conditioning, and cars. If you worked hard, you got rewarded, and seemingly in a fair way: there was no massive variance in salaries, so there was little income inequality.

The statistics bear this out in an illuminating way. In his study of American growth—to which we will often refer—*The Rise and Fall of American Growth*, Robert Gordon points out that what economists call "total factor productivity" (TFP), which is to say economic output divided by input (labor and capital—how exactly to define these, and do the sums, is beyond the necessity of this work) grew massively in the period around the war. The ten-year average growth of TFP for the 1940s, for example, was almost 3.5 percent; for the 50s, about 1.5 percent and similar for the 60s, before languishing since then at around half that figure, or the same as the TFP of the 1890s (p. 547). America grew massively in the period around the war. And it did so fairly. Again following Gordon, we can note that the income growth rates for the top 10 percent, the bottom 90 per cent, and the overall average, for the period 1948–72 were almost equal (2.46, 2.65, and 2.58 percent per year respectively). By contrast, for 1972–2013, the top 10 percent income grew by 1.42 percent, the bottom 90 percent fell by 0.17 percent (p. 609).

It's worth sticking with Gordon to consider a question these figures suggest: Why? What led to such impressive and fair growth? One of Gordon's main and most interesting findings is that the war has a large

2. Explainer: The Economics of 1946–1974

part to play. In addition to mobilizing a gigantic amount of inputs, both of labor and capital, it also increased the skill level of the typical worker. Even when the war ended, the factories, suitably rejigged so as to produce peacetime goods, and their employees, used to putting in many hours for the nation's good, continued producing (pp. 562ff). A more long-term factor that plays part of the role, and which will be important later, is the second industrial revolution, of which Gordon emphasizes the importance of the internal combustion engine and electricity. Here it is worth heeding the point made before: by the 50s, these developments had made, in many respects, the typical day-to-day life and household of the postwar citizen remarkably continuous with ours. If you compare a house in, say, 1965 with one in 1915, then with one in 2015, it will resemble the 2015 house more closely than the 1915 one.

All this is to say that the postwar period can easily seem like a golden era, and a central theme of this book will be this seeming fact. Indeed, the point can be strengthened. There's a strain in contemporary thought associated with people whom one might group as classical liberals or neoliberals which would point out that the onward march of capitalism from the U.S. out rapidly changed the *world* for the better. For the most part, the United States' role in world events will be passed over in this book, but there's a good case to be made that the period between the war and the new millennium has seen the greatest improvement in worldwide human well-being ever. For just one[1] of many figures the reader can peruse at their leisure on ourworldindata.org, in 1955, GDP in East Asia, in 2011 dollars (and adjusted for intercountry differences in prices and inflation), was $1,366. In 2016, it was $10,287. In Africa, the numbers are respectively $1,748 and $4,680. Infant mortality and per day caloric intake reflect similar trends. To what extent this should be attributed to the U.S. is of course an open question, but there's a strong case for saying that the postwar U.S. economic tide lifted not only its own boats but also those of the world, and indeed the world beyond Western Europe.

However, it's worth already noting that this perspective is exclusionary. If you belonged to a minority, such as Black or gay people, or if you were a woman, things weren't so good, as we'll to some extent see in a later chapter. And the point about the rest of the world needs to be hedged with the familiar observation that the sweatshops (at least in East Asia) that led to increased GDP didn't obviously lead to increased well-being, as well as the cynical thought that the Marshall Plan aid that the U.S. lent war-torn Europe was partly self-serving.

Nineties to Now

Moreover, if lives looked somewhat like ours, the security that many of us consider central to a comfortable life—protection against injury, age, and unemployment—wasn't present. This began to change only later in the 60s, when then-president Lyndon Johnson introduced his idea of the Great Society, introducing various aspects of what we would recognize as the modern welfare system, such as health care for the unemployed and elderly and unemployment insurance. Moreover, in those years, if things were bad for many, they at least *seemed* to be getting better. Johnson claimed to have an interest in securing racial and social justice, and even if progress was slow, there was some progress.

The war in Vietnam, which we'll discuss in some detail later, to some extent belied this. If America could think of itself as a hero of World War II and, moreover, as a leader of the free world in the years after (as it, relatively economically untouched by the conflict, was willing and able to inject vast sums of money, in the Marshall Plan to the rebuilding of the war-torn Europe), with the drawn-out, ugly, unmotivated war in Vietnam, this self-image took a battering. However, even then, people were fighting, and the voice of the people seemed to be being heard, Nixon being elected in 1969 on an antiwar platform which he (kind of, as we'll see) carried out.

In sum, then, a good case can be made that in the U.S. as in Western Europe, the period from roughly 1946 to 1973 was a time of perhaps unrivaled goodness.

Moreover, and this is important because this book is concerned not only with the facts but with their ideological interpretation and presentation, what underlaid the economic prosperity was a theory of capitalism according to which it was inherently a fair process, or at least one the unfairness of which could be assuaged by correct management by government. On this theory, capitalism worked best when people, or at least the economic system they formed, were taken care of, and it was in the best interest of the system as a whole that, in hard times, such as the recessions and depressions capitalism has periodically faced, the government intervene to make things easier, either by having more money pumped into the system or, similarly, by having the government introduce programs to help the unemployed or simply by creating government jobs for them to occupy.[2]

This is the theory of Keynesianism, whose nature, rise, and fall it is necessary to say a little about. John Maynard Keynes was a British economist whose most enduring contribution was his analysis of what to do when a capitalist society breaks down or otherwise struggles.

2. Explainer: The Economics of 1946–1974

The greatest breakdown in the 20th century was the depression following the stock market crash of the late 1920s. People—ordinary people—started investing in the stock market in a big way, and the stock price of the companies listed became artificially inflated. Eventually, this bubble popped, and an awful chain reaction was set in motion: the value of stocks plummeted, yet because many of the stocks were financed by loans, this essentially meant that people knew they would be unable to pay back their loans by selling their stocks (because, say, they'd taken out a loan to buy stocks at $x, but now the stocks are worth only $x/10), and this in turn meant banks knew, in that eventuality, that they would have lost this money. This in turn made people worry about their savings—if banks have all those loans that they're not going to get back, what if they've loaned out my money? So there was a "run" on the banks, where people all tried to get their money out at the same time, and when they couldn't, a large number of banks collapsed, bankrupting some and denting the economic confidence of all.

It will be useful, before going on, to explain what I mean by that last sentence: why *couldn't* banks give people their money back? As any introductory economics textbook will tell you, the terminology, and images from television, are very misleading. We call putting money in a bank "depositing" it and have this idea that in so doing, what happens is the teller or the machine takes our money and puts it behind large doors, for safekeeping, in a vault.

This is not how banks work. After all, most of us don't pay fees to our bank. If they just sat on your money, where would they get the money from to operate?

Instead, banks use the money they are given to give out loans to others, on which they earn interest. They put your money to work, and then give you a smaller bit of the interest. There is no requirement that they have the cash equivalent of all the deposits made; instead, they have some much smaller amount of cash on hand, say 3–4 percent of the total money deposited in the bank (what is known as "fractional reserve banking").

This is no problem, under normal circumstances: provided not everybody tries to get their money out at the same time, that 3–4 percent will be perfectly adequate, and no problems will arise. But problems *will* arise when everybody tries to get their money out. The banks won't have the money on hand, and unless they can get it from elsewhere—and if everybody at all banks is asking for their money at the same time, it seems as if this will not be possible—they will be forced to deny their customers their money. And that's what happened.

With that said, let's return to our story. After this, the economy settled into a depression. People didn't trust banks anymore and so were more inclined to hold on to their money rather than deposit it. Moreover, banks were so battered they couldn't offer particularly good interest rates, so it simply wasn't worth the risk to deposit it, in case the bank later collapsed.

But this simple and indeed highly understandable behavior has large knock-on consequences for the economy as a whole. If people hold on to their money, neither depositing it nor, fearing more unpleasantness later on, using it to buy things, the whole economy clogs up. If they don't buy things, say combs, that means that the demand for combs decreases, and so the comb producers won't be able to afford to keep on their comb makers. These comb makers now become unemployed, but then *they* will become equally unwilling to buy whatever they want—shoes, let's say. One person's decision not to buy will have knock-on effects.

Of course, one way to get past this problem would be for the comb producer to *borrow* some money to temporarily get over this problem, enabling him to keep making combs in the hope that things will improve. But because our original unemployed person has decided not to put his money in the bank, either, and since the bank depends on deposits to make its loans, that will be more difficult.

This, known as the paradox of thrift, was what caused the depression to be so dramatic, at least according to one theory. The economic vicissitudes had spooked consumers, and the spooked consumers responded by ceasing to desire to spend or invest their money. That is, their *demand*, and thus so-called aggregate demand, decreased.

But then what is to be done? Keynes's big idea is that we need to find some way, when economies find themselves in this slump, to jolt them out of it. He suggested, through the course of his writings, several such methods, but the one most associated with him is the idea that, in such circumstances, the government should in one way or another put some money in the pockets of our suffering comb makers and shoemakers, enabling them to buy what they want. And if things are really bad, and one is faced with widespread unemployment, then the government can choose to create public-sector jobs for the unemployed by, say, undertaking infrastructure building or repair.

The key point is that one can't just let nature take its course:

2. Explainer: The Economics of 1946–1974

because of these quirks of human psychology, this essential irrationality (after all, by not spending, the first person is essentially contributing to a worse economy, which will hurt him), economies will find themselves in these irrational positions from time to time, and it takes intervention to fix them. But the government can come to our aid.[3]

Keynesianism was, at least in practice, the dominant approach up to at least 1970. Even the presidents—of whom there were many—who didn't like the idea, who thought that it smacks of irresponsibility and that a government, like a household, should tighten its belt when times are hard rather than extravagantly spending nevertheless, time and again, resorted to government spending to get out of a recession (the Wapshott book cited in endnote 2 is a good source for presidents' attitude towards Keynesianism).

There is something fundamentally nice about the Keynesian theory. If it were true, that would be good: if somber economic rationalism (even if that rationalism was premised on the fact that humans can be counted on to be *ir*rational in a recession) called one to help out those who suffer at the hands of that very economy, that would be a nice feature of reality. And its seeming empirical success in dealing with slumps seemed to suggest that this nice thing was, in fact, a feature of reality. The child of the 50s and 60s—at least the white, middle-class child—could well be excused for thinking that capitalism was a fair system.

In the 1970s, however, a problem arose for the Keynesian theory, and an alternative theory which seemed more fitting to the data came to the fore. The problem is known as stagflation, and properly to explain it requires some more technical background.

I said above that governments, on the Keynesian theory, put money in the system to stimulate demand during recessions. But now a problem arises. There is more money in the system than before. But there are the same amount of goods and services for sale. That means, at least in theory, that prices will rise too. We put money in the system to recover from depression, to put people back in jobs, but we see that putting too much money in the system will raise prices.

Data suggested that this bit of a priori reasoning tracks an empirical regularity. The New Zealand economist A.W. Phillips collected data that showed, indeed, there was an inverse relationship between unemployment and inflation: lower unemployment, more inflation. A sensible goal of economic policy then, given both unemployment and inflation are bad, would be to find the sweet spot where neither is at an unacceptable level. This gave Keynesian economics a constraint within which to operate: they should seek as high employment as possible that won't give a ridiculous amount of inflation.

However, in the 1970s, this relation was seemingly shown to be false, as we were faced with rising inflation *and* simultaneously rising unemployment. This was not explicable according to any feature of the Keynesian theory, but it *was*, however, explicable according to the rival theory of Milton Friedman and was the first step in the replacement of Keynes by non–Keynesian policies which aimed, in various ways to be described later, at fine-tuning the economy in another way.

First, though, I need to present some of the basic features of Friedman's theory (I'm relying here on Krugman 1994 pp. 34ff). The theory associated with his name is monetarism and is based on the idea that the money supply is a crucial macroeconomic variable apt to explain the big features, such as recessions and depressions, that blight our lives. Monetarism, in fact, didn't last very long—it was tried out for a couple of years at the end of the 80s to little great success—but I think it's fair to say that it has cast a long shadow, and the inflation-targeting policies of the 90s are well understood in terms of it.

The Federal Reserve can try to control the supply of money. Indeed, that was one of the reasons it was introduced. As Friedman tells us, in the start of the 20th century, there were similar bank runs, and so the Federal Reserve was created to prevent such failures of confidence. In the case of a run, it could simply create more money which it could give to the banks.

The Depression was the Depression, according to Friedman, because the Federal Reserve failed to do its job in controlling the supply of money (see his account in Friedman and Friedman 1980: 90ff). It should try to avoid putting too much money into the system, because that will cause inflation, but, in tough times, as after the collapse of the stock market, it should be willing to add to the supply. If it had done that, then the commercial banks would have had more money, so they could have loaned it out cheaper and this would have encouraged demand. If money were very cheap, our comb maker wouldn't worry so much about borrowing some and this is how the economy could be jump-started. We needn't have the government intervene by dumping in money or creating new jobs: simply make resources available to private enterprises and then rely on the wisdom of markets.

So let's return to the early 1970s. We've been doing the Keynesian thing for a while, and because that involves creating money, things have been mildly inflationary. For the Keynesian, we could cut back on

2. Explainer: The Economics of 1946–1974

the inflation, if we so wished, at the cost of some jobs. Not so for Friedman. Think of it like this: the comb maker now has money, and he can buy and sell as before. But there's more money in the system, so there's going to be more inflation, so goods and services will come to cost more. So, if he's being sensible, he will up his prices. But now think of the shoemaker: he's got some created money, and is up for buying some combs, but then the comb maker ups and raises his prices, and he can't afford them.

According to this logic, the Keynesian solution shouldn't work. On realizing that there's more money in the system, people should revise their prices (including the price they charge for labor) up, negating the effects of the stimulus. The only reason this didn't happen, Friedman thought, was because people were ignorant of this logic.

But only for a while: while it might work for a bit, this system will eventually cease working, as our comb maker and shoemaker start to take account of inflation in setting their prices. And once that happens, to retain a constant level of unemployment will require more and more money to be pumped into the system, and the Phillips curve will break down.

And this happened: the great thing (from the point of view of the theorist, anyway) is that Friedman *predicted* stagflation, already in 1967. But it's not just a wonky econ fact. Think of *being* an American in the early 70s, watching prices rise vertiginously and being told, by the government, to eat animals' brains and hearts (see Perlman, *The Invisible Bridge*, pp. 162ff), or being told that gas was now scarce and expensive (*ibid.*, p. 183). Or indeed, think of being an American in the late seventies: in 1978, when consumer prices were rising at 12 percent a year, or as the weakened dollar, which traded at $200 an ounce (gold) in 1977, traded at more than four times that at the start of 1980 (Frum, p. 302).

A theory that told you why this was and how to get away from it—suffer through the unemployment your inflationary policy has caused and then leave the market be, would be attractive. Government intervention can't solve our economic woes.

Note that purports to be a *technical* matter of fact. It's not normative: it just says how things work. It suggests that we ought not do Keynesian economics because it'll lead to inflation and then eventually either more inflation or stagflation. But it doesn't say that that's a *good* thing. It could be that it's a very bad thing, to be bewailed, just as we might think, had Keynesianism been true, it would have been a good thing, to be celebrated.

But this technical, somewhat wonky claim about macroeconomics was and is redolent of more normative, ethical claims. In particular, it seems to support the idea that the government shouldn't butt into citizens' economic lives and that the economy will do best left to its own devices, even if that is painful for some.

And this normative claim persisted even as monetarism went out of fashion. That a small state was morally and economically the right thing to do persisted in the supply-siders who made up Reagan's advisors. Kind of. The supply-siders (so named to indicate their differences from the Keynesian theory that economic woes were caused by a failure of demand) thought we could have our economic cake and eat it too. In particular, at the heart of their theory was the idea that lowering tax rates could actually in the end increase tax income, as well as strengthening the economy in general. The thought was taxing penalizes success, so the less taxes, the more people will be willing to work hard. This is a respectable enough idea, although the extent to which it's a panacea is widely doubted. But regardless of its success, it certainly, at the level of ideology, was important. It suggested greed is good, that the way for an economy to succeed was for the government not to stick its nose in and to let the businessmen business (Reagan famously didn't heed in practice this advice, spending an obscene amount of defense spending that no doubt helped the economic performance).

And this ideological point continued. Partly because of Reagan's profligacy, Clinton inherited a massive deficit when he was elected president in 1992 and, claiming the era of big government was over, pledged to balance the books. Not only that, but it appeared that he did well to do so, as the weak economy he inherited improved in the early 90s.

Indeed, the 90s as a whole was a remarkable period of economics. At its heart lay the famously gnomic chairman of the Federal Reserve, Alan Greenspan who, bizarrely—central banking hardly being a glamorous occupation—is arguably one of the iconic figures of the era. He presided over what was, until July 2019, the longest period of continuous growth in history, and his semiannual Federal Open Market Committee meetings to decide monetary policy became the sort of thing the newly rolling news channels covered feverishly. He was viewed—to use the title of a biography of him—as *The Man Who Knew*, who, by fine-tuning the economy to help it out of slumps by making money cheaper, or by—well, at least theoretically, he was later to be much criticized for not in fact having done so, leading to the 2000s dot-com boom—making

2. Explainer: The Economics of 1946–1974

money more expensive when the economy looked like it was going to overheat.

(For Clinton's financial policies, and how much luck as opposed to underlying sound ideas led to their success, see Joseph Stiglitz, *The Roaring Nineties*, W.W. Norton, 2003. For a fascinating inside story about Greenspan and his times, the biography mentioned is warmly recommended).

If you looked at the financial papers, the 90s were a time of unmatched prosperity. But already in these good times bad times were lurking. In what former Federal Reserve chairman Ben Bernanke would call "the great moderation" (the period from the mid–1980s to 2007), macroeconomic volatility decreased, and interest rates could be kept low by central bankers like Greenspan, thereby juicing the economy (low interest rates encourage consumers to bring consumption forward, to take out loans because the rates are so good for houses, cars, home improvements, even holidays), because of the free movement of capital. At a worldwide level, many countries, such as China, were savers, and they outweighed spendy countries, with the result that there was more money than people seeking it, and thus interest rates were low. It was widely thought that the problems of economics had been mainly solved. In words that aged extremely not well, famous economist Robert Lucas, in 2003, said that the "central problem of depression-prevention has been solved, for all practical purposes," but in the experience of many (remember the facts about growth and income inequality) that must have been, to those who heard it, cold comfort.

And herein lies the problem that will take us up to the crisis (and indeed beyond). The decline in volatility and in interest rates encouraged an ever-more unrestrained "search for yield." No longer could one make a good passive income from more mundane savings, and so stock market whizzes, with the help of fancy math, started developing complicated financial products, products which, as we'll later see, played a big role in the eventual collapse of the global economy in one of the epochal events separating us from the 90s.

That, then, is the economic world the citizens of the 90s inherited and lived in: neoliberalism reigning supreme, greed being good, the rising tide, ostensibly, raising all boats. Over the ocean communism seemed to have failed, and it would have been hard not to think that there were no political places to seek comfort. There were Clintonian third-way Democrats and Republicans, and both seemed to be undergirded by a free-market, small-state capitalist agenda. Together these gave a sense of a society which didn't particularly care about the unlucky and which, on the other hand, was happy enough helping the already rich. A society that somehow, the data tells us, had stopped growing, except if you belonged to the upper 10 percent, in which case things were looking rosy. This depressing state of affairs, I claim, can partly explain the political apathy and cynicism we find in 90s work.

3

Lynch and Tarantino

This chapter is concerned with arguably the two most interesting filmmakers of the decade, David Lynch and Quentin Tarantino. My aim here is to introduce a theme that will be central to the rest of the book: the question of realism in art, and what form that must take in the late 20th century (and, later, in the 21st century). How can we best depict postindustrial life? Must it be postmodern? And what is postmodernism, again?

A brief look at 90s culture and today's suggests that our answer to that question has changed. Much of the best work of the 90s is, to use an expression we'll try to get clear on, postmodern. *The Simpsons* is perhaps the clearest case, a generic nuclear family sitcom filled with arcane allusions to classical literature or film, a show in which clever parodies of politics intermingle with abject stupidity and physical comedy, and all presented in primary colors and jerky animation. Here we see many features of postmodernism we'll discuss in detail in the next chapter: a blurring of high and low culture, allusion for its own sake (what Jameson calls "pastiche"), an interest in mass media (the Baudrillardian "hyperreal," perhaps), and an obsession, perhaps, with form over content.

By contrast, the best work today is not postmodern, or so I shall argue. Starting perhaps around the turn of the millennium we've entered the era of so-called "prestige" or "long-form" television: shows that are, in a sense (although again this is something we'll question) realistic or classical. What's good about *The Wire*, for example, is just that it has good plots, characters, acting, and so on. It doesn't rely pretty much at all on formal playfulness and allusion. McNulty is a drunk cop who'll sometimes break the rules to get results, goddamnit: the ultimate movie cop cliché. But that he's a cliché isn't intimated or played with at all: that's what not makes *The Wire* entertaining. Examples can be multiplied: *Breaking Bad*, *Game of Thrones*, and *Westworld* each derive their effects from plot, characters, cinematography: from classical cinematic virtues, and not from clever deconstructions thereof.

It even shows up in comedy. As I'll discuss at more length later, the last 15 or so years have seen a gradual "depostmodernifying" of mainstream comedy: from *Arrested Development* through *30 Rock* and *The Office*, to *Parks and Recreation* and *Brooklyn Nine-Nine* and *The Last Man on Earth*, comedies have become less formally playful and more straight. One of my central questions here and in the remainder of the book, then, is to try to explain the reason for this evolution in popular culture.

Before doing that, though, it will be useful as well as, hopefully, interesting, to look in some detail at some examples of the best and most memorable 90s dramas. I opt for two that seem representative of the age, apt examples of the 90s' playful, allusive genre-bending drama. In each case, though, I want to make a—hopefully—interesting claim, namely that these works, although they may indeed be well described as postmodern, actually are, in a good sense, realist. We fail to see this because they each attempt to portray certain aspects of life typically overlooked by classical art. This is important, for the following reason: one of the aims of art, one might hope, is to portray the world as it is. I will claim that the playful style of these auteurs, although it might seem unrealistic, is in fact apt for the representation of a strange world, and that the more straight novels, films, and TV shows that began to appear around the turn of the millennium are less apt depictions of 20th-century life.

That Lynch and Tarantino are kinda sorta realists might sound daft. After all, the one is most commonly described as surrealist, and the other's films are a complex web of allusions and stylish genre-defying fun. Neither seem concerned to depict the world we live in, as opposed to the world of extra-dimensional dancing little people and wise-talking gangsters. However, that's a mistake, I'll argue. Lynch, the arch surrealist, is best viewed, to my mind, as a realist, but one hard to understand as such given the history of film and television. And Tarantino arguably presents a realistic account of one who spends all their time watching movies: postmodernism is a form of realism in a media-saturated culture, I'll claim. A consequence of this we'll see later is that contemporary art, to the extent that it's neither Lynchian or Tarantino-esque, flees realism, and I think that's borne out: our most popular shows are to a large extent fantasy.

Let's start then with the work of Lynch. I will concentrate mainly on *Twin Peaks*, a TV series that aired on ABC in 1990 and 1991, although

3. Lynch and Tarantino

I'll take into account also his earlier (1986) *Blue Velvet*, which presents the Lynchian universe arguably in its cleanest form.

Twin Peaks is ostensibly a murder mystery set in a small town in the Northwest of the United States. A girl, Laura Palmer, is found washed up dead, wrapped in plastic, and FBI agent Dale Cooper comes to town to resolve the mystery. Its popularity was a result of its quirky humor, lovable characters, and surreal intrusions. Twin Peaks is a town where a lady carries around and talks to a log ("the log lady," naturally), where the resident psychiatrist has a strange obsession with Hawaii, where a police interview is interrupted because there's a ... fish in the ... percolator. Cooper is a Zen Buddhist–inspired, coffee-pie-and-donut-loving agent who comes to a town of pillar-of-the-community local doctor types, coffee shops, young lovers and bikers and schools where everyone knows everyone, where there isn't a cell phone or McDonald's in sight, or indeed any trace of modern business or politics. Or ... any Black people. Or many sexually empowered women (Audrey certainly counts as sexually empowered). *Twin Peaks* is like the nostalgic misremembering of the 50s by an older, conservative person in the 90s (speaking initially of the music in *Blue Velvet* Lynch says "yes, it's a fifties thing. Banal in a way. But it's kind of removed from that also. Misplaced, almost. A fifties/nineties combo was what *Twin Peaks* was all about" p. 134, *Lynch on Lynch*).

And all this against a genre-defying and extremely playful soundtrack that conveys whimsy and melodrama and goes somehow to make up the sense of distance, of the town and its inhabitants living in a world of their own, where slightly different rules apply.

Despite all the superficial charm and eccentricity, though, the story is extremely dark: the murderer is the girl's father who sexually abused her. Even prior to that revelation the show touches on drug addiction, incest, and prostitution. Rewatching the first episode, what strikes one overwhelmingly is not the quirky stuff, but just how much crying there is: how shots linger over Laura's mother, or the principal of the school, or Laura's friends, sobbing, to an extent that feels, at least to this watcher, voyeuristic in a way unexpected of fiction.

Another aspect of the charm also, one might surely think, is its cute allusions to past works. An inexhaustive list: the actor who plays the one-armed man, for example, is also in a show featuring as a central character a one-armed man (other castings are similarly allusive); there's a show within the show, a bad soap named *Invitation to Love*, which at times roughly traces what's happening in the series, and the whole work, as with others of Lynch, is studded with allusions to *The Wizard of Oz*.

In light of this, one might think we're dealing precisely with the postmodern. We should understand the donut-loving, meditative Cooper as defined against the more traditional presentations of law enforcement on TV and in film. We should understand the eruptions of surreal humor as trying to chip away at the mystery genre, or the prime-time soap genre, or the cop show.

This can't completely be denied. There is clearly some of that going on, and any analysis must recognize this fact. But, that notwithstanding, I think a strong case can be made that Lynch's vision is, contrary to what it seems, much more classical and realist than we typically think. Lynch is weird in many ways; but so is reality.

To make this point, I want to focus on four aspects that I take to be crucial to Lynch's work, aspects which, taken together, lead him to be branded postmodern or downright surrealistic, and show instead that they are in service of a new sort of realism. The four aspects are: (i) a concern with focusing attention on the expression of genuine sentiment, (ii) a particular sort of dark humor, (iii) an infatuation with disturbing or aberrant sexuality, (iv) dream-like surrealism.

So let's take them in order. The first is the straightforward expression of true sentiment. In Lynch's world, we see teenage love and a mother's grief, small-town friendliness and family lunches, loving dotty grandmothers and dutiful sons, compassion, bravery, heroism. We see it, for example, in the Hayward family in *Twin Peaks*: in the doctor father asking his daughter if she'll be up for church in the morning, making awkward but ingenuous small talk with that daughter's boyfriend.

A very neat example of this comes from the final scene of *Blue Velvet*. Against beautiful Julee Cruise music, Jeffrey, the male protagonist, wakes from a nap outside to see a robin (which, per a dream of Sandy, the female protagonist, symbolizes love), and is called in to dinner, stopping to shout over to his dad in the neighboring garden who, having had a heart attack at the beginning of the film, is now recovering. They share the following utterly banal, utterly realistic dialogue:

JEFFREY: How you guys doing?
FRIEND: Hey Jeffrey
DAD: Hey Jeff. Feeling much better now Jeff.
JEFFREY: Good for you dad.

3. Lynch and Tarantino

He goes in to where Sandy's aunts or someone are waiting, tells them lunch is ready, and they smilingly tell him it sounds good. In the kitchen, Sandy and her mom are looking at the robin, who is eating a bug. The grandmother expresses displeasure at this and they look at her warmly and then, two clean cut American youths, at each other. The film cuts to a man on a truck waving, to roses in front of a white picket fence and then to a boy with a conical hat walking upscreen toward his mother, into whose arms he falls, and she smiles, albeit with a slight look of worry.

We should read all this as straightforward: Lynch is concerned to present these nice, happy feelings, a family and a young couple sharing a lunch. It can be hard to read it like this, though: it seems too earnest and overly sincere. It can be very easy, when faced with the first sort of thing, to think that Lynch is being "ironic." That all those things are passé in our modern era. That even if at one point people spoke like that, and filmmakers captured their speaking like that, those times are gone. Those moments of innocent sentiment have been permanently destroyed by, among other things, repeated presentation of them in the media of the previous era.

There's a famous and very useful quote by Umberto Eco on this that bears reflection:

> I think of the postmodern attitude as that of a man who loves a very cultivated woman and knows that he cannot say to her "I love you madly," because he knows that she knows (and that she knows he knows) that these words have already been written by Barbara Cartland. Still there is a solution. He can say "As Barbara Cartland would put it, I love you madly." At this point, having avoided false innocence, having said clearly it is no longer possible to talk innocently, he will nevertheless say what he wanted to say to the woman: that he loves her in an age of lost innocence [Eco, Postscript to *The Name of the Rose*, pp. 67–68].

Faced with this, and now returning again to *Twin Peaks*, consider the following scene with biker James and Maddy, Laura's cousin (played by the same person who plays Laura, in a playful bit of casting), from season 2 episode 6:

> JAMES: If you really love someone, it's like this bright light is shining on you all the time. You're right in it and it's great. But I just don't think you can be that way all the time.
> MADDY: Sure you can.
> JAMES: Well, I want to try to make the way my heart feels last forever. Pretty weird.

James, it seems, hasn't read his Eco. And nor, then, has Lynch. He isn't portraying how people actually talk, because we're all postmodern. We don't say things like that, at least not without Cartlandian prefaces. And so, you might think, that we shouldn't take this sort of talk, or the *Blue Velvet* scene, seriously. It's instead ironic. Lynch is channeling, by pastiche, Cartland. He doesn't mean it.

I think this is wrong. I think one *ought* to take it sincerely: Lynch does mean it. In an interview with Chris Rodley, he was asked about this very thing:

> Q: Some of the dialogue, far from being naturalistic, seems either exaggerated in its naivety or ironic
> LYNCH: Well, it's only as naive as small-town America
> Q: Another non-naturalistic part of Blue Velvet is the opening sequence of shots: an impossibly blue sky, a pristine white fence, redder-than-red flower, etc., through to the dark, wet insect battles beneath that beautifully green lawn.
> LYNCH: That's the way America is to me. There's a very innocent, naive quality to life, and there's a horror and a sickness as well. It's everything. The look of it was inspired by my childhood in Spokane Washington [*Lynch on Lynch*, p. 139].

I think we should take him at his word. These scenes are not ironic pastiches of earlier melodramas, but are meant to be a more or less realistic snippets of life.

And the thing is—Lynch is completely right. Life does have that naivety to it. Young people fall in love and look at each other meaningfully, people love their grandmothers and express that love. People make emotional goodbyes at the airport. Life is naive in that way. The trouble for artists—and indeed people—is that because the dumb, big blockbuster films, TV series, and romance novels traffic in this, and we're wont to make fun of such things, we are apt to view any "serious" work that attempts to portray it as ironic. But that's on us.

It's understandable, though. Because here's a bit more of *Blue Velvet*: the mother of the final scene just been reunited with her child, having been kidnapped by a psychopath who cut off her husband's ear and who sexually abused her after huffing gas and screaming, "Daddy wants to fuck," soundtracked, during one pivotal scene, with Roy Orbison's "In Dreams." It's weird.

Not only that, but while he's doing so, the hero Jeffrey is hidden in the closet watching, and later he himself, the small-town, wide-eyed boy, will have violent sex with Dorothy. You might think against this

3. Lynch and Tarantino

backdrop the final scene can't but be ironic: that in the face of such things, innocence is gone irrevocably. I take it that Lynch's thought is that that isn't true. That innocence can coexist with horror. That beside the abusive house of the Palmers there's the healthy house of the Haywoods.

I don't want to claim that the Lynchian world is an adequate representation of the complexity of life. But I do want to make the simpler point that naive sentiment exists, it must find its place *somewhere* in our representation of the world, and Lynch's work provides an example of how to do it (just do it!) and the pitfalls associated with it (it'll be read as ironic).

Now, obviously there are issues here. It's more than a little glib to end on such moments as opposed, say, to the years of psychological trauma Dorothy and her child will encounter. If there *are* such moments of innocence and joy even in the darkest situations, which there surely are, there are many moments *not* like this, when the dark wins, and you might think that any art which fails to represent this fact is being disingenuous and, in fact, unrealistic. The same thing holds for the exculpation of Leland, the father, in *Twin Peaks*: his abuse is transformed too neatly into him being the victim of evil spirits and going peacefully into the Tibetan afterlife. In general, for someone whose work so often turns on sexual violence, Lynch does nowhere enough to present all sides of it (although I think he does do better than many others, for whom rape seems to function as merely a plot forwarder. Lynch at least does try to take the victim's perspective, as in *Fire Walk with Me*, an almost unbearably hard to watch film). We will return to this extremely important point shortly.

The second aspect of his work I want to look at is humor. There's a very distinctive sort of Lynchian dark humor, of which the following are merely a couple of examples. In almost the very first scene of *Twin Peaks*, Pete Martell has found the body of Laura Palmer and phones up to speak to the sheriff. His receptionist answers:

> LUCY (TO THE SHERIFF, RIGHT BESIDE HER): Sheriff, it's Pete Martell, up at the mill. I'm, I'm gonna transfer it to the phone on the table by the red chair—the rec chair against the wall—the little table—with the lamp on it—the lamp we moved from the corner. The black phone, not the red phone.
> HARRY: Morning, Pete.
> PETE: She's dead. Wrapped in plastic.

Or, again, there's the scene in which Cooper and Truman go to visit Ronette Pulaski who is in a coma after being attacked by the killer, and whose terrifying flashback/nightmare of Laura's murder had ended the previous episode. They go into the hospital room of the traumatized girl and ... they struggle, slapstick style, to maneuver the awkward swivel chairs to sit by her beside.

Again, it's just a fact of life that sometimes funny things happen when sad things happen: so-called gallows humor. At least, it does in my life. You learn whatever close family member has whatever terminal illness as you're stuck in whatever foreign city desperately looking for a bathroom in which to perform whatever acutely pressing bodily function. This happens.

Art frequently avoids such things, because, typically, there is serious art, and there is funny art, and even in things that can mix them, to mix them in the very same scene is generally not done: it's a somewhat weird fact of the way we perceive art that a funny scene can contain sad things and remain predominantly funny but it's harder for a sad scene to have comedy while remaining sad. But Lynch doesn't care for such facts, and it's to his credit. The key point to note is that what seems aberrant, a divergence from standard drama, is, in fact, something which leads to realism. The point, obvious when you think about it, is that what we call realistic drama isn't so: it isn't filled with the banal clichés and pratfalls that make up our lives. Since Lynch's work does contain banal clichés and pratfalls, it's more realistic in this respect.

Let me now turn to the third feature, the treatment of sexuality. One issue a lot of people have is that women are treated badly in Lynch's work, and it's typically in a fetishized, sex-laden way. He is the auteur who most of all, you think, gives us a direct access to his sexual subconscious, and that's filled with rape, pedophilia, and hot lesbians kissing.

All of this is right. It does seem like we are viewing some male fantasies; these male fantasies are destructive and misogynistic, and, when we get ourselves in the frame of mind that we think art ought to be representative of the range of human life, we have reason to quarrel with Lynch. Presenting, and adulating, these visions of sexuality is ultimately impoverishing and perhaps destructive.

Again, though, I'm kind of tempted to think that it's, in a sense, realistic. Everybody watches porn, apparently. The person sitting opposite you in a work meeting, the single mom drinking a coffee in Starbucks, the middle-aged guy in the gym—the quiet solitary moments of their lives are filled with things I typed out but then deleted because it

3. Lynch and Tarantino

sounded, a bit, well, pornographic (did you know incest porn is one of the breakout trends of the last third of the 2010s? Google "what's up with all the incest porn?"[1]).

We carry about these desires in our head, and most of us are very reticent to put our name to them, for obvious reasons. Lynch doesn't have this reticence, and again it's to the benefit of realism. The problem still remains, of course, that it's a realistic portrayal only of one aspect of one old white dude's weird sex stuff, and that's a serious failing.

In fact, I think the regressive Lynchian attitude toward sexuality is a crucial phenomenon for understanding our pop culture. Lynch's world is full of fetishistic sexual violence against women and pretty much devoid of powerful female characters. It is highly regressive in this respect, and I think that's part of the reason why his worlds have so many elements which recall previous eras. His world winds the clock back to before *Roe v. Wade*, before the statutes recognized marital rape, before birth control and premarital sex were taken as a given—before women attained the power they have today, and could be more easily diminished and treated as objects. Just as the *Generation X* people look back beyond 1974 to economically healthier times, Lynch looks back to that era as a time unmenaced by sexually liberated women, and his retro style lets him sneak this theme past the watcher (and onto network television!). That is to say, we see the nostalgic theme of 90s art, but put to a more nefarious use, to center misogyny and regressive attitudes toward women, that one might have hoped would be less acceptable after the women's rights movement. A crucial question we'll ask later is whether things have changed in pop culture in this respect.

Finally, there's the surrealism. There are obvious examples and less obvious examples of this. The more obvious ones are things like the black lodge that features first in Cooper's famous dream at the end of episode 3 of the first season, or again the weird substance that Frank huffs in *Blue Velvet* (which would have been ever more surreal had the idea, which was apparently considered, to have it be helium, been taken up). These sorts of things show up with increasing frequency in Lynch's work, which come to rely more and more on disjointed, hard to understand narratives and bizarre characters (think of the diner monster in *Mulholland Drive*, or the alien in *Lost Highway*).

It can seem hard to square the outright surrealness of much of Lynch's work with the idea that Lynch is a realist, and certainly I don't want to say that my story is perfect. Some of it, especially the later work which experiments with very nonlinear inexplicable story lines, doesn't seem in any meaningful sense realist.

But. Here's a feature of our life: dreams. Dreams are a very important part of the human experience, and dreams have that same sense of strangeness. Dreams aren't, you might think, these negligible things: properly to account for a given person's experience—perhaps especially early in the morning—you need to account for their dreams. Most art doesn't do that, or if it does it does so so very inadequately—people tell their dreams which have some sort of obvious intelligible significance and which further the plot in some way.

That's not how surrealism in Lynch's work functions. Think of Cooper's dream. While it does further the plot, its elements, exegetes notwithstanding, have no symbolic significance. Why the little man? Why the talking backward? There's no answer for this, I take it, at least if we look to Lynch's intentions.[2] But it works—it feels right. It captures something of the weirdness of dreams, and since that weirdness is a part of our lives, it is faithful to that part.

Overall, then, I think there's a good case to be made for the claim that the four aspects which we think of as typical Lynchian are, rather than postmodern or surrealist, instead hyperrealistic. They present features of life we tend to gloss over rather than presenting something other than life. We live in a Lynchian world.

Before moving on, however, let's note the consequences of the work of Lynch for the overall argument of the book. His work *clearly* looks back to the 50s as a mythical time, a time of innocence. Twin Peaks, and the Lumberton of *Blue Velvet*, are typical American small towns: their worlds don't contain rap or Pepsi or yuppies; instead it's milkshakes in diners, gas station owners, and bikers playing guitar. It seems that his idea that the world contains beautiful things is the idea that the 50s existed, and in other places in the interview series he expresses a strong declinist sensibility, that things are messed up now as they weren't then. So Lynch, I would want to say, is another prime example of a nostalgist, but in a sense he goes further than Coupland: Coupland's characters yearn for the 50s, whereas Lynch just transposes the 50s world to the modern day: as he says, *Twin Peaks* is a fifties/nineties mash-up.

So, that's Lynch, on my view: not a surrealist but more like a hyperrealist. The second filmmaker I'm going to consider has some noteworthy similarities to Lynch: he is also interested in characters who subvert stereotypes, in the use of music and especially music from the 50s and 60s, and in stylized and frequent violence. Indeed, this has led David

3. Lynch and Tarantino

Foster Wallace, to be discussed in a later chapter, to say that Tarantino copied the Lynchian style and cleaned it up a bit and made it mainstream (in "David Lynch Keeps His Head," collected in *Consider the Lobster*).

That's not my view though. If Lynch is a realist, we should think of Tarantino as the theorist of the postmodern par excellence: his work is playful and self-consciously genre subverting, stylish but ultimately emotionally empty.

In order to see this, let me consider *Pulp Fiction*. It's a story about gangsters and thieves and crooked boxers, filled with drugs and violence. It has a complicated temporal structure: the film, for example, begins and ends in a café, but the action it recounts neither begins nor ends there. The details aren't so important: what is important is the *style*.

There are certain key Tarantino themes. The first is obsessive reference to other films. For a viewer like me, who is not particularly au fait with the French new wave, these go over my head, so I rely on the internet to tell me, for example, that the very first scene, in which two crooks come up with an apparently new scam to make money by robbing places where many people congregate, is straight from one of the earliest films, 1903's *The Great Train Robbery*.[3] This same page reveals it's absolutely *full* of references to TV programs of the fifties and sixties which again age and nationality mean I haven't seen.

Not only that, but visually we have the same thing. Everyone has a retro look: simple black and white abounds, labels aren't to be seen. There are few gadgets, and the settings include a 50s-themed restaurant and a diner, the bastion of small-town community, and probably much more. Moreover, and perhaps most effective for a stylistic point of view, is the use of music from the era, perhaps most memorably the 1960s "You Never Can Tell" in the famous dance contest scene. A key thing to note is that this iconic scene is pure style, no substance, at least assessed relative to classical dramatic standards. Very long, it furthers the plot at best slightly, but it's compulsively watchable. So, then, a lot of 50s/60s referencing in *Pulp Fiction*: this is a film of nostalgia too, but like Lynch's films, it's "misplaced."

It's worthwhile performing a thought experiment at this point. Think of the things you watched, wore, and listened to as a child, and now imagine a TV show or movie absolutely packed with references to them. Or, again: look at the TV shows and movies you like these days. Are *these* packed with such references? Some are, no doubt—depending on your age, things like *GLOW* or *Stranger Things* may bring back the past to you. But most aren't. It's fundamentally quite odd, we should realize, to have such a form of art. But it's nevertheless a central feature of Tarantino's work, and the other postmodern highpoint of the decade, namely *The Simpsons*, and to the extent that these works are seen by many as typical of the 90s, it's a central feature of 90s style in general. Not only do we have nostalgic characters, as in *Generation X*, but we have a nostalgic style.[4]

Let's turn to a second aspect of Tarantino's style. Lynch, I argued above, traffics in genuine feeling. It's somewhat hard to get this—because it is so extreme and one-dimensional and moreover because it invariably comes packaged up in the signifiers of the 50s and the small towns of the era, but it is, I claimed, there. Not so Tarantino. Vastly entertaining, *Pulp Fiction*, at least to this watcher, isn't in the business of making anyone *feel* anything. Then what does it do? It tells an entertaining story, it has funny dialogue, great music, it experiments with form, it subverts convention. This absence of feeling, this hipness, should be seen, I think, as marking a real feature of the 90s mood. As with (some parts of) *Generation X*, and as we'll see with some later works, one gets the sense of a great abstract intelligence, in this case one that has seen and analyzed every movie and knows the rules for making them by heart, meeting emotional numbness.

Let me focus briefly on one such aspect, namely the witty dialogue. Here is a famous scene, spoken by Samuel L. Jackson and John Travolta, both dressed in sharp black suits, on the way to kill some people:

VINCENT: But you know what the funniest thing about Europe is?
JULES: What?
VINCENT: It's the little differences. A lotta the same shit we got here, they got there, but there they're a little different.
JULES: Examples?
VINCENT: Well, in Amsterdam, you can buy beer in a movie theater. And I don't mean in a paper cup either. They give you a glass of beer, like in a bar. In Paris, you can buy beer at McDonald's. Also, you know what they call a Quarter Pounder with Cheese in Paris?
JULES: They don't call it a Quarter Pounder with Cheese?
VINCENT: No, they got the metric system there, they wouldn't know what the fuck a Quarter Pounder is.
JULES: What'd they call it?
VINCENT: Royale with Cheese.
JULES: (repeating) Royale with Cheese. What'd they call a Big Mac?
VINCENT: Big Mac's a Big Mac, but they call it Le Big Mac.
JULES: Le Big Mac. What do they call a Whopper?
VINCENT: I dunno, I didn't go into a Burger King. But you know what they put on french fries in Holland instead of ketchup?

3. *Lynch and Tarantino*

JULES: What?
VINCENT: Mayonnaise.
JULES: Goddamn!
VINCENT: I seen 'em do it. And I don't mean a little bit on the side of the plate, they fuckin' drown 'em in it.

Superficially, this could seem like a Lynchian sort of dialogue. Just as Lynch gives us cops who care about donuts because some cops *do* like donuts, and it's not inconsistent with tracking a murder that one stop to appreciate the trees, so, surely, some hitmen vacation in Europe and note and discuss the little differences.

But it feels different and has a different sort of dramatic purpose. I'm tempted to say that Lynch ignores genre while Tarantino subverts it. If *Lynch's* cops talk about donuts, it's because cops in fact talk about donuts. If Tarantino's hitmen talk about donuts, it's because movie star hitmen *don't* talk about donuts. Lynch looks to reality and records it, and thus defies genre by ignoring it (again, with the caveat that this isn't the whole story; sometimes he does play with genre for playing with genre's sake); Tarantino looks to genre and subverts, and defies genre purposefully. But we get, interestingly enough, something like the same thing: gun-toting people discussing high-calorie foods.

Let me end with one other feature typically associated with Tarantino and prima facie similar to Lynch: the use of netherworld things like drugs and violence. There are definite similarities, but again Lynch goes deeper, if not deep enough: he doesn't just murder the girl, he shows, in great detail, the sadness of the mother. And he shows the horror of the abuse brutally in *Fire Walk with Me*. Tarantino's violence, on the other hand, is all surface, no consequence.

And one final point before ending this whole hyperrealism vs. genre stuff. I've been claiming that Tarantino is arch-postmodernist, all surface and no content, that it's just a series of either references to other works or subversions of the conventions thereof, and so we should think of it as unrealistic. But there's another way to look at it.

Tarantino belongs to perhaps the first generation that was raised on TV and movies (he was born in 1963; I don't have an exact figure for how widespread television was then, but in 1950 it was in fewer than 10 percent of houses and in 1959 more than 90 percent, which gives you its rapid rise to ubiquity). This is an important fact: what might it do to someone to be raised on such things? This might seem an overly simplistic story, but think: prior to the invention of television, the voices one encountered, and the things one saw, for the most part, were those of one's family and surroundings. And one's family and surroundings are, typically, not all that entertaining, or at least are markedly different from the families and surroundings on television and in the movies. It's plausible to think, then, that the process of growing up is different for one growing up before and growing up after television had become a ubiquitous feature of American life. One is exposed to more and more different but fictionalized voices which drown out the actual voices of family and friends (in a later chapter we'll see concrete evidence from sociology to suggest that television does indeed play this role as a proxy for human interaction).

Now here's a thought: Tarantino's art simply reflects this fact. If one's life consists to a large extent of watching movies and television, and one wants to accurately present one's life, then one's art should somehow contain a lot of television and movies. But it would be very boring (and presumably difficult from the point of view of copyright) if one were to just plonk your protagonist in front of a screen and watch him or her watching, so one makes do with allusion.

Here's another way to put the point. Say you want to convey a particular piece of information in an interesting way. That someone is angry, for example. Back in the day, you might have appealed to some feature of the natural world. After all, before TV, there wasn't much else to do but look out the window at the weather, so it would be natural to describe someone's anger as a storm. But now, in the 90s or as a child in the 70s, you're probably in some big city, the view from your window is uninspiring, but you have Saturday morning cartoons or movies to entertain you, so it's natural to use them instead. And thus we get, for example, *The Simpsons'* writers expressing Homer's exasperation with "D'oh," which itself comes from a character in the Laurel and Hardy shorts.

On this view, the allusion-heavy style of the 90s isn't some clever deconstructionist turn away from the goals of art as we've typically considered them, which is to say as a depiction of the world, but just an updating of the means to that goal demanded by the updating in the sort of lives one leads. Rather than a deconstruction of movies, it's an attempt to portray a life lived mediated by movies.

I'll expand upon this theme—that realistically to portray a media-saturated life requires unusual artistic strategies—in more detail later in the book. However, before doing that, I want to consider a more theoretical question. I threw about the term "postmodern" above, and indeed it seems well applied to many features of 90s work. But it's

3. Lynch and Tarantino

unclear what I mean—it's unclear what anybody *ever* means when they talk about postmodernism. I'd like to take a look at the opinions of some of the most influential people here, and so in the next chapter I'll dip into what's known as "theory" to see if we can pin down this important feature of the culture.

4

Explainer: Postmodernism

Postmodernism is a word that gets thrown around a lot, both when describing 90s culture and when describing the current culture. Some people, not so seriously, have tried to trace back our current post-truth, alternative facts politics to postmodernists; more pertinently, most of the art I describe in this book would also be described as postmodern, and I will make the case that social media communication, especially memes, is a postmodern way of communicating but that current, 2021, art is post-postmodern. It will accordingly be useful to say a bit about what this amounts to.

There are a bunch of different meanings for postmodernism, one of the central features of which seems to be its resistance to definition. I'm going to look at the work of some of the most influential theorists in this area, since I think we can derive from their work some interesting ideas that will help us understand our era.

Let me begin by noting two senses of postmodernism I *won't* so much concentrate on. On one, "postmodern" is just a temporal designation, to denote the period when modernism ended. On this account any work of art which appeared—very roughly—after the 50s would be postmodern: Burroughs would be postmodern and Scorsese, and the Beatles and *Saturday Night Live*. This, I take it, is close to maximally unhelpful. Another would be less chronological but equally heedful of etymology and suggest that it's writing that responds to or defines itself against modernism. We'll see a bit about this later.

Let me then turn to the first of our writers, Jean Baudrillard. He was a French sociologist concerned with giving an account of the features of postindustrial society, such as mass media and consumerism. He later traveled to America, and most of his more famous analyses involve aspects of American culture in the quarter century or so before the millennium.

4. Explainer: Postmodernism

He remains influential to this day as one of the key thinkers of postmodernism, and indeed has some popular notoriety: Morpheus's line "welcome to the desert of the real" in *The Matrix* is from Baudrillard, and the makers of that film forced their staff (poor bastards) to read "Simulacra and Simulation," which is the essay we'll discuss.

Baudrillard is interested in what he calls the precession of simulacra. "Precession" is a technical term from mechanics which, as far as I can tell, Baudrillard uses just as a fancy synonym for "preceding." "Simulacra" is a fancy word which means, essentially, representation. To say that simulacra are precessing then is to say that representations have come to have precedence. Over what?

Well, to answer that let me present a picture of language I hope we can all agree on: there are things out there, and there are words which stand for them. (Some deny this, holding that there is no such *standing for* relation relating words and things. Words get their meaning not by making contact with some extra-linguistic bit of reality, but by the relations they stand in to other words. "Sofa" doesn't make contact with some extra-linguistic bit of reality, the sofas. Rather, it makes contact with other [intra-linguistic, obviously] words: "chaise longue," "armchair," "beanbag," and gets whatever positive meaning it has by its differences with these other words: it is not built for reclining, it is not built just for one, it would not be out of place in a dentist's waiting room, and so on. Regardless of whether or not this is true, something like the model in the text must be presupposed to understand Baudrillard, so let's presuppose it.)

The things, for most of us most of the time, are where the action is at. Gold, the metal, is much more valuable than "gold" the word. There's also a sort of temporal preceding: we have this picture of a preexisting reality, to the various parts of which we then attach names. Adam named the animals, but the animals were already around.

Baudrillard's thinks this idea—that things outvalue and precede representations—is, now, wrong. Here, in his almost incomparably awful style, is how he puts it:

> In this passage to a space whose curvature is no longer that of the real, nor of truth, the age of simulation thus begins with a liquidation of all referentials—worse: by their artificial resurrection in systems of signs, a more ductile material than meaning, in that it lends itself to all systems of equivalence, all binary oppositions and all combinatory algebra. It is no longer a question of imitation, nor of reduplication, nor even of parody. *It is rather a question of substituting signs of the real for the real itself*, that is, an operation to

deter every real process by its operational double, a metastable, programmatic, perfect descriptive machine which provides all the signs of the real and short-circuits all its vicissitudes. Never again will the real have to be produced—this is the vital function of the model in a system of death, or rather of anticipated resurrection which no longer leaves any chance even in the event of death. A hyperreal henceforth sheltered from the imaginary, and from any distinction between the real and the imaginary, leaving room only for the orbital recurrence of models and the simulated generation of difference [excerpt from "Simulacra and Simulation" in Leitch ed., *Norton Anthology of Theory and Criticism*, W.W. Norton and Company, 2001, p. 1733. All subsequent references in this chapter are to this book].

This whole paragraph, indeed pretty much the whole essay, could be reduced to the italicized—by me—line. While hardly a novel point since the so-called Sokal affair,[1] it's worth emphasizing that this is truly awful writing, and, moreover, truly awful writing that people are forced to read. This essay is widely anthologized and cited—in fully three different books on my shelf you can find it. Students all over the world read this and, probably, think that the level of insight is proportional to the verbiage and that their failure to get much out of it reflects on them. But it doesn't. Baudrillard certainly has provocative ideas that, as we'll see, provide a useful lens in understanding some features of 90s culture, but a lot is just empty words.

But maybe even if the style is bad, the idea is good? Sometimes this is true. Kant has bad style but is interesting. Frege's *Begriffsschrift* has as obscure a typography as one can imagine but reinvented formal logic. So let's continue. The idea that we've substituted signs of the real for the real itself is kind of intriguing sounding, especially in the era where some claim millennials have exchanged sex for porn, and we've got a reality TV boss for boss of the country. Maybe Baudrillard's on to something.

To illustrate his point, Baudrillard points to some features of (then) contemporary culture: Disneyland and Watergate. He thinks that in both cases there's a natural way to think about these features which is, in fact, wrong. The natural way to think of Disneyland is that it functions as a fictional, unrealistic representation of America: it's a false world within the real world of the USA. The natural way to think of the Watergate scandal is that it functions as a representation of how politics *shouldn't* be done—the scandal, by its very scandalousness, points to the non-scandalous normal nature of politics. In each case, we have a pair of distinctions: the fictional, unrealistic world of Disneyland as against the real world outside its boundaries, and the scandal and crime of the

4. Explainer: Postmodernism

Watergate break-in as against the normal, honest course of American politics.

But this is wrong, says Baudrillard. Taking Watergate first, his claim is that there is no such thing as the normal, honest course of American politics. For example, take the wiretapping of Democrats Nixon carried out: this has, it's known, long been something done or at least permitted by the political establishment (Kennedy and Truman, for example, both did it). If this is so, then if a scandal is a violation of some norms of conduct then, as Baudrillard says, there is no Watergate scandal (at least as concerns wiretapping).

Instead, the function of Watergate was to convince people there is a normal, honest course of American politics. It served Baudrillard to impose the idea that it was a scandal, that what Nixon and his gang did was indeed a break with some norms of political behavior and that therefore there was an order that was being scandalously defied. The scandal which wasn't a scandal caused a scandal and therefore brought into being the condition for a scandal!

This is an interesting analysis—whether it's in any way borne out by what actually happened is another question (we might note that Americans' faith in their institutions took a nosedive after Watergate; we might note again that Nixon's replacement, Ford, by pardoning Reagan, attached to himself some of the former's guilt). But it at least makes sense, and presents a position worth considering: that representations—the sum total of newspaper articles, books, movies, and so on—about the Watergate scandal served to bring into being what was previously lacking, namely the idea that there was an upstanding political order.

Let's consider his second example, which is a bit less clear: Disneyland. He thinks that its secret is that, although we think of it as a fictional representation of a sort of world, in fact its purpose is to hide the fact that "all of Los Angeles and the America surrounding it are no longer real … it is no longer a question of a false representation of reality … but of concealing the fact that the real is no longer real" (op. cit., 1741). Disneyland doesn't function as an escape into a fantasy world; it functions to distract from the fact that there is no actual world anymore.

What does this mean? In what sense is Los Angeles no longer real? Well, he doesn't really say. A textbook on postmodernism (*Postmodern Theory*, Best and Kellner, 1991 p. 119) suggests that the proliferation of manuals (sex manuals, DIY manuals) makes the same point for Baudrillard: we come to privilege the ideal over reality. We're not concerned with our actual lawn, or relationship or whatever, but with the expert one the specialists will show us how to create. Another example Baudrillard gives himself is of opinion polls: we think of them as registering opinion, but we know well that they *form* opinion. If you read in an opinion poll that a given party is doing better than you would have anticipated, you might then come to put your support behind what you previously took to be a lost cause.

These are all mildly interesting observations. We do seem, in some sense, to live in a time in which representations are very important, and can even sometimes have this reality-making power. Again, the tendency to just point to our current political situation is strong: the quick *argumentum ad Trumpum* can lead us to think we are definitely in a Baudrillardian world.

Still, we don't get, from Baudrillard, anything clear enough to give us a sense of postmodernism. It's obviously not the case that L.A. is no longer real, and we can note that humans have been defining themselves against ideals, and doing something because they think the neighbor does it too, for as long as there have been human beings. Baudrillard doesn't make the case that there is something particularly different about postindustrial society that warrants giving it and only it the moniker of postmodernism. So let's leave Baudrillard, although we'll have occasion to return to his observations as the book progresses.

The next person to consider is another big name, Jean Lyotard. His basic idea is that postmodernism is defined as an "incredulity towards metanarratives." In plain English—we don't believe in overarching theories of the world. For example, back in the day people believed in God, and then they believed in reason, socialism, Darwin, Marx, Freud. In general, it was thought that there was something we were heading toward, some ideal, or that at least we were progressing, and that, moreover, we were doing so according to an intelligible process. For Darwinism, or at least its popular interpretations, the laws of natural selection caused us to be more adapted to our environment than our ancestors, and those laws explain not only why, for example, we don't brachiate but also our little peculiarities, like why we have useless appendixes or why it's very hard to stop eating something sweet after you start. For Freud, the laws of the unconscious are what gives rise to our behaviors, from small slips of the tongue and dreams to the sort of partner we choose, and understanding these laws can enable us to free ourselves of the neuroses and anxieties with which we are burdened. For Marx, the laws of capitalism itself suggested its downfall, and, for example, for all their

4. Explainer: Postmodernism

sci-fi bizarreness, Uber's self-driving cars are just the newest working out of an underlying capitalist logic.

Now, though, what do we believe? Freud is certainly out—we don't assign any deep meaning in our parapraxes, and few would have much time for thinking that the concepts of id and ego and superego limn any psychological reality. While we're all—apart from the many who aren't—still pro–Darwin, we're also very aware of the extent to which science is sometimes irrational or can be misused or is sometimes just false (we live in an era where replication crises have undermined our faith in much social science, which appears to be p-hacked and nonreplicable). And Marx—the thought that there is some beyond of the unfettered capitalist system encountering the underside of which in Manchester influenced Engels so—that is hard to see, although it is becoming ever easier.

We are, Lyotard thinks, in an age where the thought that we are progressing in accordance with big picture and meaningful laws ought to be one held with suspicion. In Lyotard:

> Neither economic nor political liberalism, nor the various Marxisms, emerge from the sanguinary last two centuries free from the suspicion of crimes against mankind. We can list a series of proper names (names of places, persons and dates) capable of illustrating and founding our suspicion. Following Theodor Adorno, I use the name of Auschwitz to point out the irrelevance of empirical matter, the stuff of recent past history, in terms of the modern claim to help mankind to emancipate itself. What kind of thought is able to sublate (Aufheben) Auschwitz in a general (either empirical or speculative) process towards a universal emancipation? So there is a sort of sorrow in the Zeitgeist. This can express itself by reactive or reactionary attitudes or by utopias, but never by a positive orientation offering a new perspective [*ibid.*, p. 1614].

Less fancily: how can you believe in *anything* after Auschwitz? Not to mention God, but even any sort of belief that humans are progressing—how can it remain? How can we think that Auschwitz is a step along the path toward a better future (as per the Hegelian theory of history, according to which history has a pattern [and so on as in text])? We have given up the thought of progress, the idea that there is one aim toward which things tend, and have replaced it with plurality. He uses, vaguely, the notion of a Wittgensteinian language game to try to make this point. At the start of the century came the idea that there was one language which could serve as a pure vessel of logic: a language into which we could translate vague imprecise language that would serve as a universal scientific language. As the century developed, he points out, the number of different logics exploded, each apt to translate a different part of language, with no real concern for there being an underlying language in which everything could be said (a fact which one could, without too much inaccuracy, link to Gödel's incompleteness results and Wittgenstein's passage from the *Tractatus* to the *Philosophical Investigations*). There was no universal language, it seems, but different languages for different purposes: one language for talking about necessary truth, one for talking about responsibility and duty, and so on. That's where Lyotard thinks we are: there are just different local languages, local sets of rules, local ways of behaving, not to be subsumed under some big picture story of reality.

Again, a lot of Lyotard's work is vague and poorly expressed. But nevertheless, and as with Baudrillard, the thought seems worth considering. The thought that is definitive of postmodern cultures, and thus at least the 90s, that its subjects don't believe in big-picture theories of the world has some sort of appeal to it. It is noteworthy, I think, that for a decent percentage of young people the idea of religion is never even considered as an option. And it's also noteworthy that were I writing a hundred or so years ago, there is a decent chance I would be at least receptive to Darwin, Freud, and Marx, each of whom saw an order in things. Does a contemporary, moderately well-informed person, see things this way?

The idea that we're getting better is hard to take with inequality and climate change, and Freudianism has been replaced with the medicalization of the mind. At the moment, our mental lives have been stripped of their *meaning*. For Freud, one's sufferings *said* something; they tried to communicate the kernel of you that makes you unhappy. Even the smallest thing, a little slip of the tongue (a Freudian slip) was indicative of something. Now it's just serotonin and oxytocin and dopamine: we've moved from meaning to neurochemistry. Similarly, Marx had a vision of how capitalism would progress toward its own demise, but that vision doesn't seem to have come true and we have come to accept what Mark Fisher famously called "capitalist realism," the thought that there is no alternative to our current situation (*Capitalist Realism*, zero books, 2011). We can't even find repose in science. The replicability crisis in the social sciences is revealing that whole swathes of research are rotten to their core, the result of researchers inadequately versed in statistics being forced to churn out research papers for tenure or consultancies.

4. Explainer: Postmodernism

So it's prima facie reasonable to think that the mark of the postmodern is this absence of big beliefs. And when we see *The Simpsons*, I'll suggest that that sort of equivocality about metanarratives plays an important role. But it strikes me that it gives us little explanatory purchase in explaining, say, *Pulp Fiction*. It's a long way from Auschwitz and the end of belief to Jules and Vincent. So I conclude that again while an interesting thought, it would be hasty to say that this gives us the essence of postmodernism, or even something especially definitive of our era (people have often been haunted by belief's absence; and is it really true that in our era of the alt-right and identity-politics left we *don't* believe in things? I'll consider this later.).

So let me turn to another theorist, again often anthologized and mentioned in this context, namely Fredric Jameson. He both writes better and is more immediately helpful in explaining the artists we're considering. He thinks an important thing about postmodernism is the relation between high and mass or popular culture. Noting that an interest in pop culture is, in a sense, already deeply there in modernism (Joyce, for example, wrote a chapter of *Ulysses* in the style of cheap romance novels; Eliot fills "The Waste Land" with current songs alongside Latin poetry and Shakespeare references), but he thinks it has a different way of using these things.

> They no longer "quote" such "texts" as a Joyce might have done; they incorporate them, to the point where the line between high art and commercial forms seem increasingly difficult to draw [*ibid.*, p. 1961].

To make this notion of incorporation more precise, he introduces a distinction between pastiche and parody. A parody, roughly, is adopting a voice other than one's own, "to cast ridicule on the private nature of these stylistic mannerisms and their excessiveness and eccentricity with respect to the way people normally speak and write" (ibid, p. 1963).

So, Jameson says, this presupposes a sense of a normal voice, against which the parodied is measured, for example the way the Nausicaa chapter is measured against the first few chapters of *Ulysses*. But now—what would happen if one no longer believed in such ordinary languages? If a plurality of different voices was all there was, with no baseline, then to speak would involve putting on a voice, but it would not be parody. It would be, in Jameson's terms, pastiche.

> Pastiche is, like parody, the imitation of a peculiar or unique style, the wearing of a stylistic mask, speech in a dead language: but it is a neutral practice of such mimicry ... without that still latent feeling that there's something

normal compared to which what is being imitated is rather comic [*ibid.*, p. 1963].

We have seen and will see again this notion of pastiche. It captures Tarantino's aesthetic as well as the manic style of *The Simpsons*, as we'll see. It also arguably finds expression in one of the most interesting genres of music of the 90s, namely rap, which relies heavily on sampling older works.

Interestingly for our purposes, he makes the case that nostalgia is an important feature of the postmodern outlook. He points to the film *American Graffiti*, released at the height of Watergate in 1973, and looking back in an idealized way to 1962, and to some other nostalgic films and books of the era, and seems to suggest that nostalgia is a distinctively postmodern thing.

He discusses also the film *Body Heat*, an homage to certain film noirs but set in the present day (so the 1980s of his writing). It manages to pull off the homage by using a small-town setting, and thus being able to get away without representing the trappings of modern life. I suggest that this is exactly what's going on with *Twin Peaks*. And what he goes on to say will also prove highly relevant:

> It seems to be exceedingly symptomatic to find the very style of nostalgia films invading and colonising even those movies today which have contemporary settings: as though, for some reason, we were unable today to focus our own present, as though we have become incapable of achieving aesthetic representations of our own current experience.

He then goes on to consider the stylized representation of the past we find in such works. Again, think of the picturesque picket fences of *Blue Velvet*'s Lumberton, and then recall this was a decade when Black people were still forced to sit separate from whites in shops and on buses. Our retro films aren't accurate presentations of the past:

> Cultural production has been driven back inside the mind, within the monadic subject: it can no longer look directly out of its eyes at the real world for its referent but must, as in Plato's cave, trace its mental images of the world on its confining walls ... *we seem condemned to seek the historical past through our own pop images and stereotypes about that past, which itself remains forever out of reach* [*ibid.*, p. 1966–67, my italics].

This is all very interesting, and will be worth heeding. Jameson, writing in the early 1980s, diagnosed a trend that reached its height, arguably, in the 90s, with Tarantino and Lynch. He sees that nostalgia is a fundamental feature of postmodernism, and taking his suggestion, we can

4. Explainer: Postmodernism

then agree that the 90s are indeed a postmodern decade. Moreover, his idea that art has come to traffic in representations of reality rather than reality itself will become important when we consider *The Simpsons*. But I think we can suggest in advance a reason for our moving into Plato's cave. It's the same reason I suggested Tarantino was realist: the rise of television. If we're now about representation rather than reality, the reason for that is because representation was reality, for the many Americans who sat around watching television all day.

One last thinker: Michel Foucault. It is, I think, considerably harder to pull out one big, easily compressible and comprehensible idea from Foucault's writings than it is from the others. His writings are vast, organized into different periods and complicated. What I'll do is explain one part of one central cluster of concepts for which he is famous, and which are relevant for today.

These are truth, power, and surveillance. That truth, or at least what is commonly taken to be true (an important qualification, of course), is connected with power is something very intuitively obvious. We need think only of Fox News and the *Daily Mail*, the millionaires who bankroll anti–climate change research and who buy, on either side of the party political line, elections. Or again, we can think of countries in which the government straight-up censors what its citizens can encounter: again, we have a straight causal connection running from the powerful to (what people take to be) the true.

When Foucault speaks of truth and power, or, as he sometimes does, truth/power, though, it's important to note that that's *not* what he means. The power that interests Foucault is not to be found in the obvious places: not in the millionaires and the state and the media. Rather, for Foucault, power works much more subtly, constantly, and mundanely.

In order to see this, consider the following two stories about how punishment, conceived of as a manifestation of power, could be wielded. On one, you punish people when they do something really bad. When, basically, it's you vs. them: when the people rise up and try to overthrow you, say. And when you do so, you do so brutally, let's say with public executions.

There are advantages and disadvantages to this method. Obviously, it incurs risk—if the people are advancing on you, they might win. And brutal ostentatious punishments take time and money too. But it has a certain advantage: you don't have to really pay that much attention to punishment. The only time you need to have your punishment hat on is during those large and unmissable disruptions. And that in turn means you don't really have to devote time and resources to attending to your citizenry.

The other method of punishment works by correcting not large infractions, but small ones. Not assassination attempts, say, but juvenile delinquency. This has a certain advantage: if you can nip misbehavior in the bud before it blossoms into large-scale unrest, you can save the time and risk of ostentatious punishment. But it requires a lot more knowledge. You need to be paying attention to the kids constantly, attentive to their every action, so you can be attentive to their every transgression. You need to know a lot more about them—about their daily routines, about how they mouthed off to teacher, and so on. But that knowledge confers power: if you know these small facts, your capacity to punish becomes much more fine-grained, and more effective. In the words of some text about young workers in the 19th century Foucault quotes:

> The least act of disobedience is punished and the best way of avoiding serious offenses is to punish the most minor offenses very severely [ibid, p. 1637].

One of Foucault's basic thoughts is that we moved from the first model of punishment, of big punishments for big transgressions, to the second model around the turn of the 19th century. We did so partly because the individual, the common person, became an object of study then. It became important to know vital statistics like the number of children a person had, their health, the age their parents died at, and so on, in order to manage more efficiently towns and countries. With this rise in the science and practice of statistics (conceived of as measuring features of those who make up the state) the individual became an apt subject of knowledge, and this led Foucault to the study of prisons, hospitals, workhouses, and so on, all of which had this character of what he calls panopticisim—of being places the inhabitants of which are also being observed, with the knowledge culled from that observation being used to keep them in line.

Foucault's picture is an interesting one. That power is something that runs through our institutions rather than being brutally enforced upon us is worth thinking about. I highly doubt I'm the first to have made this connection, but I think one can quite clearly make a decent case for social media as panoptical, that is as a tool in which observation and the knowledge it yields serve power. Here's how it would go: you might think that power controls knowledge in social media in one of

4. Explainer: Postmodernism

two ways: either the powerful simply censor what they don't like, or the powerful make use of the data we give them to direct us in the directions they want us to—in the direction of voting for this person, or buying this thing, or simply of spending all our time on these platforms giving us their data.

The Foucault view, though, or at least the part of it I presented here, would be different, less obvious, and more interesting (this is probably an extremely cold take; if you can anticipate what I'm just about to say, skip this paragraph). It would point to the low-level practices that guide us through social media, the small incentives and punishments it offers. For example, heterodoxy, playing devil's advocate, is often not well received on social media, in the very mundane (and embarrassing-that-we-care) sense that if I were to, say, play devil's advocate and make the free market case for sweatshops then for a start no one would favorite or like my post, and it's highly possible people would unfollow me.[2] Conversely, if I were to dunk on some libertarian think piece doing the same, I would be treated better. Favoriting, retweeting, following—these are the sort of subtle bottom-up manifestations of power that Foucault would have been interested in, and rightly so. Moreover, much contemporary discourse on the left often speaks of the intermingling of truth and power, and although often such speech doesn't seem to be tracking the Foucauldian idea, part of the justification for extremely influential concepts in political discourse today like the patriarchy or white supremacy are, at least in some people's mouths, Foucauldian. One can be a white supremacist, or uphold the patriarchy, even if you confidently proclaim your liberal bona fides, because the networks of power that uphold these things are much more subtle and insidious than the more obviously egregious outpourings of racism and sexism manifest in law, obvious hate speech, and overt physical violence.

So, that's a whistle-stop tour through postmodernism. I think there are a few things worth thinking about: even though Baudrillard is unforgivably vague, this idea that we spend a lot of time focused on images seems interesting, and, as we'll see, only increases. Lyotard's idea that there's no overlying truth is also something which gets bandied about. Jameson's ideas of pastiche, nostalgia, and representation are also all very helpful (indeed, their prescience has been noted by someone we just mentioned above, the British critic Mark Fisher, who took Jameson's conceptual resources to be applicable to post-2000 UK music). There does seem to be something, according to these terms, postmodern about

Nineties to Now

Tarantino and Lynch, even if there's vagueness there. And Foucault is arguably helpful in understanding some of the politically charged discourse around identity politics today.

So we've made, I hope, a little progress. One big question remains, though: if some works of the 90s were indeed postmodern according to what these fancy theorists mean by that, are we still in a postmodern era? On the one hand, overarching ideologies are out and prestige TV has little to do with pastiche. On the other, a lot of us spend a lot of our terms watching porn, voted for reality TV boss Trump as boss of America, and communicate in memes which are perhaps pastiche taken to its limit, and are committed to the idea that we are living in a white supremacist society, despite what much law, statistics, and our conscience tells us. I will discuss all this later, considering whether we're now post-postmodern.

5

Seinfeld

NBC's *Seinfeld* (1989–1998) can be described, at least initially, simply. It's a sitcom about four New Yorkers and their lives' mundane ups and downs. It was incredibly popular: Wikipedia tells me that for two years, it was the most watched program, and its finale got almost 80 million viewers, which is to say more than one-quarter of Americans.

Not only that, it was critically acclaimed, and would today top most critics' lists of best sitcoms ever. This combination of popularity and critical acclaim is pretty rare, and so I think it's worth considering what we can learn about culture from the show. What is it that attracted both the critics and the everyday watchers so?

There are two features of *Seinfeld* that are important both for understanding the show but also for our bigger project of understanding the ideology of the 90s. The first concerns cynicism or nihilism, and the second concerns its superficiality.

We've already, to some extent, touched on these phenomena in our discussion. We noted that *Generation X* combined cynicism and disaffection with the absurdities of late 20th-century political and economic life with heart, with characters that love each other and yearn for a different era, a fact reflected in the way the book looks back to pre–74 life.

My reading of *Seinfeld* is that it marks a development of this spirit in which the cynicism remains, but the love and nostalgia have gone. *Seinfeld* is permeated, self-consciously, with nihilism and with the sense of itself as new. Where the *Generation X* gang look back with longing, *Seinfeld* looks to the current world, putting it under the microscope of the stand-up comedian to analyze its flaws, which leads to the superficiality, which is a great source, as we'll see, of humor.

Nineties to Now

So, let me turn to cynicism. I asked what brought critics and the everyday watcher together in their enjoyment of *Seinfeld*. And, well, the smart-ass answer is: nothing. Famously, *Seinfeld* is a show about nothing, and it is so in two senses. Sitcoms tend to derive humor from a particular situation: *M*A*S*H* from the Korean War, *Happy Days* from the 50s, most of the others in some variety of household. *Seinfeld* has no situation in this way. Although there are certain locations used again and again, such as Jerry's apartment and the diner they frequent, the show tends to follow them around Manhattan as they get in various adventures.

Now, we can quibble to what extent this really makes *Seinfeld* new, and how much it's really different from, say, *Cheers* in this respect. Just as *Cheers* isn't really about anything in the sense that *M*A*S*H* is about the Korean War, so *Seinfeld* isn't about anything, we might think. Fair enough: I think there's a decent case to be made that some of the "show about nothing" rhetoric the makers were fond of wasn't too accurate.

Where *Seinfeld* undoubtedly *does* differ from its predecessors, though, is the way it self-consciously subverts them. Famously, the dictum of *Seinfeld* is "no hugging, no learning." It set itself up explicitly in opposition to family friendly sitcoms like *The Cosby Show* or *Happy Days*, or shows with a sociopolitical heart like *M*A*S*H*, in which the characters are basically good, and things basically turn out well, and if they don't, lessons are learned.

The characters in *Seinfeld* are not basically good, and for the people with whom they interact, things do not turn out basically well. Take Susan Ross, George's erstwhile fiancée. She had been living a perfectly happy life before she met him, but when she did, in the space of a couple of years, she (a) got vomited on by Kramer, (b) got fired from her job because of her relationship, (c) indirectly led to her father's beloved cabin being burned down, and (d) his secret homosexuality being revealed, and finally (e) died, licking the toxic glue of cheap envelopes George skimped on for their wedding invitations.

Not only that, but this was the object of more or less indifference to everybody, including and perhaps especially George. When the gang learn of her death, after brief unmeant commiserations, and at George's suggestion, they go for coffee as they always do; the episode plays out with George phoning a woman he's interested in, asking her out and telling her that his calendar is pretty open—apart from the next day, when

5. Seinfeld

his wife's funeral is being held—and would she like to go out with him? Examples like this could be multiplied at will. Here's an inexhaustive list of things they did: Jerry stole a rye bread from an old lady in the street, snatching it from her arms and running away; when a fire breaks out at his girlfriend's mother's house, George knocks women and children out of the way in a dash for the exit; again George is concerned that his girlfriend might be bulimic not because of her well-being, but because it means the dinners he buys her are money down the drain; Elaine, pretending on the phone to be a child's grandmother, and getting sick of the call, pretends she's dying so she doesn't have to keep talking. Jerry's catchphrase is practically "that's a shame," uttered entirely unfeelingly when someone close to him goes through some misfortune.

Of course, finding humor in cruelty and inhumanity is hardly unique to *Seinfeld*—generations of stand-up comedians, and things like *It's Always Sunny in Philadelphia*, *South Park*, and *Family Guy* have made it passé.

But to analogize *Seinfeld* to these other more uncontroversially "dark" comedies is not quite right. Firstly, it's not typical dark humor. It avoids the really serious topics, such as murder, drugs, child abuse, and so on, that dark comedy tends to thrive on. There's no profanity, and any talk of sex is very euphemistic. It's filmed like any standard sitcom using multiple cameras and looks, today, very much a product of its time.

If anything, though, this makes its central lack of heart all the more cutting. We know, for example, that we're not meant to empathize with the cast of *Sunny*; we know, basically, that how Ricky Gervais gets his laughs is a very simplistic taboo breaking. But *Seinfeld*—these are normal people, just like us. That *they* are like this suggests that *we* are maybe like this—other "gang of friends" sitcoms of the age do seem explicitly aspirational: you would like to be one of the *Friends* gang. Of course, to a large extent that's just part of the humor. It goes against our expectations of the (prime-time, multi-camera) sitcom genre that its protagonists should be terrible human beings. So that's one important feature of *Seinfeld*: it's emotional coldness. To the extent that we associate coldness and cynicism with the 90s, then the massively popular *Seinfeld* is a sign of this.

If that were it, though, still I don't think *Seinfeld* would deserve all that much attention (well, apart from the fact that it's still, almost 30 years after it first aired, about the funniest sitcom there's been). What's particularly interesting about the inhumanity of the *Seinfeld* gang is its source. A recurring theme is *superficiality*: they do things, for example end relationships, for very silly reasons. They don't see the forest for the trees: Jerry, for example, breaks up with a girl because she eats her peas one at a time with a fork; George breaks up with a girl because she beat him at chess. Elaine breaks up with someone because, when leaving a note that a friend of hers had given birth, he didn't add an exclamation point. She even, in another episode, breaks up with someone because he was a "bad breaker upper":

> ELAINE: (Fast) Well, you know when you break up, how you say things you don't mean? Well, he says the mean things you don't mean, but he means them. [So I'm going to] Dump him. I can't be with someone who doesn't break up nicely. I mean, to me, that's one of the most important parts of a relationship.

For the *Seinfeld* gang, life swarms with a series of complicated minute rules that guide social behavior. But, as if they suffer from a strange sort of eye disease that magnifies the small while doing nothing to the big, they can't see beyond these rules which imprison them.

This is the way we should think of the gang: they are sort of like scientists of modern life, people stuck to the microscope who have no life outside the lab. Except they're not trying to understand cell biology to cure cancer but are working out after how many dates you're required to break up with someone in person. (The rules, in case you're interested, are that you can break up with someone over the phone provided either you've only had six dates with them OR you've had more than six [exactly how many more isn't specified] but you haven't had sex. Elaine responds to this advice with displeasure [see "The Alternate Side," season 3 episode 11]). They are frequently presented as sorts of savants of modern life, knowing precisely what modern etiquette demands, as for example in the scene (in "The Pledge Drive," season 6 episode 3) where Jerry asks George how long exactly you're meant to keep a "thank you" card for, or when the gang wonder how many sneezes can elapse before you say "God bless you" to someone in the presence of their spouse (who, naturally, has first refusal when it comes to gesundheits—see "The Good Samaritan," season 3 episode 20—for the ethics of blessing).

Or again, on how George can tell if he's got a girlfriend. It depends,

5. Seinfeld

Jerry tells George, on many variables. Normal things, like how often you see the person (every weekend? Is a date implied?), how often you call them (every day? semi-daily?). Then more subtle matters like whether or not they've left stuff in your medical cabinet. Under analysis, George's case is revealed to be a borderline one, until Jerry, like a lawyer waiting to drop the final decisive question, traps him and then sums up:

> JERRY: On many factors. Is there any Tampax in your house?
> GEORGE: (Pause) Yeah.
> JERRY: Well, I'll tell you what you've got here.
> GEORGE: What?
> JERRY: You got yourself a girlfriend.

What makes these funny, though, is the fact that the rules by which they guide their behavior don't, in fact, exist, but they assume they do. Jerry assumes that a certain phone call frequency together with other stuff implies a girlfriend, but of course it doesn't.

This is what sets *Seinfeld* apart, I think, from other comedies. After all, observing the foibles of modern life is hardly unique to it: it's a staple of most any comedy. What's different about *Seinfeld* is that it's not actually observing features. Instead, it's making up features, pretending that they exist, and then watching the clash that arises between the gang that's obsessed with those features and the rest of the world.

Although I was somewhat tepid in my enthusiasm for Baudrillard, some of his fuzzy motivating thoughts seem relevant here: recall he held that the Watergate scandal was self-creating in a strange way. It didn't accurately describe political reality as divided into the regular, moral, law-like functioning that is typical and its rupture in scandal, because there was no such regular functioning to begin with. But by suggesting a scandal, it thereby suggested the law necessary for a scandal.

So, we might think, here: there are no rules governing when one does or doesn't have a girlfriend, but by acting as if there were, one brings them into being: after his conversation with Jerry, George considers himself to be in a relationship and behaves as if he were. In a decent sense, then, we can say that *Seinfeld* is a postmodern sitcom.

Related to this is one of the other distinctive features of Seinfeldian humor, which is the use of neologisms. *Seinfeld* has given us the following, which have to some extent become part of common use:

> **high talker, close talker, low talker**: Respectively, someone who talks with an abnormally high-pitched voice, or who stands right up in your face when talking to you, or who talks very quietly.
> **sidler**: Someone who doesn't make any noise when they move and so can just sneak up on you quickly.
> **regifter**: Someone who gives as a gift something which they themselves received as a gift.
> **antidentite**: Someone prejudiced against dentists.

Another source of similar humor in the same vein is expressions like the following:

> **The pop in**: When someone is in the area and comes to your house unannounced (see also: the break out pop in, when someone escapes from jail and comes to your house unannounced).
> **The day date**: As it suggests, a date during the daytime, involving less pressure, and not requiring wine and showering.
> **The kiss hello**: The unfortunate habit of kissing someone hello when you meet them.
> **The roommate switch**: when you're dating someone and attempt to replace her with her roommate.

There's an interesting feature of these expressions which has been much studied by linguists: nouns and definite descriptions are *presuppositional*. We can think of something like "antidentite" as a sort of name, and names have this feature: if you use it in someone's company, you presuppose that your hearer is familiar with the name's bearer. If Bill is my uncle, but you don't know him and we've never talked about him before, it's very weird for me to say, out of the blue, "Bill is getting a new car." It's presupposed that if you use a name, its bearer is familiar. Similarly, if you use a phrase like "the x," it's presupposed that there is one and only one x. If we're talking about cars and I say "the guy who fixed my car was nice," you'll come to assume, if you didn't before, that one and only one person fixed my car.

Seinfeld exploits these linguistic devices to make it seem as if "antidentite" and "roommate switches" are familiar things, parts of the world as taken for granted as your friends or the president.

5. Seinfeld

That they are, in fact, to most people, including the audience, unfamiliar gives us the impression that the gang live in their own separate world where what's taken for granted is different. As, indeed, they do: we don't recognize high talkers as features of the social world, and nor is roommate switching something we are familiar with.

Here's one way to understand this. The world is a confusing and scary place, and to have a name for something, or to think that it's governed by rules, gives comfort. That's why the Greeks thought there was a God of wind whose moods determined whether their sea crossings would work, and why they gave him a name ("Aelous"). We should view *Seinfeld* as trying to do the same for the confusing and scary place that is New York City of the 90s. The problem is that that world is for all intents and purposes indeterministic as is the weather system: there are no rules they can use to bring it under control, just as we can't predict the weather too accurately.

Here's another way of understanding this humor: they are trying to *brand* the social world in which they find themselves, but they fail, because they're trying to draw distinctions where none exist. In drawing distinctions between the high talkers and the low talkers, between being in a relationship with an implied Saturday night date and one without, they are drawing distinctions that don't really make a difference, just as, so the story goes, a given factory might produce one and the same fizzy liquid, slap a Coke label on one and a Smart Value label on the other, and thereby charge different prices for them. Brands are distinctions without differences, and I think we should understand *Seinfeld* as attempting to take over this logic of brands into the social world, and making it ridiculous.

This might sound like kind of a reach. But it's notable that this sort of linguistic humor is also a central feature of another work we considered, namely *Generation X*. On the bottom of a lot of the pages of that book are little boxes with definitions, like the following:

> **Boomer Envy.** Envy of material wealth and long-range material security accrued by older members of the baby boom generation by virtue of fortunate births.
> **Bread and Circuits.** The electric era tendency to view part politics as corny—no longer relevant or meaningful or useful to modern societal issues, and in many cases dangerous.
> **Ultra Short Term Nostalgia.** Homesickness for the extremely recent past: "God, things seemed so much better in the world last week."

Nineties to Now

Occupational Slumming. Taking a job well beneath one's skill or education level as a means of retreat from adult responsibilities and/or avoid possible failure in one's true occupation.

Again, most of these aren't of existing terms, and perhaps not existing phenomena. One gets the sense that Coupland is trying, in a sense more plaintive than *Seinfeld*, to make sense of the features of the world he inhabits, and finds that existing language doesn't cut it.

Once you attend to this, you'll see that appeal to brands is ubiquitous in 90s works: Bret Easton Ellis's *American Psycho* of 1991 derives most of its little humor from juxtaposing detailed accounts of exactly what sort of suits and skin creams its hero wears with extremely graphic descriptions of rape and murder; a similar thing is found, to a similar effect, in David Fincher's *Fight Club*; David Foster Wallace's *Infinite Jest* is set in a future in which even years have brand names and his literary fiction ancestor Don DeLillo's much lauded *White Noise* is practically set in a supermarket. In *The Simpsons*, moreover, among many other examples, we find the clown Krusty giving his name to a range of products including: Krusty-brand Home Pregnancy Test, Krusty's sulphuric acid, and Krusty's Legal Forms ("hey hey they're legally binding") (I owe this list to Chris Turner's excellent 2004 book *Planet Simpson*).

Talking and joking about brands was everywhere in 90s humor (the next explainer will suggest why—this was a culture coming to terms with the brand as a new and central feature of the economy), so I don't think it's so implausible to say that something like that's going on with Seinfeldian verbal humor.

Returning to *Seinfeld*, then, the big thing about it is not that it's a show about the little things that make up our modern life. Rather, and more brilliantly, it's about the nonexistent little things that these four *think* makes up our modern life but which don't. It's also, I would suggest, about the deadening effects of knowledge, or at least the microscopic knowledge which they possess, and which seems to distract them away from human feeling. Again, compare *Generation X*: their awareness of their McJobs is tempered with hopes for a beyond, realized at the end of the novel. *Seinfeld* is monocular, focused entirely and minutely on the present, with absurd and deadening effects.

In my overall narrative, I would want to suggest that *Seinfeld*

5. Seinfeld

seasons roughly four–six mark a distinct point of development in the 90s. The move from *Generation X* to *Seinfeld* is marked by the falling away of nostalgia, by an obsessional interest with the here and now of modern life in its minute depths. And with that goes away nostalgia and melancholy, and is replaced by coldness and apathy, with the same keen eye for the ridiculousness of the modern world but without the sympathy and love to make it bearable.

6

Explainer: Branding

I've suggested that a central thread of the humor of *Seinfeld* and a range of other works ought to be understood in terms of what we could call the logic of branding. The aim of this chapter is to consider that logic, by considering the way the concept of the brand took off in the late eighties and early nineties.

The notion of brand is one I think the interest of which is dulled, to us, by familiarity: millennials like me, even in the smallish town in Northern Ireland I grew up in, are used to high streets with Subway and McDonald's, most likely pestered our parents to buy us expensive branded clothes, sought SNESs or PlayStations or Xboxes.

But to the previous generation, this wasn't so. The ubiquity of brands is a relatively recent development, understanding which can shed light not only on the works we've just considered, but on numerous features of our life today, from the different online spaces we congregate in, to the preference for craft beer and burgers on slates and jam-jar cocktails, to the burgeoning of gig economy businesses like Uber and Airbnb. By learning about brands, and by seeing them reflected in work by people less numb to them than us, we can learn about our world.

And our online, artisanal, techno-libertarian world can be seen as a consequence of what we can call, following Naomi Klein, the spiritualization of big business, whose *No Logo* (Picador, 1999), published around the millennium, I rely on extensively in this chapter. Starting from around the late eighties, companies have done their absolute best to divest themselves of the awkward physical trappings which previously were essential: of full-time workers who want benefits and decent wages, of factories which require fixing, and of products which can easily be copied by a low-budget competitor. Rather, big companies are now in the image business: a company sells a lifestyle, or an idea—that is, an intangible, immaterial thing. Of course, it can't quite—or couldn't, until

6. Explainer: Branding

recently—get by *entirely* without the physical, but it can ship it out to third-world factories, or hire people on 38-hour-a-week (or whatever is required so that the job is not, technically, full time) contracts which can be terminated instantly.

The trend away from matter is inherent to a society in which goods are mass produced, Klein notes. If I'm selling you rice but there's another guy over there also selling you rice, how do I get your business? I can cut my prices, sure, but he can cut his too. I need a way to set my product apart from his, to find a distinction in the absence of a difference. That difference was the brand.

Brands had been around for decades. Uncle Ben's, for example, had been selling rice since the mid–40s, aided by the eponymous Ben, a kindly shopkeeper who graced its packages. And advertising, as we all now know from *Mad Men*, is also a venerable institution since pioneered by Eddy Bernays, Freud's nephew, who used his uncle's psychological insights to get people to buy stuff.

Given this, one might think we're not dealing with a phenomenon particular to the nineties. But brands only really came into their own a bit later. Indeed, on Klein's telling, a very concrete sign of this dematerialization occurred in 1988, when Philip Morris bought Kraft for six times what it was worth, the thought being all that extra was for the good name of "Kraft" (Klein, p. 6). The importance of branding was revealed or perhaps better created—again, obscure old Baudrillard comes to mind—by the money that was spent on it.

But this suddenly discovered value in brands was also reflective of an underlying necessity. Because the underlying economy changed in another fundamental way with the coming into existence of big box discount stores, the prime exemplar of which is Walmart (the best book about which I know is *The Wal-Mart Effect*, Charles Fishman, 2006).

A company like Walmart uses economies of scale to crush competition: its stores are so big, and so plentiful, that they can sell things much cheaper. How can I get you to buy *my* soda when Walmart, with its economies of scale, can offer gallon jugs for cents?

Again, branding. In a sense, I cease to sell the soda, and sell instead an idea—perhaps I make an advert showing cool young people around drinking soda, conveying the message that if you drink it, you too could be friends with—indeed, be one of—these cool young people. Economies of scale don't (yet) apply to ideas.

All the big companies realized this: they realized that their product was an image rather than anything physical. Klein collects quotes in which CEOs and industry insiders are disarmingly honest about this. Starbucks tell us that people "don't truly believe" there's a difference between their coffee and others, so they must "establish emotional ties" with their brand. The owner of Diesel jeans says, "We don't sell a product, we sell a style of life." Nike claims it's a "sports company" whose aim is to keep "the magic of sports alive" (Klein p. 20, p. 23, p. 24, respectively).

This can sound like bullshit, but these *are* very successful companies, and they *are* selling things which can be got much cheaper. The simplest explanation is that a customer buying them is in fact buying something else to account for the higher tag; so why not just call that brand. If it seems a bit metaphysically heavyweight and pretentious—well, that seems to be how reality is.

These companies, anyway, certainly believe this sort of thing. It's reflected in the staggering amount they spend on advertising. Reebok, for example, in the guts of a recession, upped ad spending 71.9 percent in 1991 (Klein p. 16). It's reflected in the culture we inhabit, it's reflected in their adventures across the world, and it's reflected in the income inequality that's risen in lockstep with it.

Klein points out facts that can seem to be obscured: corporate sponsorship of events like concerts and sports and even schools first became a really big thing in the 90s. And that era saw the development of brand ambassadors, the most famous example of whom was Michael Jordan, who came to be associated with the products of Nike, and things like product placement and sponsored concerts. We're now somewhat inured to stadiums named after shoes and campuses filled with McDonald's, but it's worthwhile looking at things through slightly older eyes and seeing that this is indeed a bit weird. It's somewhat surreal and unpleasant that our entertainment should be so commercially compromised in this way, and it becomes understandable, I think, that the artists we've been looking at should be so attuned to it. And seeing that, we should focus our gaze on the surreal fact that we live in a society in which Apple launches are *events* and when a decent percentage of the people who watch the Super Bowl do so to see the new commercials.

And once we've done so, we should return to our current always-online life and be on the lookout for the invasion of advertising into our personal spaces, not only in the literal sense that we have to navigate around ads to see content, but also in the more insidious way that, chasing likes and self-censoring, what now makes up, for many of us, the bulk of our interactions, are mediated by certain brand-like constraints.

6. Explainer: Branding

Although we joke about personal brands, actually to embrand oneself, with the rigidity and blandness that that implies, is a very bad thing.

So that's the first take home: branding is important in nineties art because it was a relatively new development, and we should remain awake to its weirdnesses today, especially given how brands seem to have integrated themselves into our lives.

(I have been, and will continue to be, somewhat harsh about the notion of brands, and it can seem almost self-evident to people of a liberal persuasion that things like McDonald's can be found in every corner of the world. It's worth pointing out, though, that alongside the anti-branding sentiment there have been people who come to praise rather than bury the brand. Authors like Charles Wheelin in his 2002 *Naked Economics* and more recently Tyler Cowan in *Big Business* [2019] have argued that the predictability branding fosters—if you find yourself lost in a foreign country, you can know to expect a Big Mac and free Wi-Fi if you see a McDonald's—are, or at least can be, beneficial. Branding makes the world more predictable and is something we often value. I think this point is a good one and worth taking seriously when assessing the pros and cons of brands, and I think it also sheds light on the previous chapter about *Seinfeld*. The *Seinfeld* gang is trying to reduce the unpredictability of modern urban life by assuming that there are these repeating social patterns, that dating is as predictable as Big Macs.)

There's a second thing, perhaps even more consequential than the first, which arises from this process of spiritualization. If what you're *really* selling is an idea, then the physical world is an impediment. It's kind of a pain for Nike, if they're selling the mere idea of sport, that they have to be bothered making shoes, a process which involves workers, whom one must pay, in factories which one must provide with electricity and toilet paper and occasionally repair.

The logical step is to try and get rid of these unfortunate physical substrates, and our companies took that step. As is by now familiar, many of the goods we use are made in awful conditions in the third world, where you can pay people a dollar a day as and when you need them, and where the externalities of pollution and illness caused by overwork needn't worry you.

But it's not only that. Again as Klein is at pains to point out, it's not strictly true to say that these companies moved jobs out there—rather, they ceased to get involved in the business of making themselves. Nike doesn't own any factories which make things; rather, they make a contract with someone to supply them made goods, which they then brand

and market. Nike is just like us—the company shops around to get the best value for the products which bear its name (Klein pp. 197ff).

Of course, not *all* companies can get away with this. We can't have our Starbucks served to us from the Philippines. But still, it must be galling, if you're Starbucks. The coffee you're making is really not what you're selling, but rather it's the Starbucks idea. The barista does little toward making this idea, so it's somewhat unfair that you should have to pay them properly.

And so they don't. In service industries, which have become much more numerous since globalization moved manufacturing abroad and habits have changed, people work non–full time. These jobs offer flexibility, even if they don't offer benefits, a fact which completely overlooks the very large number of people for whom this is their sole source of income. It isn't people in school doing these jobs anymore, for the most part, it's people struggling on around the minimum wage, working essentially full time without the benefits or protections full-time work is meant to provide. Although not of the same order of magnitude, their labor is cheap, much cheaper than it is practicable. A few years prior to Klein's book, this situation was made worse by Clinton's welfare reforms which removed support for single mothers and put them into these precarious service jobs, the degrading and unlivable nature of which Barbara Ehrenreich documented in her highly readable *Nickled and Dimed* of 2001.

Of course, this has only increased, but now it's increasingly rampant, and now huge swathes of academia run on zero-hours contracts. Not only that, but the dephysicalization has, familiarly, taken a novel turn. Businesses like Uber and Airbnb hit upon the clever expedient of having no physical product at all. Their whole business is coordination and transmission of information: of matching up people who need a ride with people who have a ride, people who need a room with people who have a room. They are the apotheosis of the brand era: purely informational companies. Capitalism's flight toward the spiritual is, it almost seems, complete; crucially, though, it's a journey that's been in the cards from the beginning. Although it's obviously been made possible by the internet, the rapid change in business we're witnessing is perhaps an inevitable stage in the logic of the brand, and so we shouldn't think it's a mere accident of history that has come about because of unpredictable technological advances.

There's one more interesting lesson to be got from Klein's book (Klein pp. 129ff). Consider Walmart, he paradigm budget brand, and

6. *Explainer: Branding*

Starbucks, a—at least let's say—prestige brand. Both adopt the same methods when taking over a market: they bombard the area with stores, thereby forcing other companies out of business. Starbucks, for example, will open a range of stores in an area, even if that involves "cannibalization"—profits from any given store being lowered because of the other Starbucks in the area. Once they've moved in, they force other stores out, at which time they have a monopoly. Walmart does the same, only on a statewide scale: they only move into a certain area once they're able to open a good number of stores in close proximity, but once they have done so, they are able to essentially take over whole swathes of the county, as they benefit from massive economies of scale (essentially, as if they had one gigantic store in the territory they occupy) and are thus able to drive smaller stores out of business.

It's notable that this is more or less explicitly Uber's strategy at the moment, and once you realize that, then maybe it'll make you think again about the fact that Facebook and Twitter are free. Are they trying to get a monopoly on the internet?

All of this will be discussed more later. My aim here has been twofold: to present a bit of the history of branding in order to understand what can seem like a slightly strange and passé 90s art obsession and also the source of some of its distinctive artist maneuvers, and to understand the nature of brands today. But one final point. I hope that realizing the relative recentness of this, well, almost straightforwardly immoral form of capitalism will make us, like the heroes of *Generation X*, realize that there is an alternative, that things haven't always been this way (they weren't pre-74, so Dag thinks), and given that, they needn't always be this way: it's not an inevitability of the human condition, or perhaps even of capitalism, that things are as they are.

7

_____, Race, Gender and Representation

This chapter, which is absolutely central to my overall argument, is, as its partially empty title suggests, different. It is not about art, but about an absence of art; it is about representation and an absence of representation.

As was pointed out, a noteworthy and somewhat unfortunate feature of this book is that it's very white and male. This is in and of itself objectionable: if I am trying to tell the story of a generation, telling the story of one particularly privileged demographic of that generation is going to come up short. But it's more than that. Unless you think that I am simply wrong in my choices of the best of the 90s, it's an interesting question why it is so dominated by the work of white men. It is also an interesting question whether this domination will continue.

Discussion of that will have to wait for the final chapter. But just to at least temporarily inject some diversity, let me anticipate and note that I think this domination, at least partially, at least arguably, hasn't continued. Culture has gotten more diverse between the 90s and the 2010s, in little and big ways. A superficial, but arguably nevertheless still important metric is just to watch TV. *Seinfeld* and *Friends* are all white; in *The Simpsons*, people of color are peripheral characters (indeed, there are no serious Latin people). Crossing the border of the century, in *Arrested Development*, this remains true. A few years later, we have Tracy Jordan in *30 Rock* as a main character alongside female protagonist Liz Lemon. *The Office* and *Parks and Recreation* have minority characters playing main roles, and when we fast-forward to today, it has become de rigueur to have a diverse cast, and it's noteworthily strange if a show doesn't have a racial and gender balance that at least roughly tracks the demographics of the country (think *Brooklyn Nine-Nine, Superstore*).

The characters on TV have come to reflect, to some extent, the ethnic composition of the U.S. The unfortunate stranger whose only access

7. _____, Race, Gender and Representation

to the country was via its sitcoms would no longer be *quite* so misled about who makes it up.

The same holds of "higher" culture. In the last couple of years of the 2010s, the standout literary star has been, I think without a doubt, Sally Rooney, a young Dubliner. It is she who is the David Foster Wallace of our time in the sense of someone deemed the voice of a generation. Among cultural critics, there are people like Roxanne Gay and Ta-Nehisi Coates, who write about being Black, fatphobia, mental illness, and much else. One of the standout shows is HBO's *Girls*, written and fronted by women.

All this is to say is that someone writing, in 2040, a book about the 2010s simply couldn't list a bunch of white men, in a way that I think I can list a bunch of white men while still listing the most momentous works of the era.

Any talk of increased diversity in 2021 that stopped there would be, however, incomplete. Because not only has culture undergone a partial "dewhitening," whiteness has, like a bump in the carpet, appeared elsewhere. In politics, in the U.S. but also elsewhere, ethnic nationalists, anti-immigration campaigners, and xenophobes have become features of the mainstream political discourse, as anti-racist taboos that held sway in the last half of the 20th century (on both sides of the political aisle) have eroded, a fact that we will discuss in greater detail later.

The aim of this chapter is severalfold. Firstly, it simply attempts to put some data and history behind these observations about the varying fortunes of various non-white-male groups in the second half of the 20th century and in particular the 70s. I will also consider the various backlashes against this move, along the way showing that today's culture wars continue a debate already begun in the 90s. Having accrued some data, I will attempt to explain the cultural pattern that I claim to find, of era-defining non-white-males represented in pop culture in 2010 but not in 1990, a fact which will be puzzling once I've done the first bit. The overall message, I hope, will be that we can learn about the development of culture not only by analyzing present works of art, but also by considering what is absent and why.

***

So far in this book already the early 1970s have appeared numerous times as a focal point. On the narrative I've endorsed, which many others would also, it marks a turning point. It is the time that the economy visibly went south, with the stagflation that ushered in a new economic paradigm. With the benefit of hindsight that citizens of the 1970s didn't have, we can see that that began an era when growth sputtered. As we have seen, many of the developments that made life recognizably modern had already been introduced into homes by then (apart from the computer, to be dealt with later). And finally, it is the era when domestic politics was undermined and spectacularized by Watergate, Nixon's subsequent resignation, and his pardoning by Ford.

I have argued or will argue that these events were crucial to forming the sometimes cynical, sometimes nostalgic mindset that I have claimed shines through 1990s work. But I have so far mostly left out one other completely crucial early 1970s development: the increasing freedom of women and, perhaps to a lesser extent, people of color and gay people.

The story probably begins, as does so much of the story here, with the Second World War. Women had worked before the Second World War, but it marked something new. Female labor force participation rose from 10.8 million in March 1941 to more than 18 million in August 1944. Not only that, but it was, almost literally, empowering work. The figure of Rosie the Riveter is one of the iconic cultural figures of the time, depicted as a woman ready for work with her hair bundled up and a bulging bicep. These women worked in the factories that had quickly arisen at great scale, making munitions and related war products.

Once the war ended, the enlisted men got demobilized, and there was a move toward putting women back in the home (for details, see Susan Faludi, *Backlash*, pp. 65–70) yielding the figure of the bored housewife presented in, say, *Mad Men*, or in the work of Betty Friedan:

> The problem lay buried, unspoken for many years in the minds of American women. It was a strange stirring,—A sense of dissatisfaction, a yearning that women suffered in the middle of the twentieth century in the United States. Each suburban wife struggled with it alone. As she made the beds, shopped for groceries, matched slip-cover material, ate peanut butter sandwiches with her children, chauffeured Cub Scouts and Brownies, lay beside her husband at night-she was afraid to ask even of herself the silent question—"Is this all?" [Quoted in Zinn p. 505]

That said, the figures are impressive. The percentage of women aged 25–54 working in 1948 was 34.9; 44.5 percent in 1964; 69.9 percent in 1985 and 76.6 percent in 1999, with a decline to 73.9 percent in 2014 (Robert Gordon, *The Rise and Fall of American Growth*, p. 506). Although women continued, and indeed continue, to be underpaid relative to men (earning 77.4 percent of men's earnings in 2010, compared

7. _____, *Race, Gender and Representation*

to 58.8 percent in 1975, per Gordon), the number of high-status jobs occupied by women has also changed. Gordon tells us in 1960, 94 percent of doctors were men, 96 percent of lawyers, and 86 percent of managers vs. 63 percent, 61 percent, and 57 percent respectively in 2008. We see a similar increase in the number of female members of Congress (p. 507).

If that were all, it would still be impressive. But there was more. Cultural mores were changing to enable women to live lives that are more recognizable as lives we expect women to have today. In 1965, for example, the Supreme Court ruled it was unconstitutional for the government to prevent married couples from using birth control. As a curmudgeonly British poet—decidedly not a feminist—once wrote, "Sexual intercourse began/In nineteen sixty three," and critics have made the point that this was truly a new way of being.

And then a flurry of important legislation came along just as OPEC and Watergate did. In 1972, SCOTUS went further, announcing, "Everyone, including unmarried minors, had a right to use contraception" (quoted in Patterson, *Restless Giant*, p. 47). Opinions and habits changed too. In 1970, about half a million unmarried couples cohabited; that figure more than doubled in eight years; ten years prior that only, one a quarter of Americans thought so.

In 1972, the Equal Rights Amendment, according to which men and women should be treated equally under the law in all domains, was sent for ratification and was ratified by a good majority of states, although it remains stalled to this day. And finally, in 1973, *Roe v. Wade* was decided in the Supreme Court, which invalidated states' laws illegalizing abortion, which it argued was a matter of privacy (Patterson, p. 52).

Women made use of the newfound abilities. From Patterson (p. 47), we learn that unmarried white girls aged 19 engaging in sexual intercourse had been around 20–25 percent; it reached nearly 75 percent by 1990. From Frum's *How We Got Here*, we learn that in 1972, a survey of attitudes revealed that 56 percent of women thought premarital sex was always or almost always wrong. Ten years later, about the same percentage thought it was wrong only sometimes or never wrong. The same thing held for parents: in 1967, 85 percent of parents of college-age kids condemned premarital sex; by 1979, only 37 percent did. Only a shade more than 2 percent of women who came of age in the 1950s had slept with five or more men by 1950; 22.5 percent of those who came of age post–Vietnam had (Frum, p. 191).

Nineties to Now

It is easy to overlook—an incisive observation I take directly from Frum—but what we take for granted as the normal romantic trajectory of life for most people—a series of "relationships" that often bear many of the features of marriage—exclusivity, closeness up to cohabitation, the creation of extended families, would have been something completely alien even a few decades ago. Things decisively had changed.

While cultural conservatives might—indeed, did—bewail this, I think for many of us this changing of habits should be seen as an entirely good thing. Sex is, or can be, a good-making feature of life, and its cultural and legal accessibility to women is a mark of genuine progress, a fact especially noteworthy given the political and economic decline elsewhere in the culture.

The view that I've been more or less explicitly endorsing is that socioeconomic trends show up—are reflected in—the best pop culture of the time, according to my own somewhat narrow definition of pop culture. And on my view, the biggest positive development of the times in which the artists of the 90s came of age was the partial freeing of women to earn their own money and pursue their own desires. (I don't of course mean to say that the developments of the 70s were decisive; from the ongoing pay gap to #metoo to the 45th president of the United States, things are clearly still troubled. But if we can consider things relatively, comparing the situation before and after, there was great improvement in a way that there clearly wasn't from a macroeconomic perspective.)

Other formerly downtrodden groups also saw their fortunes changed, again at least relative to their previous lot. On the cusp of the 70s were the stonewall riots in NYC, where the occupants of a gay bar rioted when cops raided the eponymous gay bar for spurious reasons. In a different domain, a large handful of important decisions improved the lot of gay people in the 70s. Twenty-two states repealed laws against sodomy, and 50 cities introduced ordinances against discrimination based on sexual orientation. The first openly gay teacher was accredited, and the Democratic National Committee introduced into its platform opposition to sex-based discrimination, openly gay people were accepted in the church even, in some groups, as pastors. Finally, and perhaps of less overall moment than the developments just mentioned, it's shocking and worth knowing that it was only 1973 that the American Psychological Association ceased to classify homosexuality as a disorder. In all, some progress for gay people in the 70s (again, relative to their previous lot; and again, this is from Frum, pp. 205ff). Again, let's just take a step back. In our world, at least for many of us, acceptance of

7. _____, Race, Gender and Representation

LGBT+ is unthinking, not up for debate. That being gay was illegal 50 years ago, in a country with a claim to being the world's most advanced at the time, should give any of us who didn't live then pause, to let it sink in how things have changed, and indeed had changed by the 90s.

Finally, perhaps the most contentious of all, is the case of African Americans. We can start with some good news. In 1965, 72 Black people held public office in a variety of different roles; in 1978, more than 2,000 did (Zinn, pp. 465–66). Sticking with 1965, the Voting Rights Act was signed into law, and thereafter the number of southern Black people registered to vote rose swiftly, from 2 million in 1974 to 3 million in 1976 (Zinn p. 456). In 1964, the Civil Rights Act was passed.

It sounds good. But even reading Zinn's mainstream and white history is to be brought face to face with a catalogue of horror. Of protests in which Black people are killed by police or armed guards, again and again, and exonerated by courts (p. 463); of Black churches being bombed and children killed, of the everyday hatred of white words against Black people; of plots by the FBI, now famous, to hound Martin Luther King, Jr., or of President Kennedy's attempt to neuter by joining with the March on Washington. Or again, later, of the horrors and violence of busing.

Perhaps even more fundamental than this is the fear that even the prima facie impressive-sounding legislative forward marches weren't changing things at anywhere near the rate they ought to be changed, that unemployment, ghettoization, drug addiction, and violence were not much being touched. Black youth in 1977 had an unemployment rate of 34.8 percent; in that same year, median Black family income was about 60 percent of that of whites; Black people were twice as likely to die of diabetes and seven times as likely to be the victims of homicidal violence (p. 466).

How should we think of this change in society? If this piece of our social reality has so notably changed, what tools should we use to make sense of it, in the way that we used, say, Friedman's monetarism to understand stagflation? I want to suggest some answers, primarily from Black feminist theorists. I do so—as ever—for their inherent interest but also because they give us ways of assessing and understanding the presence or absence of historically marginalized groups in pop culture and in life and the challenges they might face. As it so happens, in one form or another these theorists' ideas have percolated up to the mainstream conversation about these topics, so we'll also be equipping ourselves with tools to understand today.

Nineties to Now

Black feminist critical theorist Patricia Hill Collins is one of the central figures here whose work we will consider. Standpoint theory is typically traced back to Marxist theory and is—roughly—the idea that people who occupy different perspectives on the world have different epistemic access to it—they can know different things, and in some ways know the same things better than those occupying other perspectives. Thus the proletariat might understand better than the bourgeoisie or the intellectual the nature of working life. When applied to race and feminism, this becomes the claim that one's social position, while socially disadvantageous, can be epistemically advantageous in giving one access to truths others (such as white men) can't see.

In a bit more detail, her thinking turns on what she calls "epistemologies." She writes:

> Epistemology constitutes an overarching theory of knowledge (Harding 1987). It investigates the standards used to assess knowledge or why we believe what we believe to be true. Far from being the apolitical study of truth, epistemology points to the ways in which power relations shape who is believed and why [*Black Feminist Thought*, p. 252].

This could well—and does to many—seem shocking. One might think, after all, that there are such things as science and scientific methodology, which aims at objective apolitical invariant truth. A lot of the contemporary "intellectual dark web," the "classical liberals" associated with blogs like Quillette and Areo, for example, have as their sworn enemy ideas like this, and many Twitter pixels have been spilled arguing about it.

Nevertheless, it strikes me as wildly plausible: that there is one or a small handful of dominant epistemologies that hold sway in academia, journalism, the arts, and so on that determine what gets counted as good academia, journalism, etc. And given that, as a matter of fact, all these domains have been historically dominated by white male heterosexuals, if you think it's possible that these features might influence these epistemologies—again, quite reasonable—then if you do not belong to those groups, you might struggle. As Collins writes:

> Black women scholars may know that something is true—at least, by standards widely accepted among African-American women—but be unwilling or unable to legitimate our claims using prevailing scholarly norms [p. 254].

Standpoint theory has it that these different perspectives or epistemologies should all be appealed to, and indeed should be so simultaneously. A very good example of this, in fact, is this chapter so far. I have been

7. _____, *Race, Gender and Representation*

telling an only slightly hedged narrative of progress, according to which things objectively got better for various groups. But the way I chose to do so was not by asking the people themselves, by speaking to gay or Black people and hearing their stories, but by quoting statistics and percentages culled from books written exclusively by other white men.

But that should be of concern, for many reasons. For one, there's the fact that these authors on whom I have been relying might have—almost certainly did—cherry-pick their statistics to present the story they were looking for. For a second, the recent replication crisis in social science has revealed that much of the social experimental method is, to put it politely, bullshit—fatally flawed by bad methods.

Faced with issues like this, the reader might think, sure, standpoint theory sounds good—you need a new source of knowledge, a new epistemology. Merely knowing that Black people could vote in 1965 doesn't tell you enough. You need to know about what it felt like to go up to the polling station almost certainly run by whites, to know what it's like to be routinely slurred, or even routinely looked at with suspicion or faced with microaggressions.

And, of course, the point generalizes. Collins certainly doesn't think that it's positivism vs. Black feminism when it comes to the epistemology debates. Groups proliferate, and:

> those ideas that are validated as true by African-American women, African-American men, Latina lesbians, Asian-American women, Puerto Rican men, and other groups with distinctive standpoints, with each group using the epistemological approaches growing from its unique standpoint, become the most "objective" truths. Each group speaks from its own standpoint and shares its own partial, situated knowledge. But because each group perceives its own truth as partial, its knowledge is unfinished. Each group becomes better able to consider other groups' standpoints without relinquishing the uniqueness of its own standpoint or suppressing other groups' partial perspectives [p. 270].

Now, one can—and many with great passion do!—criticize some of these ideas. You might be proudly in favor of the Western taming of reality and the scientific pursuit of truth and think that this all smacks of relativism. You might note that the positivistic methods can seemingly tell us something about Black lives. From one of the very same white male authors I relied upon above, for example, I learn that only 8 percent of some surveyed Black people thought racism was declining and that between 1968 and 1973 the percentages of Black people who felt they had been discriminated against increased steadily (Frum, p. 244).

Nineties to Now

But part of it, surely, is just common sense. Black people will know more about racist discrimination than the typical white person; women will know more about sexist discrimination than the typical man. This is hard to argue for: if you're a woman, consider walking in a part of town that feels rough and being on edge. Consider being a man, instinctively thinking you could ward off a decent portion of attackers, and not being on edge. The person to trust with regards to dangerous parts in the city, often, will be the people who suffer from their danger.

There are several reasons I have spent some time on this. For one, the idea of standpoint theory, especially as presented here, according to which there is a dominant epistemology and a series of nondominant but equally if not more (notice the absence of the above list of "white male") respectable epistemologies, is very influential, and part of the ideological underpinnings of what we today call identity politics. It will thus be necessary to bear in mind once we consider our current day. Second, I wanted to present a counterbalance to the positive views I have presented earlier in this chapter, and third, it is because issues such as racial and gender equality and inequality are central to my analysis of the pop culture of both the 90s and the 10s, and so it is necessary to attend to the voices of those who speak from marginalized positions. And we can then rephrase what we've been seeing: the artists of the 90s have been seeking to reaffirm their dominant epistemologies in the face of material and intellectual challenges by using nostalgia to look back to an era where power was all white and women were sexually unliberated housewives.

Let me consider another Black woman thinker of the time whose ideas have become very central to the current debate, as well as having distinctive lessons for us to learn about race relations in the time we are interested in: Kimberlé Crenshaw, whose concept of intersectionality is easily graspable, very influential, and hard to really challenge. The basic idea is that privilege or lack thereof is multidimensional. Or, perhaps an easier way initially to put it is to say that privilege is not additive. The disprivilege one suffers as a result of being a woman *and* being Black is not simply the sum (imagining we could perform such sums) of the disprivilege of those two identities. And privilege can sometimes offset disprivilege: neuroatypical men, for example, can often be leaders in fields despite their different and sometimes disadvantaging functioning (admittedly, this kind of speaks toward a respect in which an operation of addition [or rather subtraction] is well defined over privilege).

But we don't have to rely on guesswork. Crenshaw is a lawyer, and

7. _____, *Race, Gender and Representation*

one of the merits of her view is that she presents clear cases in which intersectionality is operative in the law.[1] She discusses a famous legal case in which a woman who wasn't hired at a company as a secretary blamed it on her being Black and a woman. The company retorted that they hire Black people and they hire woman as secretaries, and so she had no claim to being discriminated against as Black (because they hire Black people, in non-secretarial roles), *or* as a woman (because they hire women in secretarial roles), and so no claim to being discriminated against. Crenshaw thinks that cases like this show that in considering discrimination—which crucially involves considering a person's position in society—one has to take the person's various positions together: the woman has a case as Black *and* a woman.

Examples from feminist theory, critical race theory, and literary studies along these lines can be multiplied. Arguably a somewhat converse case to the standpoint theory we considered was Edward Said's extremely influential 1978 book *Orientalism*. In it he argued that Western representations of the Near East were inaccurate caricatures, images of fantasy that said more about the Western artists and thinkers who produced them than the people and cultures they were supposed to represent. One could view this as a case in which standpoint again matters, and indeed as an example of what happens when groups not in the right position to know attempt to make claims about a place. Feminist theorist bell hooks, in *From Margin to Center*, placed an emphasis on Black women, and in particular on the claim that many of the figures and proposed advantages of the new wave of feminism passed Black women by. Indeed, she begins her book by claiming that people like Betty Friedan, quoted above, were speaking only of a subset of women—mainly white and at least middle class—and that, accordingly, to call her view "feminism" as if it were speaking for all women was just inaccurate.

What all of this work tends toward is an emphasizing of particular perspectives and ways of knowing other than the dominant ones, with, in some cases, a tendency toward concentrating on lived experience, the various dimensions of discrimination, and the way our representations are shaped for better or worse by power structures. And then note that all this serves as a pretty decent gloss on one of the buzz words of our time, "identity politics."

All of this work is extremely important for understanding the general intellectual culture of the time, as it manifests on campuses but also as it has thereby permeated into the real world. I think, indeed, that this work has only really borne fruit in the sense of becoming part of the national conversation in terms of how we instinctively understand ourselves recently, to the point that Hilary Clinton attempted to name-check "intersectionality" (maybe—she seems to have got the idea so wrong it's possible it's just a coincidence), and we can read thinkpieces about whether Clinton or Sanders is a question of identity politics vs. socialism.[2]

What is the relevance of all this for our book? It is manifold: since one of the themes we've been developing is that 90s nostalgia is a means of turning back the clock on social change, we can use these thinkers of social change. Since one of our main goals is to understand the spirit of our current age, understanding its history is necessary.

Most of what I have said above is positive: it presents progress. Some of that progress might indeed be in the form of positivistic misleading statistics, but, more clearly, it's uncontroversial that Black women like hooks and Crenshaw and Collins wouldn't have had the opportunity to develop their theories of how they were overlooked and have those theories reach the mainstream were it not for the advances in racial justice the last century saw.

But it's worth noting that the moral arc of the universe has never bent straightforwardly toward equality. To show this, I want to do two things: first, to present some of academic responses to some of the academic work just presented, then to show how, both in the 90s and now, even among progressives, there has been dissent about the value of this sort of work. Along the way, I will try to answer in more depth a nagging question that a reader of this book almost certainly has: how can I defend the fact that (in terms of the pop culture I consider) the voices in this are solely those of white males? Am I not committing exactly the sort of mistake Said castigated the Orientalists for, namely painting with a single and Western male brush a whole decade?

Before that attempt at self-defense, though, let's consider some of the conservative intellectual work produced around the start of the 90s. We can start with the two Blooms, Allan and Howard, both of whom produced influential books that can, more or less, be seen as responding to the work we've just considered, and indeed as responding to it with disdain.

Thus, Howard Bloom, in a book defending the Western canon of literature, bemoans its attack by

> Feminists, Afrocentrists, Marxists, Foucault-inspired New Historicists, or Deconstructors-of all those whom I have described as members of the School of Resentment [*The Western Canon*, p. 20].

7. _____, *Race, Gender and Representation*

He goes on to say that

> The Western Canon does not exist in order to augment preexisting societal elites [*ibid.*, p. 36].

And that the reason we read and teach the same progression of dead white men is that they are aesthetically enjoyable and enriching, and cultural politics is simply a side issue. He writes:

> Whatever the convictions of our current New Historicists, for whom Shakespeare is only a signifier for the social energies of the English Renaissance, Shakespeare for hundreds of millions who are not white Europeans is a signifier for their own pathos, their own sense of identity with the characters that Shakespeare fleshed out by his language. For them his universality is not historical but fundamental; he puts their lives upon his stage [*ibid.*, p. 39].

Shakespeare speaks for everybody, per Bloom, and so the denial of universal voices—whether from Collins, from Said, or earlier from Lyotard—is no good. And many agreed: the cover of my copy informs me it was a *New York Times* notable book of the year and a national best seller.

A similar book, at a similar time, by a similarly named person, is Allan Bloom's *The Closing of the Western Mind* (1987). He straightforwardly complains that the Black Power movement has sought "black identity, not universal rights" (p. 33), and it's pretty clear that, looking at his students' attitudes to sex ("it's no big deal," he quotes one as saying [p. 99]) he thinks that something has been lost, a sacredness and seriousness to sex, and he is happy to pin the blame for this on feminism. And yet a third bugbear for him, as the opening of his book attests, is the supposedly endemic relativism infecting campuses.

Of course, it's not very surprising that not everyone should be on board with the feminist and anti-racist views we sketched earlier. Arguably more surprising is that people with otherwise clear progressive bona fides, then and now, have questioned whether the emphasis on these epistemological questions concerning representation, misrepresentation, and who gets to speak should be the motive force in politics.

In particular, consider this line of reasoning. Said, or Collins, points out that we must emphasize other voices when considering certain topics. The conservative critics argue back: there is a canon of work that once and for all tells us about the human condition. People argue back, trying to decolonialize the syllabus and get marginalized people represented in academia.

Then there's a slide from the people doing the representations to the representations themselves. It's bad to create representations of people from the Persian Gulf as passion-ruled savages, or of Black people as criminals.[3] It's bad to say such things, and in general you should be very careful about what you say and what you watch, because these, via fancy theories like postcolonialism and standpoint epistemology, are places where discrimination works.

A certain species of leftist, both in the 90s and now, has looked on this debate as one less important. Regardless of whether you accept my speculative genealogy of political correctness in the last two paragraphs, there have been people both then and now who think that the main questions we need to be considering are about the actual socioeconomic structures (typically of capitalism) that inhibit equality and the sort of world we want to live in. Thus consider Naomi Klein, whose work we considered in a previous chapter, talking about the futility of campus politics:

> In the outside world, the politics of race, gender and sexuality remained tied to more concrete, pressing issues, like pay equity, same-sex spousal rights and police violence, and these serious movements were—and continue to be—a genuine threat to the economic and social order.
>
> But somehow, they didn't seem terribly glamorous to students on many university campuses, for whom identity politics had evolved by the late eighties into something quite different. Many of the battles we fought were over issues of "representation"—a loosely defined set of grievances mostly lodged against the media, the curriculum and the English language. From campus feminists arguing over "representation" of women on the reading lists to gays wanting better "representation" on television.... But by the time my generation inherited these ideas [i.e., roughly the sort of ideas we presented above, I think], often two or three times removed, representation was no longer one tool among many, it was the key. In the absence of a clear legal or political strategy, we traced back almost all of society's problems to the media and the curriculum, either through their perpetuation of negative stereotypes or simply by omission [*No Logo*, pp. 107–8].

Or consider one of the leading voices of the British left, the cultural critic Mark Fisher. In a famous and very controversial post called "Exiting the Vampire's Castle" from 2013, he wrote:

> The privilege I certainly enjoy as a white male consists in part in my not being aware of my ethnicity and my gender, and it is a sobering and revelatory experience to occasionally be made aware of these blind-spots. But, rather than seeking a world in which everyone achieves freedom from identitarian classification, [some online leftists] seeks to corral people back into identi-camps, where they are forever defined in the terms set by dominant

7. _____, *Race, Gender and Representation*

power, crippled by self-consciousness and isolated by a logic of solipsism which insists that we cannot understand one another unless we belong to the same identity group.[4]

Note again the hitting of all the key buzzwords. For Fisher, the emphasis on identity and difference occludes the possibility of what is most necessary in class struggle, namely solidarity. And consider, more or less exactly 20 years after Klein, the book of the vanguard of the contemporary left, *Chapo Trap House*:

> In the absence of real political power, liberals and lefties stumbled into a pathology where we only hold power over—and wage struggles for—the realm of fantasy ... [incorrectly thinking] that a nation's culture is self-reinforcing and affects all other walks of life, so if you change the culture, you can change the political reality [p. 205].

Replacing culture with representation on syllabus, you see again that debates are going on 30 years after *Black Feminist Thought* and 40 after *Orientalism* about the importance of representation in contemporary political life, and importantly, opposing voices come not just from conservative critics like the Blooms, but also from clear and bona fide leftists like Klein, Fisher, and the Chapo gang.

And so a dialectic has arisen where there are on one hand the people concerned with social position and privilege; on another hand, conservatives who, roughly, like the status quo; and on yet a third hand, other progressives who think that we there are bigger fish to fry than race and gender, who are more focused on class or economics as the site of political conflict. One sees this dialectic everywhere today: in Clinton vs. the GOP vs. Sanders in 2016, or in Biden vs. GOP vs. Sanders in 2020. We see "woke" people squabble with, on the one hand, the conservatives, and on the other their leftist almost comrades. The key thing to realize is that this is old, and it stems from the debates we've considered in this chapter, which debates in turn stem from the political and social developments we traced at the start.

Now, I've gotten a little off course here—but with reason—so let's refocus. There were legal and material benefits to marginalized groups, who became the object of much influential scholarly work around the 1980s. There was a backlash among some intellectuals, such as the Blooms, as well as, more surprisingly, leftist people like Klein. And, moreover, we can see this backlash replaying itself today. As if it were something new, the blogosphere and social media are packed with people making fun of this race-centered critical theory work. And these people come from widely different parts of the political spectrum: there are people who call themselves classical liberals who are generally pro-science and who deplore what they take to be the unscientific aspects of such theories and—as a sort of necessary accompaniment—the idea of different epistemologies (isn't, they think, the epistemology of empirical science enough?). These people tend also to be skeptical of sayings like "discourses have power." There are the alt-right who might be straightforward actual capital "R" racists, but at minimum are pro–Trump. And there are the leftists who disagree with this line of thought, thinking class and economics is where the real fight must be fought. The important point is that much of these pressing current debates are well traced back to, and in some cases recapitulate, old history. The novelty, really, is Trump and the alt-right, and they will be discussed in another chapter. But the overall point is that, in an era when economically and politically the country seemed to stall, the position of previously trodden upon groups improved, and realizing this can help us understand some puzzling features both of the pop culture of then and now, and of the more general cultural conversations we are involved in.

Before moving on to the next chapter, it's time to pose a question that has already perhaps been on the reader's mind: am I not falling into the same canon-philia as the Blooms? Am I not, even in the pitching of this book, suggesting that some can speak for all, that there is a privileged set of geniuses whose voice we should all heed, and which happen all to be white men? And, a second question, assuming an affirmative answer to the first: why should anyone read such a book?

My answer is basically as so. Yes, I am in essence arguing for a canon of 90s elite pop culture that I think is both deserving of our aesthetic attention and notably white, middle class, and male. What that means is that the Zeitgeist I aim to be describing will indeed be one that more accurately represents the concerns of that demographic.

That's not ideal, I grant, nor do I think it's fatal to my project. The project will be successful if I succeed in presenting a picture of the era that seems recognizable—that, when people think of the 90s, my work accurately captures it. Moreover, I must come out as, at least in part, a canon defender. While I do certainly think it's a bad thing—a very bad thing—that the vast majority of voices esteemed as canonical have heretofore been white and male, I don't think that fact detracts from the quality of the work in the canon (it just shouldn't be the whole canon).

7. _____, Race, Gender and Representation

Similarly, I don't think my all-white, all-male lineup speaks against the quality of the work I discuss—that *The Simpsons* is a peerless work of late 20th-century art is a hill I would die on.

Moreover, I feel especially not uncomfortable writing this book because I think that the 90s might have the interesting distinction of being the last era for which a canon is even conceivable. The lessons of the thinkers we've considered in this chapter have been adopted in a profound (if, as we've just seen, not unanimous) way by young people today such that creating a diversity of voices is a central concern of the people in power. So, in a sense, while I do come to praise the pop culture canon of the 90s, I do so because I think I am thereby burying the idea of pop cultural canons. It is certainly *not* the case if one were attempting to give the Zeitgeist of the 2010s that one could do so speaking only about white men. Telling *that* story will require, as we will see, reference to shows written by and to represent girls called *Girls*, that is viewed by many as one of the breakout shows of the era; it will require discussion of cultural commentators like Ta-Nehisi Coates and Roxanne Gay, the obligatorily multiracial cast of the contemporary sitcom, and it will require mention of things like identity politics and intersectionality.

But there's more. As I've said, central to my analysis is that the 90s is an interesting case study in how issues to do with minority representation get taken up into the wider culture—part of what my book argues is that the very white-maleness of the 90s canon is itself responsive, in a negative way, to the liberating movements of the 70s we've discussed in this chapter. In a sense, then, I am entirely on board with someone like Patricia Hill Collins who thinks that white people will reproduce white epistemologies—David Lynch, for example, on my reading, is someone who does this by recourse to nostalgia. In the same way, as we'll see, the staging of *The Simpsons* in a pseudo-50s small American town can be viewed as an artistic strategy for avoiding coming face to face with the uncomfortable fact that the main characters are mostly white, the women mostly conforming to stereotypes of the era before *Roe v. Wade*. We'll even see this continue to this day: although contemporary media features more representation of minorities, it is questionable how deeply this goes, and I will suggest that the move toward fantasy and sci-fi in recent prestige drama can well be read as an attempt to avoid facing the modern world in which the voices and perspectives of people other than straight white men are valued. One way to read this book, thus, is as an extended "worked example" of critical race-theoretic concerns, one that comes to bury the canon of 90s white art (while, admittedly, praising it). Accordingly, if this book is in a sense defending a canon, it is doing so in a very different way than the work of Bloom, and in the service of other aims and motivated by different concerns, most important among which is trying to locate the marginalized in pop culture.

Interlude:
The 90s in Ten Events

In this chapter, I want to take a step back from my overall argument to consider, briefly, some of the more memorable events of the decade, in order to show how the important concepts we're focusing on revealed themselves in history and at the same time present that history either as a reminder or as an introduction.

1990. In the summer of 1990, after a prosperous 1980s which saw consistently good GDP growth, America went into a recession. The causes of it are somewhat contested and obscure, but that summer people started, in the way we've learned happens periodically, tightening their purse strings and holding on to their money. This had two key effects: firstly, they put an end to George H.W. Bush; in 1992, he was replaced by Clinton whose campaign's unofficial slogan was "it's the economy, stupid." But secondly, it forced or at least nudged Clinton toward the policy he took of deficit reduction. The deficit had risen sharply under Reagan (ironically given he at least claimed to want the state to spend less), and Clinton and his advisers thought they had to bring it under control. And they did so, but by another irony, that meant the Democrat Clinton adopting the fundamentally conservative policy of reducing government spending. Not only that, it at least appeared to work: with Clinton, the economy started booming. And this, in turn, would naturally encourage the thought that that conservative foreign policy was the right one and that Clinton was just more of the same (in fact, it's likely that this rests on a misunderstanding: as liberal economic commentators like to point out, the economy was already recovering when Clinton took office). Regardless of the facts, this recovery must surely have further cemented the ideological domination of neoliberal economics in the citizens of the 1990s.

1991. In February, the Gulf War ended. It had started eight months earlier after Saddam Hussein invaded Kuwait, and its purpose was, depending on who one asked, to protect the allied Kuwaitees against the supposedly Hitler-esque Hussein or to secure George H.W. Bush's presidency and to reinvigorate American faith in the concept of war, a faith which still hadn't really recovered after Vietnam. A particularly noteworthy feature of it was the way it was televised, with live footage airing on the news, of Baghdad at night being lit up with bombs, and the news anchors acting as cheerpeople for the war and its weaponry (one CNN anchor speaking of the "sweet, beautiful sight" of a rocket[1]). Again, it's not hard to think of this as epochal: the same device that brings you even *The Simpsons* brings you jingoistic war footage. How could that fail to cause in one a distanced cynicism?

1992. History ended on December 31, 1991, when the Soviet Union was dissolved. The earlier fall of the Berlin Wall had prompted conservative intellectual Francis Fukuyama to announce that the Hegelian-esque progress of history had reached its final point with the triumph of democracy over other forms of government like socialism, and he expanded on this thesis in a book called *The End of History and The Last Man*, published that year. In the earlier essay he pointed to the globalization of culture: television sets in China, McDonald's in Prague, and so on. He could also point to the economic triumphs of the Asian tiger countries, which, having at least in theory moved toward something like a market economy, had known great prosperity. On that basis, his theory wouldn't have seemed too implausible in the early 90s. How it stands up now, with climate change, economic stagnation and inequality, terrorism and radicalism, is another story, but one can easily imagine the informed citizen of the 90s feeling pent in: if this is the acme of history, and this isn't great for me, what can I hope for?

1993. This year saw two events to remind people that even if America was culturally at the vanguard (as in essence this book takes as motivating premise), and—if one believes Fukuyama—even world-historically so, it remained an extremely backward country. Rodney King was a Black man who was pulled over by police for drunk driving and subsequently brutally beaten by four LAPD officers. It so happened that someone caught the beating on film,[2] but the subsequent trial of the officers resulted in their acquittal, which in turn provoked the 1992 LA riots. In 1993, King gave testimony at a federal trial and then, at last, at least two of the officers were convicted, but the time it took for justice to be done, combined with the brutality of the footage, served to make salient that the system remained fundamentally tilted against minorities. This message was reiterated a few months later when the continuing plight of gay people was made manifest by Clinton's introduction of "the don't ask, don't tell policy" concerning the military, according to which, while being discovered to be gay or bisexual was sufficient grounds for being kicked out of the army, provided it never was discovered, there was no problem. If one was gay, one shouldn't let it be known—and others shouldn't ask. The first draft of this book was written in 2017, after Trayvon Martin, Philando Castile, Sandra Bland, Tamir Rice, and others, and with Trump trying to institute a trans military ban. The third draft was written during the 2020 Black Lives Matter protests. It is easy to think America has barely become any less backward.

1994. On April 8, Kurt Cobain, lead singer of Nirvana, killed himself. He had been suffering from heroin addiction and depression in addition to severe stomach problems the causes of which were unknown. Nirvana's 1991 *Nevermind* had been one of the surprise breakout hits of the early 90s, reaching number one in the charts partly on the strength of its first single, "Smells Like Teen Spirit." The grunge aesthetic of Nirvana and related bands undeniably forms a central part of most people's conceptions of the 90s. This is neatly encapsulated in the much-watched video for "Smells Like Teen Spirit": the general apathy connoted by ripped jeans, unfussy jumpers and cardigans, and lank hair; and the armless catatonic dancing are icons of the era. What is interesting is the surprise factor: the record company would have been happy with 250,000 sales for the album, but in fact sold over 10 million in America. This would suggest that Nirvana and their disaffection struck a chord with the young people of the 90s. (It's a notable and strange fact, pointed out, for example, by Mark Fisher, that there doesn't seem to be anything like that since at least the millennium.)

1995. On August 24, Windows 95 was released. The 90s was the era that the personal computer became a household item. Although the internet wasn't yet mainstream, sales doubled from around 20 million to around 40 million between 1990 and 1994 and then almost quadrupled up to 140 million by 2000. Moreover, a range of software that we still use today was first introduced, the most famous example being the various Windows operating systems. These drastically improved the user-friendliness of PCs, which even a few years ago ran only DOS, a command line operating system. In addition, software like Microsoft Word and games like Doom, which have gone through different versions, remain popular today. Absent the internet—and that's of course a very big absence—a computer in 1995 would be just about useable to a younger millennial in a way that a computer of a decade earlier wouldn't have been.

1996. On August 22, 1996, Bill Clinton signed PRWORA, the personal responsibility and work opportunity reconciliation act. This bill drastically reduced the resources available to those who were jobless, ostensibly in a bid to get them to work and thus to reduce welfare dependence. It removed, that is to say, the safety net instituted as part of Roosevelt's New Deal. And remove it it has: it now serves one-third fewer people than it did in 1996, and yet the amount of people in poverty has increased by a bit under a third and the amount of people in deep poverty has increased by 50 percent—so, as a main resource for helping the poor, it doesn't work.[3] That's kind of hard to appreciate, such big numbers. The fact is that it made more people poor. Poverty itself can be hard to appreciate, and to help understand the effects of the act, which targeted primarily single mothers, and disproportionately Black people, the journalist Barbara Ehrenreich went to find work in such jobs, laying out the various paradoxes of poverty: that if you're poor you're forced to buy poor-quality things which will break and require you to buy them again. Buy cheap, buy twice: but if you have only the small amount of money, you can't do anything but. Her *Nickled and Dimed* showed the different world the poor inhabit, that the elites are happy to condemn millions to, and arguably, along with Michael Moore and Klein and others whose work appeared around the turn of the millennium, served to make the generation following X more sociopolitically aware. Not only that, this bill was enacted by Bill Clinton, a Democrat—the Republicans wanted to pass much crueler reform. In short, it's exactly the sort of move that would disgust a person, to which the only reaction is Simpsonian snarling.

1997. On September 15, 1997, a couple of PhD students at Stanford University, Larry Page and Sergey Brin, registered the domain google.com. It wasn't the first internet search engine, and for a while it wasn't the only one—older readers will remember AltaVista, Yahoo, and AskJeeves, and younger readers probably still know, as an irritation, Bing—but it was and remains the best. Moreover, the company that they formed has, as is very familiar, expanded to a multibillion dollar operation that may well bring about the next evolution of the human animal (or at least so this author, who is an AI true believer, thinks). Even if this somewhat extreme prediction doesn't come true, nevertheless it remains the case that the next step forward in human history began to be taken around the end of the 1990s. (This book was written without access to a decent university library, and as such depended to a large extent on being able to quickly access PDFs of books and newspaper articles that seemed relevant; this chapter, moreover, benefited greatly from Wikipedia. For all its flaws, the internet does seem to represent a quantum leap forward in our ability to carry out research.)

1998. On December 19, Bill Clinton was impeached (and subsequently acquitted). The exact details of the story are complicated and somewhat interesting, but it would take us too far afield to go into them (Wikipedia is helpful). Is it remembered (and memorable) for the exposure of Clinton's affair with intern Monica Lewinsky, his lies about which being the only thing the independent prosecutor could get enough evidence to make a case against him with? What is particularly relevant are certain explicit details of that affair which were revealed, along with Clinton's slippery attempt to avoid admitting guilt. As to the former, the report the prosecutor wrote up (easily available online) is replete with semen-stained shirts, cigars in vaginas, and "brief genital-to-genital contact." As to the latter, Clinton famously attempted to lawyer his way out of trouble, quibbling semantics. Clinton was asked to consider an affidavit which had Lewinsky saying "there is absolutely no sex of any kind in any manner, shape or form, with President Clinton" and which Clinton's defense team endorsed but which certainly seemed to be false. Wasn't it false? Clinton replied:

> It depends on what the meaning of the word "is" is. If the—if he—if "is" means is and never has been, that is not—that is one thing. If it means there is none, that was a completely true statement.[4]

And this formed the water cooler discussion, like Watergate 25 years previously (and like "grab 'em by the pussy" forms the contemporary equivalent of the water cooler, the Twitter thread or the article comments section). It's easy to think that this scandal somewhat inured American politics to bad behavior, so that once someone really bad came along, the political sensibility was too numbed to really appreciate it. (As I write, Trump has just been diagnosed with COVID-19, just after holding a superspreader event announcing the nomination of the Supreme Court justice to replace Ruth Bader Ginsburg. It is unclear, at the time of writing, who all he has imperiled with this particular instance of his dreadfulness. This is about the fourth time I've revised this paragraph; every single time, there's a brand new Trump story for this parenthesis.[5])

1999. In November of this year, the Gramm-Leach-Bliley Act repealed part of the earlier Glass-Steagall Act of 1933. This latter act was introduced after the stock market boom and bust of the twenties in an effort to prevent things like the 1929 crash occurring, essentially by separating off the more speculative, high-risk/high-reward sort of banking, traditionally done by what are called investment banks, from the more mundane banks which deal with the savings of ordinary people. On one telling, this repeal had important consequences for the 2008 crisis: according to many, it led to the commercial banks coming to take more risks (in essence behaving more like investment banks) in order to gain better profits. This is a controversial interpretation of that crisis, but nevertheless is important at least symbolically as one of many deregulatory movements that occurred under Clinton (and his predecessors), which all too often imperiled consumers and workers while strengthening big business and the already rich.

8

The Simpsons

In this chapter, I consider *The Simpsons*, to my mind the high point of 90s culture (not that I've done anywhere near experience every work to be able to make that judgment) and, I think, one of the greatest works in any medium in any time.

Let me just lay present some background facts before trying to make this impossible case. I take it all my readers will have some familiarity with the show but I want to try to make it strange, to enable us to see it as it was seen then, and how we, 20 years on, should see it. (I speak in the past tense advisedly: as everyone knows, *The Simpsons* has been bad for ages. It was good roughly from season three to season eight, so 1991–97. It has now run for over 30 seasons; my understanding is that the reason for its continued existence is that it pays the staff's mortgages.)

So, first, it's an enormously popular, mainstream, prime-time animated comedy (it's not the first such show, that honor going to *The Flintstones*). It debuted in December 1989, and it follows a nuclear family, consisting of a mother, father, and three children. The father is impossibly stupid, gluttonous, lucky, sometimes likable, and prone to extremes of elation, despair, and anger. The mother is kind, prone to worry, long-suffering. The son is cheeky, the daughter bookish, the youngest daughter still an infant. They live in a small town that nevertheless contains multitudes, and the series is populated with shop-owners, businessmen, doctors, religious people, TV and radio stars, and so on. Homer and Marge are high-school sweethearts, Marge doesn't work and cooks dinner like pork chops or meatloaf every night, and they have an old fashioned TV with an aerial on the top of the set. They shop in convenience stores and not megamarts, they go to church, and Homer congregates in a local bar with his friends from work.

So far, so ordinary: indeed, so far, so 50s. As we've seen, these are not features of American society any more: the Kwik-E-Mart would have been driven out of business by a big box store, Marge would be in work, they would have video recorders and fancy televisions, they wouldn't go to church, and Homer would probably spend even more time getting drunk alone in his home. Depressing, yes, but factual.

That notwithstanding, from this by now typical retro-nostalgic conventional premise, all of American society is captured (well, a *lot*, at least, of American society. There's isn't much *youth* in *The Simpsons*, with the attendant youthy things of sex, drugs, rock and roll, and passion, nor are there any prominent out gay characters,[1] and the only Black person is conspicuously middle-class, a nod to Bill Cosby's unthreateningly Black doctor in *The Cosby Show*).

Every postwar American president features in the show, some many times. Indeed, name a political event and it'll be here, in a flashback or a dream sequence, in an old TV show the family watches, or in the voice-acting of one of the ancillary characters. Similarly, most every TV show or movie or celebrity also finds themselves, by direct or indirect parody, in it.

Just as—to introduce the unfortunately pretentious but I hope critically helpful analogy I'm going to want to push—Joyce's *Ulysses* captures early 20th-century life by capturing a day in the life of the normal, sane, fully grounded Bloom, so *The Simpsons* captures American history and culture via a twisted version of the traditional family sitcom by means of the techniques of parody and impersonation learned from things like NBC's *Saturday Night Live*, a live action sketch show which regularly features parodies of events of political and cultural significance.

Hearing this, if one is unfamiliar with the show, you might wonder what the fuss is. It's just a parody of a traditional sitcom with some political material thrown in. But it's so much more. One of the claims I want to make is that central to its being so much more is the fact that it's animated. This unavoidably sounds overblown, but the rediscovery of animation as a medium for serious art is monumental.

The reason for this is that it allows for an extreme freedom otherwise impossible. Say you want to make fun of a TV show: for example, a show like 1990's *Cops*, a precursor to reality TV which followed police around. There's something, obviously, inherently ridiculous about such a thing, that any commentator—novelist, poet, playwright—on society

8. The Simpsons

should want to capture. So how *can* we capture it? Say you're working in prose. You can *try* to write about it.

> I was watching Police Cops, a show in which we valorise the repressive force....

But that's a bit serious. Trying to funny it up a bit:

> I was watching Police Cops, that show where we follow around that cross-section of society who get to solve problems

That's not good. Or, let's try to do one of the actual gags about this from *The Simpsons*:

> I was watching Police Cops, and Springfield's finest were on the trail of a cattle rustler. They came to the address on 844 Evergreen Terrace, and, not confused by the lowing and hay bales from the adjacent house, broke the door down, to be faced with a reverend saying this is 842 Evergreen Terrace, not 844.

Maybe that's on me, but it seems to me it just doesn't work. It's hard, I think, to try to parody TV in prose. And that's not too surprising—TV is after all a whole other medium. It should strike us as implausible that we could parody TV in prose, just as we think it's implausible that we could parody prose in TV. Try to think, for example, of a TV show that parodies the style of Hemingway or Jane Austen. I just don't think it can be done.

In a sketch show like SNL, on the other hand, it would be reasonably easily doable. Indeed, if you've ever watched a sketch show, you know that such parodies are its bread and butter. Again, it is possible, I suggest, because TV permits one to parody TV.

But, and unlike the novel, it would cost time and money. Any new sentence can transport a reader anywhere. A sketch costs, though. You've got police uniforms, maybe guns, you have to find a place that can serve as the criminal's house, and so on. But if you have to do that, then there's strong economic pressure, having gone to that hassle, to make the most of the scene, and have it play long. So parody is possible on TV, but economics compels one to make the most of it.

For animation, though, there's no sets, no need for actors. To draw a cop is no more complicated than to draw a street. For that matter, it's no more complicated to draw outer space, or *Game of Thrones*, or President

Trump than it is to draw your protagonist. Like the novel, animation has the freedom to go where it wants.

Unlike the novel, though, animation is a kinetic visual medium. It thus doesn't need to describe, as I attempted to describe, the show. It can merely present it, and because of this economy, it can do so very quickly without having expended huge resources. It can allow Homer to be flicking and to come across *Police Cops*, show it for a second or two, quickly make fun of it, and then be moving on.

What goes for TV shows goes for anything. Want to portray the moon landing? Easy. Reagan? The Beatles? Easy, easy easy easy. This freedom to go wherever one wants dramatically widens the range of topics economically viable to discuss, and it's this widened range that partly accounts, in my view, for the range of *The Simpsons*.

Indeed, continuing the Joycean analogy, we could say that the discovery of animation is somewhat similar to the use of stream of consciousness in Joyce. Consider this famous passage from the third chapter of *Ulysses*:

> Ineluctable modality of the visible: at least that if no more, thought through my eyes. Signatures of all things I am here to read, seaspawn and seawrack, the nearing tide, that rusty boot. Snotgreen, bluesilver, rust: coloured signs. Limits of the diaphane. But he adds: in bodies. Then he was aware of them bodies before of them coloured. How? By knocking his sconce against them, sure. Go easy. Bald he was and a millionaire, maestro di color che sanno. Limit of the diaphane in. Why in? Diaphane, adiaphane. If you can put your five fingers through it is a gate, if not a door. Shut your eyes and see.
>
> Stephen closed his eyes to hear his boots crush crackling wrack and shells. You are walking through it howsomever. I am, a stride at a time. A very short space of time through very short times of space. Five, six: the nacheinander. Exactly: and that is the ineluctable modality of the audible. Open your eyes. No. Jesus! If I fell over a cliff that beetles o'er his base, fell through the nebeneinander ineluctably! I am getting on nicely in the dark. My ash sword hangs at my side. Tap with it: they do. My two feet in his boots are at the ends of his legs, nebeneinander. Sounds solid: made by the mallet of Los Demiurgos. Am I walking into eternity along Sandymount strand? Crush, crack, crick, crick. Wild sea money. Dominie Deasy kens them a.'
>
> Won't you come to Sandymount,
> Madeline the mare?
>
> [*Ulysses*, Oxford World Classics, p. 37].

It represents the consciousness of Stephen, the novel's young, bookish hero, as he walks along a beach, and Aristotle, Dante, riddles, a German

8. The Simpsons

playwright, Blake, and popular songs go through his head. The point is that this flitting of attention is realistic—it marks out the way our mental life goes. Joyce's unconventional method, doing away with standard narrative, enables him more realistically to portray the life of his character.

Animation enables something like the same thing: in the late 20th century, our minds are as flitting as they were in Joyce's day, but in different ways. Indeed, for Stephen, there was a sense of peace in the external if not the internal world: while he's thinking these thoughts, he's presented with the self-same patch of beach.

However, for the person in the late 20th century, we can't guarantee this. In particular, for the channel flipper of 90s hundred-channel cable television, attention is constantly diverted this way and that. Properly to convey that requires a medium that has the same fluidity. And animation is precisely that.

I want to make a similar, and hopefully similarly paradoxical-sounding, claim that I made for David Lynch: that *The Simpsons* is *realistic*. It's a realistic depiction of the 90s person who, apparently, watched a staggering number of television hours each day. Again, postmodernism collapses into realism, because the intertextuality of postmodernism captures the media-saturatedness of our day-to-day lives.

My argument for the claim that we should view *The Simpsons* as a form of realism apt for the stereotypical late-90s watcher of a lot of television goes as so. Here are three features it's relatively uncontroversial to attribute to the watcher of a lot of television of the 90s—three states of mind that watching television fosters. Firstly, a sense of detachment and irony—one knows what one is watching is dumb, the plots are formulaic, the emotions mawkish, and so on, and that the shows are mere lures to cause you, a demographically valuable person, to watch the advertisements which make up a third of each allotted half an hour or hour segment. Yet you still spend all this time doing it. Second: a sense of being drowned by many voices—the sheer quantity of different shows available to someone with cable TV was and is immense: from news reports to comedians, from people going through real to people going through imagined catastrophes, old films and music videos, all laced between advertisements. Third, and related to this, an instability of attention—not only are you exposed to all these different voices, but you are exposed to them rapid-fire, within minutes. Not only could one go from a televised Gulf War to a rerun to *M*A*S*H* to an ad for a weed eater, one could do so more or less instantaneously, by flicking through the hundreds of channels available.

I will claim that these features are common between the watcher of TV and the user of the internet. But first I want to show that they are mirrored in the style of *The Simpsons*, which thus functions to represent the televisual mind. First, a detached and ironic attitude toward television is as ubiquitous in *The Simpsons* as in the watcher of TV. Examples could be trotted out ad nauseam, but think, for example, of the scene in "The Front" (season 4 episode 19; almost all the examples that follow were found by selecting more or less at random an episode and either watching it or reading the script, and as such could be multiplied). Bart and Lisa are walking through the corridors of a studio which makes cartoons—past water filters, cleaning ladies, and so on—asking a producer about the costs of making animations. The producer says that sometimes they cut corners, for example by reusing backgrounds. As he says this the background of the scene is itself reused—the same water filter and cleaning lady reappear, emphasizing to the audience that what they're watching is just another cheap cartoon like Itchy and Scratchy. Or think of "Bart Gets Famous" (season 5 episode 12), which begins with Bart walking down the stairs whistling *The Simpsons*' own theme. The nature of TV is something *The Simpsons* is concerned with, and in that it is similar to the jaded 90s channel hopper.

The second aspect is the plurality of voices TV drowns you in. I think this is reflected in one of the central sources of humor in *The Simpsons*, in which characters say things that are, well, out of character. It is extremely common in *The Simpsons* for characters to speak in voices other than their own. Thus in "The Day the Violence Died" (season 7 episode 18) Bart channels a disgruntled middle-aged sitcom conservative or contemporary "heterodox" thinkpiece writer in telling Liza that Generation X needs a war like Vietnam to toughen them up. In "Homer's Barbershop Quartet" (season 5 episode 1), he is chided by Homer for speaking like a "grizzled 1890s prospector." He is not, it's fair to say, speaking in any way like a normal 8-year-old boy in these instances. We see the same thing for Homer. Few fans will forget his famous Scarface-referencing speech about the vicissitudes of his ad hoc sugar business in "Lisa's Rival," season 6 episode 2. In other episodes he displays unusual intelligence (and not only because he has a crayon stuck in his head as in "The Way of the Dog," season 1 episode 9).

8. The Simpsons

Examples like this—if copyright permitted—could be multiplied ad lib. Of course, a lot of this is just played for laughs, but I think there's a point behind it: the source of these voices in which the characters speak must, surely, be television. We should think of these strange outbursts as the characters' internalizations of the disparate voices they hear; just as one learns to speak from one's parents, so the 90s person learns to speak from television, and this is portrayed in surreal out-of-character dialogue like above.

The third feature of the TV addict is their instability of attention. This is reflected in the fundamentally digressive style of *The Simpsons*—the way the show constantly cuts away to imaginings or scenes from the past or surrealistic futures, to news reports or a character's imagining.

Think, for example, of the following sequence from "Homer Badman" (season 6 episode 9). Homer has been wrongly accused of sexual assault and records an interview to clear his name, which gets edited absurdly to make him appear guilty; we then cut to his reaction, which cuts to his famous sung suggestion that the family escape their troubles by going to live "under the sea." We then cut to footage filmed outside his house, followed by more TV: *Gentle Ben*, a talk show like *Oprah*, the presenter of which is a grizzly bear. Incredibly, this all occurs within about three minutes, and while this is perhaps an extreme example, this rapid cutting between markedly different scenes is undoubtedly a central feature of *The Simpsons'* style (evidence for which is the way it was further developed in [clearly obviously *Simpsons*-influenced] *Family Guy* and related shows, where it plays an even more pivotal role). It should be taken, I hold, to be a staging of the instability of attention of the person channel hopping. *The Simpsons* jumps around because it represents the 90s TV viewer, whose attention itself jumps around.

We should view these features—and, again, this isn't close to exhaustive—as ways in which *The Simpsons*, despite surreal appearances, is in a sense mimetic. It portrays a mind hooked on television, and it is surreal only because to be hooked on TV is surreal. But this shows us something very important: despite the seeming obstacles, you can portray what it's like to live a in media-saturated, glued-to-your-screen culture. You just need to use nonrealistic artistic techniques. *The Simpsons* shows us how.

So that's the first thing that I think is of value. Just as the stream of consciousness lets us see into consciousness of a well-read turn-of-the-century Irishman, so the style of *The Simpsons* lets us see into the modern American mind.

But not only the mind of the 90s. As will to some extent become apparent later on, television today is considerably less formally playful. But that comes with a cost: it is less able adequately to depict the fact that we spend so much of our lives staring at our smart phones. On our smartphones we work, we socialize, we date, we learn—everything. If anything, the internet plays an even bigger role in our lives than TV did in the lives of Generation X (and as we'll see immediately below, TV was very important for them). And it's an artistic failing of contemporary art, in my opinion, that none has really gotten the depiction of smartphone-saturated life right. Although in an increasing number of novels, such as those of Sally Rooney, to be discussed below, the page is increasingly taken up with inset text messages and emails, and although an increasing number of TV shows have at least managed to find a way to depict texting (the message tends to appear on screen in a bubble), no art, as far as I can tell, adequately captures quite how weird it is that for many of us, the online places we congregate are simultaneously singles bars, newsrooms, and offices, and how we somehow effortlessly move between these three different ways of living from tweet to tweet. By contrast, *The Simpsons* **does** adequately capture the multivoicedness of media-saturated life, and so while it's most accurate as a representation of 90s life, I think a good case can be made that it also captures life in the 2020s.

Let me at this point take a step back and speak a bit more about the importance of television as a feature of the culture of the 90s. We relate to television differently today. Most notably, we consume it via streaming services like Netflix, but also television itself has changed: it's gotten good. We're in, people always tell us, a golden era of television. Finally, television is familiar. People seldom, at this point, theorize about the perils and pleasures of watching a lot of TV. This is because we realize that it's clearly been usurped as the central object of culture by the internet. Instead, we're today much more likely to ask what spending all this time on the internet is going to do to us. We thus don't think about the dangers inherent in TV, and thus are apt to overlook it as a critical feature of the 90s.

That would be a mistake. I think one more or less can't overestimate the importance of the role television must play in our attempt to give a story of the 90s. I follow in this Harvard sociologist Robert Putnam, whose famous 2000 work *Bowling Alone* (Simon and

8. The Simpsons

Schuster) presents a disturbing picture about the destructive role the rise of television played in shaping the fabric of postwar American society.

The take-home message is simple: television erodes social connectedness and civic participation. Civic participation takes many different forms—for example, voting, running for office, PTAs or neighborhood watch programs, workers' unions and other professional organizations, playing or watching sports, volunteering or other charity work, or simply hanging out at a bar with friends.

These sorts of things, Putnam tells us, are crucial to the healthy functioning both of society and of individuals. Consider a vivid example he gives (p. 288):

> I want to send my daughter to school, but the only school in the area is run-down. I could pay to send her to some private school, or could pitch in to help rejuvenate the local school. If I do the latter, everyone who goes to the school will benefit. But I need other people to help: I can't do it myself. It'll only work if there are strong social connections in my community, precisely the sort fostered by doing the sort of things listed above. That is, having such social connections enables you to do more: in essence, one can reliably count on the strength of your community to do things you yourself couldn't do. Having these social connections, in this particular case, saves the cost and disruption of sending my child to a private school out of town.

Not only that, but you will receive other benefits. Continuing with the example, Putnam goes on:

> say I, confident in my community's neighborliness, set up the group, and 17 people join. Then, worse comes to the worst, I make new friends. And maybe then the next time I find myself in tough times, I have people I can rely on. People who'll babysit when my grandmother across country takes suddenly ill, or who'll have leads if I find myself unemployed.

Not only that, but social connections correlate with health. The more connected we are, the less likely we are to experience "colds, heart attacks, strokes, cancer, depression, and premature death of all sorts" (327). These are well-established findings—"statistically speaking, the evidence for the health consequences of social connectedness is as strong today as was the evidence for the health consequences of smoking at the time of the first surgeon general's report on smoking" (loc. cit.).

Why this digression? Because social connectedness plummeted

from the 1960s on, more or less, and it did so just as television became ubiquitous. I refer the reader to Putnam's meticulously documented book for these claims (just one quick fact: in 1950, around 10 percent of homes had TVs, while in 1959 90 percent did, a gigantic rise [p. 221]). But not only that, "in a correlational sense ... more television watching means less of virtually every form of civic participation and social involvement ... dependence on television for entertainment is not merely *a* significant predictor of civic disengagement. It is *the single most consistent predictor* that I have discovered" (pp. 228–31).

We have here another, perhaps, key part of the puzzle of the 90s. Not only did the economy tank around the early 70s, and not only did Americans lose faith in politics, but they lost faith *in each other*, and came instead to replace time at the bowling alley or the bar or the town hall meeting with nights in front of their TV. And given that, it's a matter of vital importance that an accurate representation of the end of the 20th century represents life in front of the television and that, I claim, is why *The Simpsons* is such a vital work of art.

That's all well and good, I hope, but I fear it doesn't give an accurate sense of the most important thing about *The Simpsons*: its *funniness*. There are other smart shows out there which fall short in terms of the wall-to-wall belly laughter offered by *The Simpsons*.

To understand *Ulysses*, these days, one really has to read it in an annotated edition. Analogously, and always bearing in mind the risk of dissecting humor, I'll try to annotate a somewhat typical episode of *The Simpsons*. It was picked *somewhat* at random, although not completely (I was looking for an episode that would highlight the extent of the political references in *The Simpsons*).

It's called "Sideshow Bob Roberts" and was aired in 1994. Already the title refers to a film of 1990 about a conservative politician's bid for election, and apparently some of the shots in the episode mirror shots in the film. Sideshow Bob is a recurring guest star in *The Simpsons*, voiced by the distinctively voiced Kelsey Grammar; his long-term aim is to kill Bart after Bart got him in some legal trouble.

The episode begins, simply, with an establishing shot of a radio station, while a silly jingle plays. It's worth pointing out however that in this simple, half-a-second clip one already sees economy points. Here's an obvious point: if one were actually filming this, one would have to get a location scout to find a building, get a props

8. The Simpsons

person or set designer to make it look like a radio station, and so on. It would cost money. And then you'd have to ask yourself whether the money it costs is worth the half-a-second and the very weak pay-off of a slightly funny jingle. The answer is probably no, but with animation, there's no problem, and so this quick gag becomes economical.

The scene shifts to the powerplant where Homer works. He, Carl, and Lenny are listening to the same broadcast whose jingle we heard. The disk jockey is introduced as Birch Barlow, the author of "Only Turkeys Have Left Wings," a figure clearly meant to call in mind conversative pundit Rush Limbaugh. Homer's objection to listening to his show is not his politics, but the fact that he thinks voting is, I quote, "fruity."

At the risk of dissecting things overmuch, we're only about thirty seconds in but a lot has happened. Conservative talk radio was a new and increasingly influential feature of the political(-entertainment) scene in the 90s, and with great precision *The Simpsons* manages to parody it, along with throwing in a joke about Homer's stupidity. The juxtaposition of very smart and very not-smart that is in many ways a hallmark of the show is present here. In the modern day, Homer would offer a ringing endorsement of Tucker Carlson or whomever (in fact, he probably wouldn't; the political situation has changed in such a way that these people have a power unanticipatable in the 90s; now such a thing wouldn't ring funny as opposed to dark).

The point is: we're under a minute in and we've already got like four to five jokes, along with numerous references to politics as well as the first stages in setting up the plot.

> BARLOW: You know, there are three things we're never going to get rid of here in Springfield: one, the bats in the public library—[scene switch to man opening card catalog and screaming as bats fly out]
> —two, Mrs. McFierly's compost heap—
> [scene switch to huge compost pile and Mrs. McFierly rocking nearby with a shotgun, cackling]
> —and three, our six-term mayor,
> [scene switch to Quimby watering a marijuana plant]
> the illiterate, tax-cheating, wife-swapping, pot-smoking, spendocrat Diamond Joe Quimby.
> [cut to Quimby in a bath tub]
> QUIMBY: Hey: I am no longer illiterate.

Again, note the throwaway visual jokes that would be impossible in any other medium. Next, consider Diamond Joe Quimby. His voice and also character (aptly described by Barlow) are based on JFK. Next, Sideshow Bob phones in. He makes one of his many regular guest appearances; what you need to know is that he's a well-spoken, well-educated former clown's assistant who has long desired to kill Bart and is currently imprisoned for it.

He tells the story of his incarceration, to the sympathy of Barlow and the horror of Bart, who is listening on a Walkman (that also gets talk-radio?) in class. Barlow promises to get him out of jail, and that having been done, Bob is free to run for office against Quimby, which he duly does, campaigning on the platform that Quimby is soft on crime— after all, he let out Bob, twice convicted of attempted murder! We see a TV ad for Bob making this point, which visually calls to mind the infamous Willie Horton ad used by Bush in the run up to the 1988 election to imply that his opponent was weak on crime. Much more information on this can be located on the internet. Again, the relevant current day analogy—if there is one, which is unclear to me—would be something like the famously nonsensical GOP response to Barack Obama once wearing a tan suit.

Time passes, and the campaign is getting tight. Bob and Quimby have a televised debate. The latter is sick and appears uncomfortable and sweaty, making a bad impression on the audience. This is yet another reference to American politics. This time, it is to a 1960s presidential debate between John F. Kennedy and Nixon, in which the latter's tiredness and distractedness, people claim, won it for the former. Note again, though, that this was about 25 years old at the time of airing—a similar reference today would perhaps hearken back to something we've considered in this book (perhaps Clinton's impeachment). In any event, it's a further indication of the demands *The Simpsons* places on its audience.

It's Election Day. Homer steps behind the curtain in front of a voting booth and has to decide whether to vote for Bob or Quimby. This isn't as easy a decision as one might expect, and Homer weighs up the pros and cons of the candidates. On the one hand, Bob tried to kill his son. On the other hand, Bob tried to kill his hated sister-in-law Selma. He votes Bob. Krusty the Clown, whom Bob tried to frame for robbery, also has to decide. The fact that Bob might lower tax rates for high income people lets him overlook their past run-ins.

This scene is instructive. I spoke previously about how some humor

8. The Simpsons

is based in reality, especially this sort of dark, Lynchian humor. Much of *The Simpsons*' humor is not at all based in reality. Homer's behavior—voting for someone who runs on killing his son—is simply absurd. One of the distinctive features of *The Simpsons* is that it's not afraid to push physical and absurd comedy alongside smart material, a feature which again the animation probably makes possible (it's hard to imagine a live action series managing these jokes about child killing on primetime TV). Krusty's line, meanwhile, captures in one throwaway absurd sentence the motivation for countless millions of Republicans (not all Republicans, I somehow feel compelled to add).

Bob duly wins. But Lisa can't believe it: "I can't believe a convicted felon would get so many votes and another convicted felon would get so few." She goes to the register of voters to see if there's any funny business and is slipped a note by an anonymous stranger. They meet in a dark carpark, with Bart comparing them to Woodward and Bernstein and with Homer in the car reading Archie comics. The stranger, revealed to be Mr. Burns's assistant Smithers, whose closeted gayness is a running joke (and perhaps one which hasn't aged very well), gives them some information, a lead to chase down, and does so because he has issues with Bob's social conservatism. Smithers gives them a name, whose identity will uncover the whole thing. They spend hours in the courtroom looking, but find no reference for this person, and leave exhausted and despondent.

Before going on, just note the allusiveness. Woodward and Bernstein are the documenters of Watergate, to be discussed in the next explainer, which is to say an event 20 years before the air date. Although it's of course an iconic event of American postwar life, it's interesting to note the demands *The Simpsons* makes of its watcher: we've seen references to politics from the 60s, 70s, and 80s, already. It's a show which requires and trades on a well-informed audience. And worth noting again is its immediate blending of high and low, with the political reference followed by a reference to a cartoon, deflating the reference or inflating the comic, so that they end up on the same level.

Back to the story. As Bart and Lisa leave the courtroom, Bart spots something: from the window, a cemetery. And in that cemetery a grave for the name Smithers gave. They learn the horrible truth: "the dead have risen and are voting Republican!" Lisa corrects him: no, the Bob campaign has used committed electoral fraud, letting people cast votes in dead people's names (it's worth briefly lingering over the disturbing prescience of this. It's quite literally what Trump accused Democrats of). Not only that: he also used dead pets, including Lisa's beloved Snowball.

Thanks to the kids, Bob's plot is foiled. It seems, however, that they don't have evidence, and that he might get away scot free. But Lisa tricks him, telling him there's no way he'd be smart enough to pull off the fraud, and arrogant Bob can't take that, and ends with this monologue:

> BOB: Because you need me, Springfield. Your guilty conscience may force you to vote Democratic, but deep down inside you secretly long for a cold-hearted Republican to lower taxes, brutalize criminals, and rule you like a king. That's why I did this: to protect you from yourselves. Now if you'll excuse me, I have a city to run.

And finds himself, having been disabused of the notion that he still indeed does have a city to run, as the episode ends, back in prison, a prison depicted as exactly the sort of lax, white-color prison that people like Birch Barlow complain about.

This is, I say, paradigm *Simpsons*: there are *dozens* of episodes of this quality. Allusions to the last 30 years of American politics, quick-fire absurdist cutaway gags, snatches of TV, stupidity unsurpassed, and just incredible economy. Moreover, if I'm understanding Nielsen ratings correctly, 8.6 percent of houses with TVs had it on, which is an enormous number.

Here's something you might wonder about. I've talked up the allusive, sweeping nature of the topics covered in *The Simpsons*. As I've phrased it, and as I believe, all (most) of America is contained in it. But you might deny this for quite a fundamental reason. It's not enough just to allude to something, you might think, for something to be contained in it. Merely referencing JFK is a poor substitute for actually knowing the history and politics in question. It seems superficial. So, you might wonder, what's the point in all this allusion? There's fun in recognizing, for example, that the Bob/Quimby debate is echoing the Nixon/Kennedy one. One feels smart for recognizing it. But is that it? If all there was was this pleasure of recognition, it would be kind of hard to see the value in it.

And this gets to a lot of stuff that's already come up about postmodernism, for example in the discussion of Tarantino where it was suggested that it was all cool and no heart. What is the point of all this cleverness? Is it just showing off?

8. The Simpsons

I'm inclined to return to Joyce. Consider again the passage from *Ulysses* I quoted. Is this just an empty display? Virginia Woolf, famously, thought so. But I think we are inclined to think not because we are inclined to think that it gets at the consciousness of an interesting, if overly bookish, character. That's how some people see the world. It is a realistic portrayal of a bit of life, of a way of seeing the world.

I'm inclined to think that the same thing goes here. What *The Simpsons* gives us is the perspective of a smarter person than us on the world, someone who knows our world, who has read every paper and seen every movie of the last 30 years, and has the ability to see it reflected in the now. That, finally, is my view: *The Simpsons* is great because it's a way of *seeing* the world, casting its eye over the whole of history and TV, discerning its essence and then presenting its ridiculous side.

So that's *The Simpsons*: a new take on postmodern realism aided by the rediscovery of a new medium, animation, apt for the mass media–full world of postindustrial society. Awesome achievement as it is, however, *The Simpsons* is not all good, and I want to end on a negative note, by considering the political stance of the show. As has already been indicated, it's a massively political show. The episode I annotated above is perhaps an extreme but not overly unrepresentative example. Indeed, a webpage has collected up all the references to presidents in *The Simpsons*, and they are many. It would be hard to think of a political or social event in American history *not* represented in *The Simpsons*.

The important thing is that these references are treated no more and no less seriously than references to old movies. Indeed, despite its obsessive political allusiveness, it's also, in a sense, a highly *un*political show. You get the sense of someone vastly knowledgeable of American history but paralyzed thereby. In the next explainer, I want to suggest a reason for this attitude, but for now I want to notice that it is problematic. *The Simpsons* has a nihilism problem.

It doesn't have any positive message and, indeed, it scorns positive messages. This results in an often feeble bothsidesism according to which holding *any* view passionately puts one at the risk of fanaticism and intolerance.

The logic of the show, of course, demands this. Given that it's the anti–nuclear family sitcom, and given one of the core features of the nuclear family sitcom is the univocal voice of reason and the easy moral, it's necessary that *The Simpsons* rebel against it.

Nineties to Now

But this is not only formally demanded, it also seems to reflect the attitude of the showrunners. Having noted that the show is of a liberal bent, Al Jean goes on to say:

> If I had to say the overriding philosophy of the show, I would say it's probably nihilism, where I tend to think that government and big business are really out to screw the little guy and that, you know, it's more important, you know, to see what the feelings and emotions of a family are [quoted in *Planet Simpson*, Chris Turner, 2004, Random House of Canada, p. 239].

This gets manifest, though, very frequently as the view that in any debate, to fight too strongly for your position is a big thing. For example, in one episode (season 2 episode 9), Marge seeks to ban Itchy and Scratchy cartoons because of the effects watching that violence has on children. She succeeds, and the children go on, almost immediately, to eschew the boring ersatz replacement in which Itchy and Scratchy "love, and share, and love and share and share" and frolic outside joyfully. But then Michelangelo's David comes to town and Marge is portrayed as a hypocrite for not wanting to see it censored. Crucially, Marge *agrees* that she's being a hypocrite and that "even if one person can make a difference, they probably shouldn't."

This is bad. It's not bad only because Marge here seems to be accepting the false idea that free speech is sacrosanct but also because she backs down from her position and is presented as being right to do so. A much more admirable Marge wouldn't back down here, and it's bad that millions of homes saw this as a paradigm of decent moral commitment. Another example of essentially the same phenomenon comes when Lisa becomes a vegetarian, and becomes hostile to meat eaters, before realizing the error of her intransigent ways (season 7 episode 5).

The Simpsons much too often ends up on: you're both right. But that's generally false,[2] and this misrepresentation, determined by genre and by taste, is an influential feature of 90s distance, and a bad one.

The Simpsons, then, gives us another attitude toward the modern world. In the case of *Generation X*, cynicism and knowledge were tempered, I argued, by affection for one's friends. In *Seinfeld*, acute understanding of social minutiae seems to fill the gang's heads to such an extent that there's no room for feeling, and we see their inhuman

8. The Simpsons

relations to one another. *The Simpsons*, though, with its vast understanding of recent American culture, rests in a political nihilism, exhibits what our friend Lyotard might call an incredulity toward metanarratives, and is the worse for it, despite its many and other virtues.

9

Explainer: The Media and Recent American History

The Simpsons, I argued in the previous chapter, seems to treat American political history the same way that it treats old movies—as an object solely to make fun of. In this explainer, I want to consider some of the more salient features of that history to get a sense of why its writers might have this perspective, and thereby to show that it is, to some extent, merely a historical contingency, not an approach demanded of one everywhere and always. The flattening of politics into entertainment arose not from some deep necessity but just because of certain events in post–World War II history, and properly to understand that flattening requires a bit of detail, which I provide below, but which those already familiar can safely skip or skim.

I will concentrate on one famous aspect of domestic politics, Watergate, and one of foreign policy, the Vietnam War, showing the various ways politics was influenced by the media and made into a spectacle and why it could be the object of mockery and apathy which is so salient a feature of *The Simpsons*, but also of our society.

So let me start with Watergate. Watergate, it must be said, is a fantastic story, and has been told fantastically by Rick Perlstein, whose account (in *The Invisible Bridge*) I lean heavily on. Richard Nixon, a social conservative ("You see, homosexuality, dope, uh, immorality in general: These are the enemies of strong societies"[1]), was elected president for the first time at the tail end of the 60s—an era when young people rose up and protested against the various injustices their government perpetrated: the structural injustice and the hatred borne toward Black people, or gay people, or women, and the war in Vietnam (discussed below).

One might have thought, against such a backdrop, that an establishment conservative campaigning for "law and order" (which functioned, in 1968, against the backdrop of riots and protests, to at least to some

9. Explainer: The Media and Recent American History

extent as a dog whistle: he is going to protect the values under attack from the young, gay, Black protestors), wouldn't have done so well. But he won comfortably, appealing to what was known as the "silent majority"—the vast swathes of middle Americans, the ones not on campus or on the news, who shared his conservative values (something like the silent majority arguably reared again their head again with the election of Trump, which served to remind the world that America is in many ways a very regressive place; more on this later). Thereafter, he seemed to do pretty well in his first term and in 1972 was easily reelected for a second term

And then things started to unravel. A few months before the election there had been a break-in at the DNC headquarters in the Watergate complex in Washington, D.C. The men who were caught, it was reported, had connections to some people associated either with Nixon's campaign for reelection or with his White House staff.

Initially, Nixon himself didn't deign to respond to charges that *he* was in some way responsible for it: it just seemed, really, a bit weird. His spokesman famously said, "I'm not going to comment from the White House on a third-rate burglary attempt," and most people didn't pay much heed.

The country continued to do well: he took office again in January 1973, and, as Perlstein notes, the economy was going well and the Paris deal, putting an end to the war in Vietnam (at least ostensibly), was signed.

But there was still buzzing around the thought that the president had some connection to the break-in, and other stories of criminal behavior associated with Nixon's campaign for reelection caused a committee to be formed to investigate any illegal activity.

Fast-forward a bit, and the Watergate would-be burglars duly pled guilty, but at the sentencing, on March 23, was the first bombshell—what a fiction writer might call the inciting incident. James McCord, one of the accomplices associated with Nixon's campaign for reelection, passed a letter to the judge at sentencing, saying that perjury had been committed at the bidding of high up.

Then there was Nixon's first television appearance on April 17, where he claims he's looking into it: he's on the case. Forty-one percent of people thought Nixon was in some way guilty. It had gone from a "third-rate bulgary" to something the president addresses on screen in a few short months.

About two weeks later, the president *reappears* on television. He

Nineties to Now

notes there's been an effort to withhold facts about Watergate from the public and from he himself and announces that he's accepted the resignations of two of his right-hand men, Haldeman and Ehrlichman, *not* because they're guilty, but because being anything not above suspicion is insufficient for public trust (note how standards have fallen!).

Let's just stop a minute and try to say what this must *feel* like, to be someone watching this. Put yourself in the shoes of a 13-year-old Doug Coupland, a 20-year-old Seinfeld, a 13-year-old David Waster Wallace, a 19-year-old Groening, getting perhaps your first view into the workings of government, seeing the corruption and bizarreness involved, and moreover seeing it on the same device you watch your sitcoms on. It's unsurprising, I think, that such a person could grow up to write the for *The Simpsons*.

The parallels for the current day are also worth thinking about. We are perhaps uniquely well placed to have an intuitive sense of what the audience of 1973 would have thought and felt, as we, after all, have our own new media revealing the inner workings of power. If before it was thrilling to see a president on TV defend himself, we're now privileged enough to have access to the president's uncensored Fox News–inspired thoughts on Twitter.

Returning to our story, things don't let up. In the summer of 1973, hearings into the misdeeds associated with the reelection campaign are held and are televised on all the few channels then in existence. They are what used to be called water-cooler TV—the sort of shows everyone watches, everyone talks about.

Again, I think this is something at least the younger of us can only really strain at understanding—the idea of communal experience, and especially of the vast majority getting, in a sense, their first insight to how things work in the echelons of power, must have been overwhelming. Here they see, on one of the very first days, one of the president's men, McCord, admit, brazenly, to doing what he knew to be illegal activities, at the president's bidding.

Reaction, counterreaction: Nixon releases a statement saying that he did wiretaps, but that everybody knew it, and that he had a gang who did shady stuff, but that was for national security purposes. It seems that the more exposure there is, the more it's prodded, the more the story changes.

More details came out: how Nixon, even when vastly popular, was obsessed with protestors, how he tried a honeypot with sex workers to trap some Democrats, how he kept a famous "enemies list," how he had

9. Explainer: The Media and Recent American History

lied in his April televised statement. At this point, though, the narrative is getting a bit tiresome: yes there are all these details, but the drama has been wrung out of seeing people give testimony about the government's badness, and it's really just going to end up being their word against Nixon's.

The summer unfolds. The war is ending. The porn film *Deep Throat* has proven to be a surprise hit and is taken as a symbol of how things are degenerating. A good depiction of this can be found in Philip Roth's 1997 novel *American Pastoral*. One of the book's culminating scene is a dinner party, at which the talk is of "Linda Lovelace or Richard Nixon or H.R. Haldeman and John Ehrlichman," at which the protagonist's aging father complains of the baffling breakdown of family values and morality:

> And where will it end? What is the limit? You didn't all grow up in this kind of world. Neither did I. We grew up in an era when it was a different place, when the feeling for community, home, family, parents, work ... well, it was different. The changes are beyond conception. I sometimes think that more has changed since 1945 than in all the years of history there have ever been. I don't know what to make of the end of so many things. The lack of feeling for individuals that a person sees in that movie, the lack of feeling for places like what is going on in Newark—how did this happen? You don't have to revere your family, you don't have to revere your country, you don't have to revere where you live, but you have to know you have them, you have to know that you are part of them. Because if you don't, you are just out there on your own and I feel for you [p. 363–64].

There was a feeling in the air of sudden great change, that things were falling down, and quickly (one of the nice touches of the scene is that they're drinking a bottle of wine the protagonist stored to age five years before but which now seems to belong to an entirely different era).

Continuing with our story: a bombshell. It's revealed that Nixon has been secretly taping White House conversations. That means the key question—what did Nixon know about the burglary and when did he know it?—should be answerable by consulting the tapes. At this point, a TV show would probably cut to its post–Act II commercial break.

Nixon duly refuses to hand them over: it would undermine future presidents, he says, and anyway, previous presidents had taped conversations too. The investigators push back, Nixon offers to summarize them, the independent special prosecutor pushes back again. They want the actual tapes.

Then out of the blue, on October 20, Nixon orders the attorney general to fire the prosecutor—that is, the guy looking into his alleged criminality. The acting attorney general refuses and resigns; the next in line does the same thing, but the third in line carries out the order. And then another dramatic reversal: Nixon says he'll give over the tapes.

In April of the next year, and in the intervening time, seven of the Watergate burglars and accomplices are indicted, and the tapes are released. The insight into government is now even more magnified—not just how things are done secretly, but the very conversations, printed out: 1,308 pages, revealing a cursing president whose f-bombs were expunged and replaced with [expletive deleted]s. It becomes a bestseller, gets excerpted in newspapers and magazines; the whole country jokes about [expletive deleted].

The media-led intrusion into the president's life reaches its thrilling peak at this point. Not only do we get to see the president give his side of the story in Oval Office speeches; not only do we get to see what people said went on, but we also get to go inside the office itself, to get right up close and hear what our leaders sound like. It must have been uncanny and thrilling: I think even we, in an age in which a presidential candidate can boast about grabbing women by the [expletive deleted] and then get elected, can appreciate this, can see how that might have a formative effect on one's political outlook.

It ends, somewhat, with a bang not a whimper, like a chess game where the one in a lost position doesn't have the sense to resign. The new independent prosecutor isn't happy with the transcripts; there are mistakes and some big gaps. More tapes come out, and finally, something decisive: a recording of Nixon and his chief of staff on June 23, 1972, just a few days after the burglary. He knew about the burglary and he knew about it early. Game over: Nixon resigns.

What is relevant for our purposes? Note the dramatic ring to it: on one way of seeing it, it's a small, incidental flaw in an otherwise great—at least so the people found him—man that brings him down, like the hamartia of a tragic figure. It's filled with dramatic irony: the moralist revealed as a crook. It has the blending of high and low culture beloved of the postmodernist: it all plays out on television. Finally, it has the absurdity, the nonsensicality that makes fiction true to life: the massacre followed by the giving up of the tapes, the hard-to-make-up coining of "[expletive deleted]."

It's not difficult to see why *The Simpsons* writers should treat this as source material of the same sort as *Star Wars* or *A Streetcar Named*

9. Explainer: The Media and Recent American History

Desire. It's also, arguably, not difficult to see the future storyesque nature of American politics in the same way. It sounds like one of those things too ridiculous to be true, but doesn't it kind of seem befitting of fiction that the last two presidents should be a reality TV star and a Black guy whose middle name is "Hussein," that before that we should have a guy who got a blowjob in the Oval Office and before that an actor from the 40s hovering around senescence? One might think, all the complexities aside, that Watergate sufficed to shift the behavior we could expect from politicians in the direction of the absurd and spectacular that leads us where we are today, and where 90s America was.

Let me now turn now to an issue in foreign policy that will help us, I think, further understand the cynicism and disaffection in American political culture of the era.

One could be forgiven for thinking, no matter what one's politics, that Watergate was a good thing. It seemed to show the power of the media to get to the bottom of corruption and to let the people in on the democratic process by bringing them the evidence in the form of the televising of the proceeding and the transcripts of Nixon's conversations.

An adversarial media, then, would be one of the positive things which one could take away from the whole debacle. Indeed, looking around this positive judgment of the media would seem to be further confirmed by the role the media allegedly played in mobilizing antiwar sentiment in the case of Vietnam. A line of thought has it that, if anything, the media went too far: an influential book by *New York Times* and later *Washington Post* reporter Peter Braestrup (*Big Story*, 1977, Westview Press) suggested that it was partly the media presenting a distorted picture of the events that swung public opinion away from the war and that losing popular opinion was one of the reasons the war itself was lost.

However, a much more cynical view of the media was presented in a range of important books and articles in the 80s: Howard Zinn's *People's History of the United States* tells the American story in terms of those normally left out of history textbooks, the exploited and minorities, and Chomsky and Herman's 1988 *Manufacturing Consent* presented an account of how the media systematically misleads the public about politics, functioning essentially not as checks to government power but as furthering its official agenda. I want to consider their account of the Vietnam War as an example of how this goes, as I think it's arguable that the negative conclusions it compels one to draw can be viewed as a contributor to the nihilism and distrust of authorities of *The Simpsons'* writers and other 90s artists.

Here's how a capsule history of the Vietnam War would go. In the postwar period, the French attempted to retain control of their colony, and the Americans supported them. They wanted, in particular, to stop the spread of communism from overrunning the Vietnamese people. So they helped out with aid and so on.

However, their aims changed in 1964 with the occurrence of what's known as the Gulf of Tonkin incident. The story that was told was that an American boat in international waters was fired upon by North Vietnamese fighters. Naturally, then, the Americans needed to respond to this provocation, and so they did. The Americans then waged a war, still with the noble aim of stopping the spread of communism, but now also to respond to the hostilities they were faced with. This continued for a few years, but during this Americans, who saw the fighting on their TV screen, became increasingly unhappy about the cost of and motivation for the conflict. This culminated in the presentation of a particular battle, the Tet Offensive. The media, it's claimed, showed the failure of the Americans here and swung opinion away from the war, and that, in turn, led to the fall of Lyndon Johnson. Eventually, several years later, Nixon signed the Paris Peace Accords, according to which the Southern Vietnamese non-communist government's rights over the whole country were recognized; in the aftermath, the North Vietnamese, however, treacherously didn't heed this agreement.

Now, people don't really believe this anymore. But, if you were to have followed the popular media of the period, that's what you would have heard. But it fundamentally rests on false assumptions. In Chomsky and Herman's words, the crucial fact is this:

> The United States attacked South Vietnam, arguably by 1962 and unquestionably by 1965 ... media coverage ... that does not begin by recognising these essential facts is mere apologetics for terrorism and murderous aggression ... from the point of view of the media, or "the culture," there is no such event in history as the US attack ... the US aggression was unrecognised ... these facts reflect the overwhelming dominance of the state propaganda system and its ability to set the terms of thought and discussion, even for those who believe themselves to be taking an adversarial stance [p. 184].

That's the fundamental fact: the U.S. functioned as the aggressor, and we should view them just as we view, say, Russia invading Ukraine. They document how the American establishment knew that the North Vietnamese, led by Ho Chi Minh, were popular, and that accordingly they

9. Explainer: The Media and Recent American History

couldn't get rid of him by political means, and so they had to try to create a conflict.

This was the Gulf of Tonkin incident. According to Defense Secretary Robert McNamara, a U.S. ship was operating in international waters when it attacked. This is dubious: on August 3, the *Maddox* was in North Vietnamese waters and, when challenged, was shot at one time. On the fourth, it was claimed that it was shot at again, causing Johnson on the fifth to complain.

However, the evidence that anything happened on the fourth doesn't really exist, and yet on the basis of one shot Congress passed a resolution to take any measures against it.

Chomsky and Herman go on to say how the American interpretation was furthered in the media, and how some even "provid[ed] vivid and dramatic accounts of the August 4 incident which apparently never took place" (they note also that it's not like the evidence wasn't out there—international media reported both sides—see p. 209). The key worry here is not so much the lies of the government (though that is obviously bad), but the failure of the media to account for it, and the suspicion and cynicism this would create in the American learning this.

Moving on, the war continued. People began to get unhappy with it, and this escalated in the Tet Offensive. Things get complicated here, but note: the point Herman and Chomsky make is that the media is in the service of the government. However, there was an opposing, conservative voice that said the complete opposite: that the media weakened the war effort by misrepresenting the outcome of the offensive. According to the already mentioned Peter Braestrup, the incompetent presentation of the war changed people's perceptions about it and caused them to go off it. Chomsky and Herman show how this is completely wrong, but it goes to show the levels of distrust and suspicion someone growing up at that time would have had.

The final thing to note is the Paris agreement. This was meant to ensure that both north and south had a role to play in the governing of Vietnam, but American immediately and obviously interpreted it in a completely different way as saying that only their side had a role. Again, the media didn't push back against this.

It doesn't seem ridiculous to think that Chomsky's anti-imperialist analyses of Vietnam and other wars, which in 1988 (when *Manufacturing Consent* was published) had already been going on since 1962, influenced the intellectual culture (indeed, he was on Nixon's enemies list) and was a determinant of the apolitical cynicism the period is marked by.

These are but two episodes in a long history, but arguably crucial ones for understanding the 90s: someone around 1990 could look back not just to an economic period of tranquility before 1974 but, just at the edge of memory, they would find the 50s and (some of) the 60s, where both domestically and from the point of view of foreign policy things seemed much less corrupt and ridiculous, where they could trust government and the media. Instead, they faced a government which lied about war and extremely close-up portraits of their cursing leaders.

Not only that, but the 1990s were essentially more of the same: the televised Gulf War in the early 1990s, to which one could tune in to hear anchors going into paroxysms about the technical specs of the weaponry, and the pornographically detailed near impeachment of Clinton a few years earlier, a scandal if anything more lurid than Watergate.

And things have continued: the current worries about fake news, one might argue, are just another instance of a case which shows the importance of controlling the media, and Trump's presidency, which is mostly scandal, mostly spectacle, seems to represent a continuation of a trend in American politics stretching back decades. But here's the key point: even though it's perfectly understandable that one born into and living in such an atmosphere would retreat to nihilism, if we take a step back and view both the 90s and today as merely the outcome of some contingent historical events (it's not like postindustrial society *demands* a ridiculous, scandalous politics, because many—indeed most—postindustrial societies don't have such politics), we can realize that the nihilism is also contingent, and things can change.

10

David Foster Wallace as Religious Poet

A theme that has built up over the course of the last few chapters has been the role that intelligence plays in the works we've considered. I suggested when discussing *Generation X* that something distinctive of its generational namesake was a surfeit of intelligence, especially when compared with the low socioeconomic status of the McWorker. This, I claimed, was productive of the 90s cynicism. *Seinfeld* we should think of as a paralyzing science of the modern, where feeling is gone, replaced by knowledge of precisely how many days one should wait to call someone for a date. And in *The Simpsons*, the panoramic view of the absurdities of postwar history lead to nihilism.

This trend reaches its peak, I claim, in the work of David Foster Wallace, who is concerned to show the destructive power of reason not as a tool for understanding the world outside oneself, but as an internal guiding light. Reasoning, Wallace claims, leads one to the horrors of drug addiction and to feelingless cynicism. The only escape is to renounce rationality: human flourishing seems to consist, in his world, in not listening to one's rational self, and instead following the advice of people in substance abuse support groups, which makes no sense. Or human flourishing consists in top-level athletic performance, of training beyond fatigue and in developing reflexes that work faster than thought. Or yet again, it consists, most simply, in overcoming the tedium of doing one's desk job (dealing with people's tax returns, in his posthumous *The Pale King*).

Another, new trend, very important for understanding our current plight, also receives its most compelling treatment in Wallace's work: the increasing ubiquity of mental illness. Mental illness casts a shadow over 1990s culture. In music, Kurt Cobain's heroin addiction and suicide is just the most remembered example of a definite trend (we could think also of the Smashing Pumpkins, or Nail Inch Nails, or Marilyn Manson), a trend expressed also in the literature and film of the era (we can think of Elizabeth Wurtzel's 1994 *Prozac Nation,* or again of Susanna Kaysen's 1993 memoir *Girl, Interrupted,* or its 1999 film version). Such was its cultural saturation that by 1999, TV's golden era was introduced by a show whose pitch could be given and understood in four words: mob boss on Prozac. In the next explainer I will give a bit of the history of the development of the concept of mental illness and addiction in postwar America; for now though I want to consider how it's reflected in Wallace's work.

His work presents a fundamentally *religious* vision of the world, a Commedia in which the hell is being addicted to drugs or alcohol or whatever; purgatory is finding oneself in rehab or at AA meetings, entirely out of one's own control and yet responsible for the wrongs one committed while high or drunk; and heaven is being in one's own control, being in control of one's body and mind in the way professional athletes or the longtime sober are. Doing something hard very well is the goal, that control of the self most associated with elite athletes is heaven for Wallace. But it's also something like elderly recovering alcoholics, toothless men with disgusting wet cigars in their mouths and no teeth who committed who knows what atrocities, who are not particularly *attractive* people to interact with for the normal person but have attained that same transcendence of their flesh that Wallace attributes to elite athletes like Roger Federer.

This might seem a bit uninteresting, in particular if one doesn't happen to have substance abuse problems or isn't an elite athlete (Wallace, incidentally, had or was both). But I think that we can safely take them nonliterally: addiction is just a particularly vivid way of presenting the lack of control that is, in essence, the fundamental ill religions tell us about, whether that be the lack of control of one's urges that the saints Augustine or Paul get worked up about, or the Buddhist thought that suffering is essentially craving. And the platitudes of AA, as we'll see, are just a way of dramatizing the banality, the irony, of truth.

But then *that* might seem uninteresting, in particular if one doesn't have any real sympathy for religion. Maybe you're not troubled like the Buddha was or the fathers of the church were. But, well, that seems doubtful. The statistics suggest that we are troubled people indeed—as we'll see in more detail in the next chapter, mental health and drug addiction are epidemic-level problems.

The reason Wallace is particularly valuable, I think, is that he spiritualizes our trouble and suffering, but also because he presents ideals:

10. David Foster Wallace as Religious Poet

ways to live. This is especially important today when, as I'll show, the biological model of psychic suffering has won the day. We tend to think of our sufferings as neurochemical imbalances, but this tends to make us passive with regards to them, and anyway, as we'll see, the neurochemical imbalance theory is based on dubious science (that's not to say one should stop taking any medicines one is taking—it's true that if you're depressed and take an antidepressant, there's a strong chance you'll feel better, which is a good reason to take it, neurochemistry notwithstanding).

That's how I think we should read Wallace. There's hell, and there are creatures above, and we can be either. This is all very interesting, but what *especially* makes him interesting, given the narrative developed in this book, is his diagnosis for what the road to hell is, and what the road out of it is: thinking, and not thinking, respectively, and especially irony and its opposite, sincerity. The addict is a fine instance of the irrationality of rationality: what he or she does, after all, is act only to avoid pain, but in so doing, causes massive pain. Moreover, the only way to get over it, for Wallace in *Infinite Jest*, is by attending AA and going through the rituals, even if it makes no rational sense. Similarly, to achieve mastery of tennis or any other athletic activity requires year after year of thoughtless labor, which requires as much mental as bodily control. In the narrative of this book, Wallace presents us with a vision of the world that is fundamentally serious and high stakes and to which irony is an unfitting reaction, and thus represents a distinctive step away from his hip and witty, but often heartless, 90s predecessors. But at the same time, stylistically he retains many of the elements of formal playfulness of some of the earlier works, and so he is an apt object of study.

Before making these points by considering some texts of his, first let me say a bit more about Wallace and perhaps attempt to mitigate any preconceptions one may have about him. In a sense, he's easy to dislike. He is a super mega genius, and a tortured one at that. He seems pretentious: he uses words like "prenominate" where "already mentioned" would do just fine, or "anent" where "about" would be fine. His characters often talk kind of similarly, as do his narrators: a sort of sitcom wittiness abounds. *Infinite Jest* is *way* too long.

Moreover, his fans are even worse: pretentious without the talent. I was such a few years ago. I was the guy who *insisted* you read him, that here was something fundamentally new that you can't not encounter. That tends to rub people the wrong way, especially when combined with the other unappealing traits of the affluent young middle-class types who form his fan base.

I also have the sense that he's disliked perhaps because "confessional" writing has been around for a decent enough time, in people like Plath and Sexton down to the personal essay writers of today, and it's at least to a large extent a female practice, and perhaps these people resent men presenting his work as if he, in talking about feelings, is doing something new.

Which he's not: the new(ish)[1] thing in Wallace is the literary fictionalization of mental suffering. What David Foster Wallace did is made it okay for uptight highly educated literary sorts of people to talk about, or at least to read about someone talking about, their feelings. And he did that through using big words and Derridean deconstructive techniques and Pynchonian "big" narratives that told you nevertheless this wasn't *just* talking about feelings but was in fact high-quality art. And this might justifiably piss people off by the implication that confessional sort of writing in itself isn't good enough. I sometimes get the sense that he's disliked by people who write confessional things because his fans think he invented talking about sadness, when he just repackaged it for a certain type of man.

All this is by way of preface, and kind of an aside. If Wallace's value were exhausted by the fact that he wrote entertaining books about sadness for sad white men, then it would be exhausted indeed.

But it's not. He has things to teach us about how to think about the world. At least so I'll try to show, by considering first *Infinite Jest*. The plot of *Infinite Jest* is big and complicated, and I don't particularly wish to explain it (there's a decent summary on Wikipedia). It's set in the mild future, in which years of names (like "1942") have come to be sponsored, as in "Year of Whataburger." People use somewhat futuristic entertainment devices which play cartridges, one of which cartridges, containing a film known as *Infinite Jest*, is so compelling that watchers are unable to look away. I hope this already rings some thematic bells about branding and the media.

Some people look for the cartridge, in order to weaponize it, or deweaponize it. The main action concerns residents at a tennis school and a halfway house for people recovering from addictions to drug and alcohol in Boston: the school and the halfway house are close by, and it tells the story of one such tennis player, a very smart but addicted to marijuana guy named Hal, and several recovering addicts, first among whom is a guy named Gately.

10. David Foster Wallace as Religious Poet

Stylistically, in terms of what we've discussed before, it has some interesting elements. There is a lot of more or less gratuitous violence: cats are killed, congested people with gags in their mouth die horrific of asphyxiations, tongues are bitten off by fitting epileptics, and a central scene involves a shockingly brutal fight with the hero. There are a lot, also, of scenes of people in various stages of affliction or depression talking about it, and there is also a lot of witty, sitcom-esque dialogue by many characters who kind of sound the same, and the narrative voice is colloquial and fast paced with a self-conscious tendency to use big words. The overall effect is that it is fun and easy to read, even if the plot is convoluted and the sentences long.

Fundamentally, as I said, the novel is about addiction and the powerlessness of thought. In its first few hundred pages we get the backstories of the addicts: we hear in minute detail of seizures on trains, of a guy desperately waiting for his dealer, of a girl smoking enough crack to kill herself, of a clinically depressed girl talking about the depression, and about the gruesome death that puts him in the halfway house. That is, we get hell in its varieties.

But we learn that all these varieties are, boiled down, the same story:

> Fun with the Substance, then very gradually less fun, then significantly less fun because of the like blackouts ... then dread, anxiety, irrational phobias ... what Boston AA calls losses ... seizures ... formicative bugs ... then eventually a terrible acknowledgement that some line has been undeniably crossed, and fist-at-the-sky, as-God-is-my-witness vows to buckle down and lick this thing for good ... then a slip ... repeated slips ... then unemployability, financial ruin, bloody vomiting, incontinence, neuropathy ... and you now hate the substance, *hate* it, but you still find yourself unable to stop doing it ... you all of a sudden see the substance as it really is ... the substance you thought was your one true friend ... has finally removed smily-face mask to reveal centreless eyes and a ravening maw, and canines down to here, it's the Face in the Floor.... You see now that It's your enemy ... you're in the kind of a hell of a mess that either ends lives or turns them around [*ibid.*, p. 226–28].

And then, you go to a meeting. And in that meeting, "crocodiles"

> old twisted guys ... with hideous turd like cigars under a framed glossy of crocodile or alligators sunning themselves on some verdant riverbank somewhere ... these old guys cluster together under it, rotating their green cigar in their misshapen fingers ... with their varicose noses and flannel shirts and brown teeth [*ibid.*, p. 235].

Tell their own personal stories of addiction, and tell you the key to sobriety is to go to these meetings, and—a much debated about feature of such programs—pray. And rationally, you are puzzled by this, because you don't believe in God and what good would going to a meeting do:

> You ask the scary old guys How AA works and they smile their chilly smiles and say Just Fine. It just works, is all; end of story.... Gately couldn't for the life of him figure out how just sitting on haemarroid-hostile folding chairs every night looking at nose-pores and listening to clichés could work [p. 230].

It goes against every rational impulse:

> at the start, you just know, deep in your gut, that they[substances]'ll never let you know; you just know it. But they do.... And then this goofy slapdash anarchic system of low-rent gatherings and corny slogans and saccharin grins and hideous coffee ... this unromantic, unhip, cliche thing ... is so lame you just *know* there's no way it could ever possibly work [*ibid.*, p. 231].

But that's not so bad, because thinking isn't to be trusted:

> That 99% of compulsive thinkers' thinking is about themselves; that 99% of this self-directed thinking consists of imagining and then getting ready for things that are going to happen to them; and then, weirdly, that if they stop to think about it, that 100% of the things they spend 99% of their time and energy imagining and trying to prepare for all the contingencies and consequences of are never good ... 99% of the head's thinking activity consists of trying to scare the everliving shit out of itself [*ibid.*, p. 198].

But at this point, thankfully, you've given up on rational impulses, you've given up on the thought of yourself as a locus of control:

> you have no faith in your own sense of what's really improbably and what isn't, [and they tell you to pray even though you don't believe in God] and like a shock-trained organism without any kind of independent human will you do exactly like you're told ... your personal will is the web your Disease sits and spins in, still ... you have to Starve the Spider: you have to surrender your will [*ibid.*, p. 231].

And that, apparently, works. And does so just fine.

There are several things I want to note here. First, and just to repeat, this is essentially a religious view of man: Christianity tells you that we are fundamentally broken, fallen creatures, and Kierkegaard tells you that you just have to make a leap of faith to accept its fundamental, unprovable tenet of Christ and Him crucified; Buddhists tell you that the essence of existence is suffering, and its Zen school councils that, to get away from it, one should just sit and attend to meaningless parables. This is Wallace's view. The very core of what it is to be a human—if we follow Aristotle in thinking that human beings are *zoon logon echon*, creatures with reason—is messed up.

10. David Foster Wallace as Religious Poet

That's the second and related point: it's a fundamentally anti-humanist view of the world. For Descartes, there were fundamentally two features of man: the will and the intellect. Wallace's lingering on addiction, as presented in the above passages, suggests that the proper functioning of each of them leads to death: after all, you desire to do fun things, and it preeminently rational that if it's okay to do a fun thing on one day, it's also okay to do it the next. But that, pursued in a way that admittedly few people, thankfully, do pursue it, leads to the hell presented above.

The third thing is that even if we are fundamentally warped, nevertheless there is a way to live. It's not by, as an analytic philosopher of action would tell you, consulting one's desires and computing the most rational way to affect them, it's by heeding some simple cliché truths ("Why," Wallace asks elsewhere, "is the truth usually not just un- but anti-interesting?" [p. 239]) and putting in effort, and in particular doing something you don't want to or don't believe will help.

Now—I don't know. Maybe this picture of the world is wrong. Maybe we're all fundamentally okay, our humanity won't missteer us in most cases; maybe we just need a little tweak, such as can be provided by the right medicine. Maybe our various woes are just chemical imbalances. That's *a* picture of the world, certainly, and indeed it seems like it's kind of the ruling one. But I think it should at least be open to question, and we should ask ourselves whether perhaps this extreme, ill-formed world that Wallace gives us is perhaps the one in which we live.

Wallace's religious way of viewing the world makes him open to seeing the good along with the bad. If there is hell here on earth, then Wallace thinks there is also heaven: indeed it's precisely because he's so attuned to hell that he's also attuned to heaven. For him, it's Federer, but more generally I think it's a vision of Things Done Well, the sense that our actions reach toward an ideal. Here's how he puts it. In one of his several essays on tennis, he writes that the beauty of the athlete encapsulates

> human beings' reconciliation with the fact of having a body.... Rather like certain kinds of sensuous epiphanies, great athletes seem to catalyse our awareness of how glorious it is to touch and perceive, move through space, interact with matter. Granted, what great athletes can do with their bodies are things that the rest of us can only dream of. But these dreams are important. They make up for a lot.... Inspiration is contagious and multiform—and even just to see, close up, power and aggression made vulnerable to beauty is to feel inspired and (in a fleeting, mortal way) reconciled [*ibid.*, p. 940].

And the fourth thing is how we should think of all this in terms of the narrative I've developed. I suggested that a key feature of nineties sensibility was a sort of knowledge-induced paralysis: from the Generation X-ers who realized they were indirectly enslaving the third world to the *Seinfeld* gang and their microscopic science of everyday life to *The Simpsons* writers trapped in the absurd past. David Foster Wallace could be seen as this taken to its extreme limit: that looking out onto the world with cleverness and distance fundamentally blinds one to the truth and leads one to hell.

And the fifth thing concerns our old friend realism and sincerity or non-irony. This is in fact something Wallace has written about extensively, but we can see the problem already in the above passage. Recall our discussion of Lynch: one of the sources of what I called his realism was that he presents the melodramatic bits that make up our life but that other artists eschew as corny. We can see Wallace wrestling with this in the above: what are we, as thinkers or artists, to do with the fact that the truth is fundamentally banal, cliché, uncomplicated?

It causes a bind. In an essay written three years earlier, he wrote about the dangers of viewing the cliché truth *as* cliché: of taking precisely the sort of distanced stance of a *Seinfeld* or *The Simpsons* (interestingly, he views this distanced stance as brought about by too much television, but discussing that would take us too far afield). If the truth is cliché, and we want to avoid cliché, then we're forced to avoid the truth. In another passage from *Infinite Jest*:

> What passes for hip cynical transcendence of sentiment is really some kind of fear of being really human, since to be really human is probably to be unavoidably sentimental and naive and goo-prone and generally pathetic [*ibid.* p. 298].

This is an interesting variation on the theme: just as *presenting* sentiment carries risks for the ironizer, so merely feeling it does too. To be human is to be undistanced and uncool.

Infinite Jest can be seen, in part, as an attempt to get through this problem, to, at times, risk being seen as mawkish or sentimental in order to say the truth. The earlier essay alluded to above ended with this famous injunction for American writers to

> dare somehow to back away from ironic watching, who have the childish gall actually to endorse and instantiate single-entendre principles. Who treat of plain old untrendy human troubles and emotions in U.S. life with reverence and conviction. Who eschew self-consciousness and hip fatigue. These

10. David Foster Wallace as Religious Poet

> anti-rebels would be outdated, of course, before they even started. Dead on the page. Too sincere. Clearly repressed. Backward, quaint, naive, anachronistic. Maybe that'll be the point. Maybe that's why they'll be the next real rebels. Real rebels, as far as I can see, risk disapproval. The old postmodern insurgents risked the gasp and squeal: shock, disgust, outrage, censorship, accusations of socialism, anarchism, nihilism. Today's risks are different. The new rebels might be artists willing to risk the yawn, the rolled eyes, the cool smile, the nudged ribs, the parody of gifted ironists, the "Oh how banal." To risk accusations of sentimentality, melodrama. Of overcredulity. Of softness [*ibid.*, p. 707].

This is what Wallace tries to do in *Infinite Jest*, and I will suggest that it's been quite influential. Wallace's work forms sort of a pivot, or is the (or, rather, an) end point of the cynical ironic 90s attitude, after which art to some extent changes.

Moreover, in any event his conclusion, quoted immediately above, remains important. In *Infinite Jest*, there is feeling, the risk of sincerity, the recognition that there is bad in the world and there is good, that the bothsidesism of *The Simpsons* is no world view.

In sum, then, Wallace is the most extreme exemplar of the thought that knowledge leads nowhere good, but by virtue of that extremeness he manages to come out the other side and ends up both recommending and practicing sincerity and anti-irony. In so doing, he is able to inject value and a concern for value back in the world, for the thought that to be human is to be subject to extremes of high and low navigating which gives meaning to one's life. The idea that there is a Good to which we can strive to attain (whether that be tennis, taxes, or sobriety) but which fundamentally requires effort and doesn't come naturally is a useful corrective to the currently popular view that our sufferings are largely a function of our neurochemistry with the concomitant idea that when a pill fixes our serotonin levels we'll be fine. In the next chapter, I'll tell the story about how this view came to be popular: how the medical model of psychiatry came to reign supreme in the late 20th century. I hope in so doing yet again to show that this currently engrained idea is merely the product of contingent historical circumstances.

11

Explainer: Psychiatry

In this explainer I want to consider the strange history of psychiatry in the 20th century. Its growth, and the direction of it, has been marvelous: worth marveling at. A couple of centuries ago, if you were feeling low, you might have attributed it to sin working in you, to your actions being out of step with the omnipotent, omniscient creator of the universe. A century ago, a sophisticated Viennese might have attributed it to a Freudian neurosis: some childhood trauma that you hadn't got over that works itself out of you in even the strangest oblique moments of your life, writing itself over such things as your dreams and the words you struggle to pronounce.

Now, most likely, you're liable to think it's a serotonin imbalance and you will be, almost certainly, very happy to take a pill to correct it. And the pill may well help, some: a lot of people, after taking an antidepressant, do get better.

But there are consequences to this. In making our suffering a question of biology or neurochemistry we risk devaluing it, in the sense of thinking that it's not a value-laden, distinctively human part of our experience. We don't think this about other things: about joy, about courage, about wit and intellect, or cruelty and arrogance. If we're so confident that it's serotonin we're lacking we may become blind to other things we're lacking, that all would be good were it not for our pesky neurotransmitters.

Maybe we should just accept these consequences. Science increasingly holds sway over these parts of our lives, and if we have a good medical theory, then we should accept it. In tracing the development of psychiatry, we'll get to see whether we *do* have a good theory of depression. Spoiler: we do not.

On one telling, the rise of psychiatric drugs is a wonder story. In 1975, in the UK, there were 9 million prescriptions for antidepressants. In 2016, there were 64.7 million.[1] The same goes in the U.S. Roger

11. Explainer: Psychiatry

Whitaker, whose 2010 book *Anatomy of an Epidemic* is one of my primary sources in this chapter, points out that the number of Americans in receipt of disability benefits for mental illness is six times what it was in 1955. Prozac is now, perhaps, the most recognizable drug brand in the world, with a cultural weight and a raft of associations attached to it. How did we get to here in the last decades of the 20th century? Well, seemingly how we get to most things: by luck and by money.

To see this, let me introduce the basics of brain science (I rely here on, in addition to Whitaker, Irving Kirsch's *The Emperor's New Mind* [pp. 82ff], and E. Siobhan Mitchell's *Antidepressants [Drugs: The Straight Facts]*). The brain is made up of things call neurons, which are like wires which transmit information from one part of the brain to another. There are billions of these spread across the brain, and information is transmitted between them. A neuron transmits information by an electronic signal; however, no neurons touch one another, but rather are separated by a small space called a synapse. Think of neurons as paths in forests frequently broken up by deep valleys, and think of the electric signals as objects moving along the paths, but moving slowly enough that they lack the energy to get out of a valley having gotten into one. A natural question then arises: how does the object continue along its path? How do we transmit a message from the first neuron to the second? How does it get across the synapse?

The answer is that neurons can produce chemicals which can fill up the synapse and transmit information. These chemicals are called neurotransmitters. Serotonin is a neurotransmitter, as is dopamine, both of which you have heard of. Together they, as well as some others, are called "monoamines."

So this is what happens: a neuron has a message, it squirts out some neurotransmitter into the synapse which conveys that message, which the other neuron receives. After it has done that, some of the neurotransmitter gets destroyed by enzymes, a process called oxidation, and some goes back up into the sending neuron (reuptake), but some remains.

The prevailing medical model of depression is then simple to state: depression comes about if you don't have enough of a given neurotransmitter in your synapses, and antidepressants work by increasing that amount.

At this point you might wonder—why? What is the connection between our mental suffering (not to mention the many and often bizarre physical symptoms of depression) and these chemicals? Ideally, medical science would proceed as so: we find a problem in the body, and then we develop drugs to fix that problem.

That's not what happened with depression though. Rather, what happened was that we found, purely by chance, that some drugs, developed for a completely different purpose, had antidepressant effects, and then we saw what those drugs did, and on that basis we concluded that the bits of the brain changed by the drug must be where the depression is at.

In particular, people noticed the following: that the drug iproniazid, which was developed to prevent tuberculosis, and the drug imipramine, which was developed to treat schizophrenia, both seemed to cure depression.

They then worked back and had a look at what these drugs did, and found the following. Iproniazid prevented the process which causes the neurotransmitters like serotonin from getting removed from the synapse. That is, in the lingo, it inhibits monamine oxidation, hence the name MAO(I), Monamine Oxidation Inhibitor, for a class of antidepressants of which you might have heard.

Imipramine, on the other hand, works by stopping the process of reuptake. So, in both cases, the drugs bring it about that there's more of the neurotransmitters in the synapses, and in both cases it appeared that patients treated with the drugs ceased exhibiting signs of depression, and so, naturally enough, people came to think that depression is the result of not having enough of a given monamine in your synapses.

This seems clean and neat, and in the late fifties and early sixties a range of other psychotropic drugs—first-generation antipsychotics, and tranquilizers—were developed and marketed. The discovery of these together made news—and money. In 1967, already one in three American adults filled a description for a "psychoactive" medication, with sales totaling 692 million (Whitaker p. 62).

Most of these were probably for the tranquilizers: in 1955, Miltown, a barbiturate (something with the same sort of effects as a benzodiazepine but many more side effects) went on sale and was the subject of news articles, and a run in the pharmacies, selling out. But the other drugs made the papers too, with *Time* and *New York Times* talking about how the recently discovered antipsychotics were changing lives. Things went so far that Salvador Dali was paid $35,000 to make an exhibit expressing the effects of Miltown (p. 58).

And the doctors were pretty happy with themselves: some hailed it as "one of the most important and dramatic epics in the history of

11. Explainer: Psychiatry

medicine itself," and "treatment and understanding of [mental] illness will forever be altered ... and in our own way we will persist for all time in that small contribution we have made toward the Human Venture" (quoted in Whitaker, p. 62).

It's not difficult to see the appeal here. Is not suffering, in one sense or another, the defining feature of life? It was the Buddha's experience of dukkha that made him discover enlightenment. Horny St. Augustine was very upset he couldn't stop himself having causal sex and thus developed Christianity. If we could solve that with a pill, well, that would be pretty great, and would more than warrant the doctors' big words.

There were, unfortunately, some problems. All these new drugs had pretty serious side effects. The MAOI type drugs, of which iproniazid was the first, in addition to affecting the levels of serotonin in the synapses, mess with a bunch of other things. They cause, for example, a failure to break down another thing called tyramine. It has no role in the brain, but it affects blood pressure: too much tyramine can be very dangerous. Unfortunately, some common foods contain tyramine, such as cheese and wine, and so if you take an MAOI, you must be careful to avoid them. The drugs of the type of imipramine also have some pretty bad side effects and can lead to one feeling jittery and restless, as well as having more serious side effects like heart problems.

The tranquilizers had problems too, people realized. In effect mimicking the sedating effects of alcohol, they were similar in another way: they led to withdrawal symptoms when stopped, because the body comes to expect them. In the 1970s, this led to a reduction in prescribing.

However, the biggest problem was that the science behind them was bad. Recall the theory: if depression were just abnormally low levels of serotonin in the synapses, then one should be able to induce depression in the nondepressed by sucking out their serotonin. And there were drugs which could do that—but people didn't get depressed. The theory was falsified by experiment.

That would be fine, if regrettable: many theories get falsified, and on that basis we develop new ones. The next stage in the story is when things get messed up. In the late 1970s, the psychiatrists' association, the APA, was going through a dark time. It was their particular raison d'être to prescribe drugs, so they were invested in the biological model of mental illness. It's just that their theories were wrong and their drugs only dubiously effective. People lost faith in medicalized psychiatry and sought other cures, and this led to a two-pronged, rear-guard action by the APA.

The first was the creation of DSM-III, the third edition of the *Diagnostic and Statistical Manual of Mental Disorders*. This listed a range of putative disorders, as well as diagnostic criteria for them. According to one person, "The ascendance of scientific psychiatry became official ... the old [psychoanalytical] psychiatry derives from theory, the new psychiatry from fact" (quoted in Whitaker, p. 239). This new book was meant to present all the wondrous discoveries of psychiatry, to be a bestiary of all the sufferings we undergo.

You are probably familiar, at least at third or so hand, with the content of this, but let's just consider an example. The entry for major depressive disorder, for example, begins with this wall of prose:

> The essential feature is either a dysphoric mood, usually depression, or loss of interest or pleasure in all or almost all usual activities and pastimes. This disturbance is prominent, relatively persistent, and associated with other symptoms of the depressive syndrome. These symptoms include appetite disturbance, change in weight, sleep disturbance, psychomotor agitation or retardation, decreased energy, feelings of worthlessness or guilt, difficulty concentrating or thinking, and thoughts of death or suicide or suicidal attempts. An individual with a depressive syndrome will usually describe his or her mood as depressed, sad, hopeless, discouraged, down in the dumps, or in terms of some other colloquial variant. Sometimes, however, the mood disturbance may not be expressed as a synonym for depressive mood but rather as a complaint of "not caring anymore," or as a painful inability to experience pleasure... [p. 210].

Before going on to give a checklist, any four of which, for a period of over two weeks, suffice for a diagnosis:

> poor appetite or significant weight loss (when not dieting) or increased appetite or significant weight gain (in children under six, consider failure to make expected weight gains) (2) insomnia or hypersomnia (3) psychomotor agitation or retardation (but not merely subjective feelings of restlessness or being slowed down) (in children under six, hypoactivity) (4) loss of interest or pleasure in usual activities, or decrease in sexual drive not limited to a period when delusional or hallucinating (In children under six, signs of apathy) (5) loss of energy; fatigue (6) feelings of worthlessness, self-reproach, or excessive or inappropriate guilt (either may be delusional) (7) complaints or evidence of diminished ability to think or concentrate, such as slowed thinking, or indecisiveness not associated with marked loosening of associations or incoherence (8) recurrent thoughts of death, suicidal ideation, wishes to be dead, or suicide attempt.

11. Explainer: Psychiatry

But this, as many note, is questionable. What exactly is the discovery here? When you manage to tick off four of the above, when before you only had three, do you undergo some deep change? What the DSM makers did, it seems, is provide a map of the domain of mental suffering. They didn't do anything like give us a neurological basis for this. They didn't say: well, some people exhibit borderline behavior. Moreover, when we looked at these people, we found this biological malfunction. Instead, they just pointed out the surface phenomenon. That's like a zoologist coming across a range of new species, describing them superficially, and saying they'd developed a theory of them (this line of argument is from Whitaker p. 239).

The second prong of this attempt to medicalize psychiatry was marketing. The APA set up a marketing division and spent a lot of money getting the message out there that mental illness was a biological phenomenon. What they really needed, though, was a killer app—a product that would *show* what they said to be true, that would provide some help in taming the bestiary of mental disorders collected in the DSM. Enter Prozac.

Prozac is a different sort of antidepressant to the ones we've considered earlier, but only slightly. It blocks the channel that prevents the reuptake of serotonin by the neurotransmitters, leading to a pile up of serotonin in the synapses. The body realizes that this is too much, and so compensates by producing less. At the same time, the serotonin receptors decrease in number, and so fewer messages telling it to produce less get through, and so the brain comes to produce more. So the brain starts to produce more serotonin than before, making up for the lack of it that apparently leads to depression.

The continuing marketing power of psychiatry made sure the public knew about this new discovery, telling people that mental illness was a disorder and not a weakness. On December 1989, the pill graced the front of *New York Magazine* with the title "A New Wonder Drug for Depression"; others followed in other big magazines (p. 258).

After this, things speak for themselves. Prozac became its first billion-dollar drug in 1992; from 1987 to 2000 Eli Lilly's value on Wall Street rose from $10 billion to $90 billion. *Prozac Nation* eloquently presented the sheer pain of mental illness, as did Kurt Cobain and his tragic life. And with that, arguably, we get to where we are today, with the ascendency of the biological model and the fact of Prozac being one of the symbols of the 1990s.

Why does all this matter? Well, there are a few reasons. One is simply, as mentioned above, that mental illness casts a long shadow over both 90s culture and today, and so understanding the genealogy of mental illness concepts helps sharpen our focus on what is distinctive about these different times. But less abstractly, our mental lives define us: our joys and our sorrows are, for many of us, the most important thing about us. And so changes in how we think about our mental lives are bound to change how we think about ourselves and what matters to us. David Foster Wallace, I suggested, is someone whose work grapples with these issues head on and is particularly and painfully alive to the meaning of mental suffering, as *The Simpsons* was particularly alive to political spectacle and television or Klein to branding. And so as we turn toward today, toward the opioid epidemic which in the years around 2015 saw U.S. life expectancy slightly decline, something unprecedented and bearing comparison to post–Soviet Russia (although not nearly of the same magnitude), toward the increase of "deaths of despair" and the threefold increase in deaths by drug overdose between 1999 and 2017, we might think—especially when we note the extent to which the epidemic was exacerbated by immoral relationships between drug manufacturers and doctors—that 90s writers and thinkers are well placed to help us explain today.

12

And Then ... 9/11, the Financial Crisis, the iPhone, Trump

I pitched the 90s in the introduction as a useful society to study because it is close to us yet also far, separated by the epochal events of the 2000s, namely 9/11 and its various aftermaths, the financial crisis, and the release of the iPhone and more generally the development of social media.

The overall aim of this part of the book is to consider contemporary culture through the lens we have built up in the course of the book so far. To do that, however, I need to say a bit about the three events mentioned above. One of the reasons for this is simply that contemporary culture is partly a product of them—properly to understand today you need to look at what made today. Similarly, the theories that I have developed in the preceding chapters are sharpened by considering how the factors I pinpointed as explanatorily relevant to 90s culture—economics, political, social—exploded in this era. Partly they are of inherent interest and importance and while no doubt (perhaps over) familiar to many readers, I hope there will be some for whom the material here can serve as a useful brief overview of the first decade of the new millennium.

So let's begin with 9/11 and the Iraq War. The largest terrorist attack on American soil to date happened on September 11, 2001. The details are familiar, and I will only give the briefest resume. About 20 terrorists from Al Qaeda, a radical Islamic group with extensive training and funding, boarded domestic U.S. flights from the northeastern United States. They hijacked, or attempted to hijack, the planes and flew two of them into the World Trade Center Complex in Manhattan, and one of them into the Pentagon. A fourth, which the hijackers, it is thought, wanted to use to attack somewhere in D.C., landed in a field after passengers fought against the hijackers to prevent their plan.

Nineties to Now

Famous footage, shown on a loop, has captured the New York flights. It shows, in shots that are hard to comprehend as reality, the two planes diving into the towers, which subsequently would fall. In total, nearly 3,000 people died, many thousands were injured, billions of dollars of damage done, and the country brought to something of a standstill for a number of days.

Volumes have been written and read about the attacks themselves, their causes, and their consequences. Indeed, the consequences are still arguably in the foreign affairs section of any newspaper. It is certainly a truism that the world changed dramatically on 9/11; I am more interested in the narrower question as to the consequences it had for our pop culture and how we view the world—for our Zeitgeist. In explaining the culture of today, what do we need to say about 9/11? Before trying to answer that question, some background.

There's a lot of history here, of course. Again the seventies is epochal, for at least (but not exclusively) three reasons. First, the Soviet Union, in its first attempt to expand its borders since 1945, invaded Afghanistan. Second, the U.S.-backed Shah of Iran was overthrown by Ayatollah Khomeini, a cleric who de-Westernized Iran, instituting a Muslim theocracy and pursuing an anti–U.S. and Israel foreign policy. And third, in Saudi Arabia, dissident Muslims unhappy with the decadent and not sufficiently religious royal family of Saudi Arabia stormed and broadcast their demands: "the adoption of Islamic, non–Western values and thus the rupture of diplomatic relations with Western countries ... the royal family would be thrown out of power ... oil exports to the US would be cut off, and all foreign civilian and military experts would be expelled from the Arabian Peninsula" (I quote from *The Looming Tower* by Lawrence Wright, who is also the source for much of the below, p. 106).

Against this backdrop, Osama bin Laden appears. A wealthy Saudi, whose father had helped build the country after oil was discovered there around the 1950s, he grew unhappy with the decadence of his home country and the foreign threats of the Soviet Union in Afghanistan, Israel nearby, and the U.S. looming large. Using the resources at his disposal, he engaged, with varying success, in fighting in Afghanistan and bombings of American embassies in East Africa and Saudi Arabia, and maybe in the 1993 bombing of the World Trade Center.

Thanks, at least to some, to insufficient information sharing between the FBI and the CIA, the ever-larger threat bin Laden posed wasn't tracked, even as he trained up and sent in mujahideen to the U.S.,

12. And Then ... 9/11, the Financial Crisis, the iPhone, Trump

even as those mujahideen enrolled in pilot lessons, even as intelligence reports indicated an attack involving plane hijacking was on the cards.

I'm not a student of international relations, and so don't want to embarrass myself, but I think it's worth pointing out how, especially to millennials or younger, what can seem like deeply baked-in features of the world are in fact relatively new. It hasn't always been the case that a sect of Islamist extremists have terrorized the West, and although, in what might seem like prescient work, thinkers had suggested that the post–Cold War world was going to be marked by a clash of civilizations (I take the phrase, of course, from the infamous 1996 book of the same name by Samuel Huntington), for the observer of the 90s, this fact would not have been apparent. More generally, this very brief resume should keep us alive to the fact that things can change deeply and dramatically, that old verities—like that history is over, or the U.S. is the world leader—can change quickly.

As significant as 9/11 was for changing how Americans thought about themselves and their country, for many young people the war in Iraq was arguably even more seminal. Let me, accordingly, say a few words about it.

It's 2001, and 9/11 has happened, and Bush Jr. is in office. Remember from the very start of the book we in passing discussed the First Persian Gulf War in which Bush Sr. proclaimed that Saddam was a Hitler and engaged him in war when Saddam invaded Kuwait on account of some disputed oil fields.

One of the hanging questions from the Gulf War was why the U.S. didn't finish the job, and why they allowed Saddam to regroup and retain control of Iraq. Whatever the reason, it was a chastised Saddam who ruled in the 90s. He had been compelled to let weapons inspectors in to make sure that he got rid of all the biological and chemical weapons it was clear he owned.

That weapons inspection program hit a snag in 1998, though, as Saddam grew increasingly restive, culminating in him expelling the UN weapon's inspectors (Patterson, p. 381). In December of that year, Clinton said that Saddam was developing weapons of mass destruction (WMDs).

Bush came, September 11 came. Although that, and the war in Afghanistan it provoked, might have been expected to take all the administration's foreign policy attention, Saddam remained a pressing problem for the U.S. Plans began being made for a war, with the result that at the time of Bush's famous "axis of evil" State of the Union address, his generals had already worked up five iterations for a plan for the invasion of Iraq (Bob Woodward, *Plan of Attack*, p. 96; I rely on this book for the following tick-tock).

With an extremely bellicose advisory team consisting in vice president Dick Cheney and secretary of defense Donald Rumsfeld, Iraq somehow quickly got popped to the top of the list. "The war in Afghanistan" prompted by 9/11 had been "easily won" (I use all these scare quotes advisedly—fighting Al Qaeda terrorism with war is absurd on its face, and bin Laden's stated aim was to draw the Americans into an unwinnable war, to let America repeat Vietnam, to make them unstuck like the Soviets had come, to change sentiment), and that, cynics might suggest, provided the perfect cover for the Bush administration to keep engaged in the Middle East and go after the much more consequential enemy that Saddam was.

Although many were itching for a fight, they were prevented on many sides. For one, they had to, you know, have a reason. The best they had, for launching a war now, was that Saddam might have WMDs that might could eventually endanger Americans. More was clearly needed, as Colin Powell, one of the few advisors who had actually seen combat, repeatedly warned (e.g., Woodward, p. 103). The hawks continued: Cheney said, without a shred of evidence, "There is no doubt that Saddam Hussein now has WMDs and there is no doubt that he is amassing them to use against our friends" (p. 164).

Cooler heads, political pressure, and institutions prevailed. The cool head was Powell's; the political pressure came from the fact that the war would require cobelligerents, who each had to get it passed their respective institutions. Tony Blair in the UK faced great problems, and massive antiwar marches happened across Europe. Finally, there was the United Nations. If the U.S. were to get the help it needed, it would need to go via the proper channels which, to the chagrin of those scrapping for a fight, meant UN security resolutions.

Bush, not having much choice (but, at least on Woodward's—perhaps unreliable—telling not resisting too much), demurred. They would seek UN support. Powell wrangled. What the administration wanted was to trap Saddam: make a resolution whose failure meant war, that Saddam was compelled to fail. They didn't quite get that.

What the UN agreed on was to reexamine Iraq for the WMDs. A careful Swede, among others, did so and reported back a few months later equivocally: Saddam is definitely up to no good, isn't being quite forthright, but we found no WMDs.

12. And Then ... 9/11, the Financial Crisis, the iPhone, Trump

Bullshit, the hawks thought. They sent Powell to the UN to present all the evidence in favor of there being WMDS; I won't list it because it's all very flimsy, and regardless France and Russia, two permanent members of the security council with right of veto, weren't on board. It wasn't happening diplomatically.

But it was happening. Saddam had technically not complied to the letter with the previous resolution: he had been evasive. That was enough: either stop being evasive, he was told, or the war is coming. And duly the war did come, on March 20, and initially the U.S. breezed through. They had most of the country soon thereafter; a few weeks after, on what may or may not have been a set-up photo shoot, TV watchers saw American troops help Iraqis pull down a statue of Saddam in central Baghdad. On May 1, Bush, in a moment that was to be mocked in TV shows we'll discuss later, spoke in front of a banner that read "mission accomplished." In October, reports came—they'd crossed a lot of land, but still ... no WMDs. In December they found Saddam, but still, no WMDs.

The war, it turned out, was the easy part. As again Powell had warned, now they had a country that had been under a dictatorship for decades to fix. That was going to take a while. American soldiers died. Perhaps around 30,000 Iraqis died. The war became and remains a source of great anger to young Americans (and others). Speaking from my own UK perspective, the large antiwar marches that were completely ignored loom large, and Tony Blair is widely viewed as orders of magnitude worse than his Gulf War–fighting neoliberal predecessor John Major.

The—to be a bit pretentious—epistemic fallout has been great. The fact that, so it appears, the war was waged on a straight-up lie, or generously on something that couldn't meet reasonable burdens of proof, was as undermining for young Americans coming up into their country, I hazard (incautiously) to guess, as Watergate was for X-er teenagers. The whole thing, in fact, is tempting to read as an erosion. Watergate was bad, sure, but it was, after all, a third-rate burglary. No Americans had death on their conscience. Young Americans, it seems to me, especially liberal young Americans brought up on Chomsky, who can tell you in great detail all of America's imperialist failings, were hit hard by the actions of their country, and that has led to a sense of alienation. And the flimsy dancing around the truth and evasions have, it is arguable, helped pave the way for our current attitude toward the media and our "post-truth" predicament.

Nineties to Now

So that's Big Event number one. Big event number two is the financial crisis of 2008. In order to introduce it, remember where we left economics. We sped through the 70s, when inflation was a pressing issue, something people feared in a way that a young person today can't really even conceive, and the target of the sort of economics that finds its way into mainstream conversation, in a way I tried to spell out in Chapter 2 (entrails for dinner, the devalued dollar).

Fast-forwarding to today, and things undeniably have changed. Inflation isn't a bogey man terrorizing the person in the supermarket; few millennials will have had the experience of massive and quick price rises. Indeed, we grew up in an era some call "the great moderation," an era in which inflation seemed no longer to be a devastating problem but one that could be and was massaged out of the economy with judicious central banking.

Not only did inflation factually become less relevant, it became ideologically less so. People wondered whether traditional economic metrics like GDP (and thus inflation) really made sense in a digital economy,[1] or even prior to that in a world of big box stores it was thought that inflation wasn't so useful a metric. Indeed, the biggest puzzle of the current era is why inflation is so low and what it means. How did we get from there to here, and what does it mean for the culture more broadly? More generally, how should we continue the story started earlier?

Any account must, of course, speak about the financial crisis that can be roughly pigeonholed in September 2008, although its causes reach back for decades, as will its consequences. You know the story in rough outline: banks made some bad and complicated bets and got entwined with one another so that the failure of one could lead to the failure of others; the government eventually stepped in and bailed the system out with taxpayer money. Partly, maybe, this was because of globalizing of finance; partly, maybe, it was imprudence on Greenspan's part to not rein in the economy at the end of millennium. (It has been said that the U.S. economy needed the housing bubble which preceded the crash to maintain the illusion that the country was still economically on the right tracks; as Paul Krugman quipped, "Alan Greenspan needs to create a housing bubble to replace the Nasdaq [dot-com] bubble," quoted in *The Man Who Knew*, p. 588.)

The causes can and will be discussed incessantly (but not in this book). But the near-term effects are clear: millions lost their jobs; no bankers faced legal problems. If history hadn't rebegun on September

12. And Then ... 9/11, the Financial Crisis, the iPhone, Trump

11, it was given, as many leftist commentators have pointed out, a fresh chance at resuscitation in September 2008.

That month culminated with then President Bush's signing the Troubled Asset Relief Program (TARP). After some negotiations about exactly what it amounted to, involving many and furious debates in New York and late-night phone calls between the CEOs of the big investment banks, the Treasury, and the securities rating agencies, it was announced that banks would take on average about $20 billion from the government, to the sum of $800 billion overall. In the words of journalist Andrew Ross Sorkin, it "effectively nationalized the nation's financial system" (*Too Big to Fail*, on which I rely here, p. 527). The government had interfered in what many associate with the acme of the private market, the greed-is-good world of Gordon Gecko and American Psycho—the world of Wall Street. And the reason it had done so was because—so the people in power thought—if they hadn't, even the biggest banks would have collapsed, and the economy would have been paralyzed.

How things got to there is a big story. Here I will briefly rehearse some of the events of that time, its bizarre (one is tempted to say postmodern) enabling factors, and its fallout.

Starting the timeline anywhere is arbitrary, but let's go for just over two weeks before, to Monday, September 15, 2008. Lehman Brothers, an investment bank (as opposed to commercial bank), and one of the biggest, announced it would file for bankruptcy, in what was and is by far the biggest bankruptcy in history. That weekend had seen furious behind-the-scenes attempts to broker deals that would sell it off, as it happened earlier that year with another of the then "big 5" investment banks, Bear Sterns. When that looked like it wasn't happening, on Sunday, there was a special market session for the sole purpose of allowing people involved with Lehman to tidy up their accounts with them.

So what, you might think. Companies go bankrupt all the time. But this was not just any bankruptcy. Two days later, on the Wednesday, Treasury Secretary Hank Paulson announced over the phone that they were living through an "economic 9/11" (p. 417), and worry was widespread that Lehman's fall would take the rest of the economy with it.

Faced with a similar problem months earlier, when Bear Stearns had failed, Paulson had intervened, guaranteeing some of their especially bad assets to buyers of the failing company in order to make them more palatable. Doing so had been, of course, politically a hard sell—Republicans quick to decry it as socialism and Democrats as pandering to irresponsible financiers—and so his policy had resolutely been to allow Lehman to fail.

But that couldn't continue. A mere couple of days later AIG, an insurance provider who, as such, was able to bypass some of the regulations (such as capital reserves) that other banks have, was looking shaky too. On that Wednesday, it found itself, around lunchtime, almost out of money.

AIG had got mixed up, in complicated ways I won't pretend to understand, as a counterparty in many trades, boosting the prices of various more or less worthless securities. If it were to fall, those securities' value would fall, and people holding those securities would be in trouble (pp. 394–95). Moreover, in their everyday life as insurer, they had policies worth $1.9 trillion, and while they were backed up by insurance, a panic in them could have ripple effects elsewhere.

And so the Treasury, which had won praise for not bailing out Lehman, changed course. It offered an $85 billion line of credit in exchange for a large ownership stake in the company (p. 401).

But even that didn't fix the panic in the New York banks. Stock prices continued to fall; ominous fears crept in everybody's mind that even Goldman Sachs might fall. A couple of days later, Goldman Sachs and Morgan Stanley, the crème de la crème, changed their legal status to receive more federal protection, in what the *New York Times* described as "a blunt acknowledgment that their model of finance and investing had become too risky" (quoted in Ross Sorkin, p. 483).

Problems remained, and problems remained after TARP was passed, with the Dow Jones industrial average losing as much as 37 percent of its value, around 10 million jobs were lost in the U.S. and Europe (Mervyn King, *The End of Alchemy*, p. 38), and, for the purposes of this book, what Mark Fisher called capitalist realism, the inability to see any alternative to the prevailing system, begun to seem less clear.

And then…? Prior to COVID-19, the U.S. economy had seen a period of growth that beats out even the one registered in the 90s, but capitalism—which was deemed to have been dealt a fatal blow in the crash—has not really recovered, at least in the minds of the opinion-setters. In *Generation X*, 40 years ago, faith in capitalism was low. In 2021, it is practically nonexistent, at least among large swathes of young people.

The reasons for this are several. For one, several big-hitting books about income inequality and economic stagnation have, to a greater or lesser extent, intruded upon the public consciousness. The most notable

12. And Then ... 9/11, the Financial Crisis, the iPhone, Trump

of these is French economist Thomas Piketty's 2013 surprise best seller *Capital in the 21st Century*, which paints a bleak picture about income inequality. The most salient lesson of this book for the modern reader—a lesson that was not so evident to our 90s predecessors—was that the thought that capitalism could be at least minimally fair, in the sense of rewarding hard work, was gainsaid. This, of course, is something that an observer of the postwar period could be forgiven for thinking, because that did seem to be an era where capitalism and reward went hand in hand. But on Piketty's story, backed up with exhaustive data, that era was a fluke rather than the norm, and before and after that period, the workings of capitalism seem to obey a rule according to which it's not so much hard work and the income it brings that determines one's position in the economic pecking order, but rather the rate of return on capital. Success in capitalism comes from owning, not from doing. Similarly, a popular—if much less so—book from 2016 (one on which I have relied extensively), *The Rise and Fall of American Growth*, makes plain, through a long view, that the U.S. has been suffering since the 70s.

Another reason for capitalism's failing to rehabilitate itself is again something that I argued was an important part of the 90s culture, namely branding and the corresponding dephysicalization of business. As is familiar, in Uber, Airbnb, and the increasing ubiquity of precarity, the spiritualization of the brand has almost reached its high point, as companies are learning to manage with as few resources, both of goods and of people, as possible. Uber is a company that gives rides without employing drivers and without owning cars; Airbnb houses people without owning properties or hoteliers. The world of piecemeal, part-time work that was already present in the temps, multiple-job workers, and fast-food workers of the 90s has steadily extended into previously more secure areas. It seems each week we hear of a new digital media venture going under; freelancing is synonymous with not being paid on time. The same thing applies to academia: about three out of four academics, per a 2016 report, are not on the tenure track.[2]

Capitalism's inherent wrongness is further impressed upon one by a simple look at the financial pages. Our new brands, our Ubers and Airbnbs, the businesses of the future ... are not profitable. As is familiar, especially Uber relies on substantial injections of venture capital money to subsidize its rides. That's why they're so cheap: the eventual aim, even mildly cynical commentators suggest, is to get rid of the businesses which actually charge the actual prices for their services and then, once they've got a monopoly, pass the savings the customer currently enjoys back onto them.

The important thing to realize, bearing in mind what we've seen in this book, is that while these developments have certainly been aided by technological change it's not as if they have come out of nowhere. It's not some historical quirk but an explicit feature of the business model of these companies that they burden themselves with as few physical trappings as possible. And given that, any strategy to fight against these developments has to bear this in mind. Merely fixing the technological underpinnings and progressing to more historically propitious circumstances is not going to solve the problem itself, because the problem—neoliberal or postindustrial capitalism—predates these changes. A message that was maybe heard in 2000 when Klein was writing is now screamed.

The failure of neoliberal economics has led to a related difference, for good and bad: the arising of politicians who claim to abjure, or really do abjure, neoliberalism and the political establishment which represent it. We can see this poignantly in Trump, who ran on an entirely absurd antiglobalizing ticket of bringing back jobs and revitalizing industry; and we can see it, more hopefully, in Bernie Sanders and people like Alexandria Ocasio-Cortez. As Chomsky notes,[3] Sanders's success in the 2016 Democratic presidential primaries is close to unprecedented, representing as it does the first time in a long time that having a decent run wasn't purely a straightforward function of money: Sanders almost got the nomination, despite having not been well funded. Similarly, as again Chomsky points out, he did so campaigning with the term "socialism." In Sanders we see the possibility of a new non-neoliberal politics that offers a new vision of what the post-crash economy might look like.

Let's turn to the final of the big three, the release of the iPhone, which I use synecdochally to mean the rise of the internet. Later, we will see the massive role the internet has to play in popular culture, but I want, in this section, to note a couple of perhaps slightly surprising dimensions in which the internet, despite its seemingly game-changing ubiquity, has not been as revolutionary as we might think.

The first thing I want to think about is economics. I will have a bit more to say below, but I want first to ask this natural question: has the internet introduced us to a new booming financial era?

It can be easy to think so when hearing about the latest unicorn (startup valued at over $1 billion) or just noticing the ubiquity of internet products in our lives. But it's worth taking a step back and looking at

12. And Then ... 9/11, the Financial Crisis, the iPhone, Trump

what the numbers say. Recall our earlier discussion of economic development in the last half or so of the 20th century: we presented some data that showed great growth around the war and falling growth thereafter, and pointed out that already in the 50s, and definitely by the 70s, many of the things we could recognize as part of modern life, from medicine to housing to food, was in place. The question is: has the internet increased our standard of living or output in a similar way that the previous industrial revolution did, which brought us electricity and the car?

Robert Gordon's answer is no. Recall we earlier saw the great increases of the period around the war. Here's another statistic from his book: for the period 1920–1970 the annual growth in total factor productivity was 1.89 percent. For 1890–1920, it was 0.46 percent; for 1970–1994 it was 0.57 percent; for 1994–2004, it was 1.03 percent; and for 2004–2014, it was 0.4 percent. The key thing to notice is the bump in the period 1994–2004. On Gordon's theory, it was here that the harvest of the technological revolution was reaped. And the notable thing is how little a bump it brought, and how short lived it was. Developments like electricity and cars brought us a half-century of innovation and growth and produced the modern world. Information technology—at least at the time of Gordon's book (2016), an important qualification—did nothing like the same. Why? The simple fact is, contrary to what our daily life might tell us, "computers are not everywhere. We don't eat computers or wear them or drive to work in them or let them cut our hair. We live in dwelling units that have appliances much like those of the 1950s, and we drive in motor vehicles that perform the same functions as in the 1950s" (p. 579). While it is true that entertainment and more generally information businesses have been changed a lot, that is only a small part of the economy, and so we should be very careful that we don't mistake the salience of the internet (especially its salience for academics) for its significance.

The same thing applies to the business model of the internet: as we have already noted immediately above, a lot of the economic model of the internet is to a large extent old wine in new skins. We had ads before, and we had dephysicalization, as this book has documented. We were already moving toward a world in which the product offered was less relevant than the idea behind it, something that seems to have reached its apotheosis in social media in which the products are simply the opinions and pictures and such of people like ourselves.

Similarly, social media has been held as a causal factor in certain (troubling or not) demographic trends, but I think again this mistakes salience for significance. The 2017 book *iGen* by Jean Twenge argued that the arrival of the iPhone and the noted rise in incidence of mental illness and various other factors such as reduced number of sexual partners and reduced consumption of alcohol that seem to have occurred about the same time were causally connected: that people have swapped out—to put it glibly—porn and Netflix for sex and beer.

The book has come in for sustained and reasonable criticism about its methods, with people dissecting her data sets, the experiments she cites, and her simplistic statistics. All of this seems right. But I would like to emphasize that the discussion of the 90s presented in this book can already shed light on some of these factors.

To see this, consider our discussion first of Robert Putnam's work on civic participation and the role television plays in impairing it that we saw in Chapter 8, and second, our discussion of mental illness in Chapter 11. Putnam suggested that the use of television correlates better than anything else with social disconnection, and we saw that the prescriptions for mental illnesses have been on a massive upswing in the 20th century. What both of these suggest to me is that the trends Twenge is pointing to—trends that indeed ought to be of concern to us—cannot be pinned neatly to smartphones, but rather are reflective of longer-lasting trends in late 20th-century life. Indeed, one can argue that it's screens in general, with the facsimile of human connection they offer, rather than the internet specifically, that are responsible for this trend.

Before going on to consider someone who has been conspicuous by his absence so far, I want to emphasize that the approach taken in this book is already bearing fruit. By placing these epochal events in their deep historical context, as, as if as an end of a seesaw the opposite end of which is 1974 and the pivot of which is 1994, we can see what indeed is new and what is not new. The event of 9/11 is new in scale and salience but is the working out of decades-long U.S. involvement in the Middle East. The 2008 crash seems to have dramatically shifted attitudes toward capitalism, but certain features of the post-crash economic scene that have played that shifting role, notably the dephysicalized model of business, precede the dawn of the millennium. And finally, the internet, although superficially so revolutionary, doesn't show up profoundly when considered from the point of view of 20th-century economic trends, and especially arguably hasn't ushered in a new era of socially alienated mentally troubled people, because they seem to have antedated it. For all its salience, we shouldn't overestimate the importance of the internet for how life is actually lived offline.

12. And Then ... 9/11, the Financial Crisis, the iPhone, Trump

A Necessary Digression: Trump

Any book attempting to speak about today would be of course incomplete without discussion of the presidential elections of 2016 and 2020, the storming of the Capitol on January 6, 2021, and their common denominator: the success of Donald Trump in politics. It can feel that with him, we are in an entirely new political era, an era of tweeted political statements, of presidents who mix utter venality with cruelty and who—and this is the really important point—command the support of very large groups of people seemingly indifferent to or supportive of this behavior. There have always been cranks and racists and incompetents in public—the bizarre thing and brand new thing is that now one of them is, among many, extremely popular.

Or perhaps not so brand new. Many people think we're somewhere we (humankind) have been before, with the shuttering of the press, the dehumanization of non-natives, the praising of a forgotten past. Even the camps where immigrant children are concentrated at the Mexican border call to mind for some the Nazi era.

Properly to say what the meaning of Trump is is, needless to say, well beyond the scope of this book on pop culture and must await much subsequent work. However, what I want to do here is to see if there's anything we've discussed that might shed some light on the Trump phenomenon.

Of course, there are some relatively low-hanging pieces of fruit that our tour through the 90s that sped back to the 70s and on through the millennium can help us to see. When we see the latest Trump scandal, if it involves political chicanery (it would, I think, date the book too much to mention the issue of the day) and misleading the public, we can simply point out that Trump is by no means the first person to do this. We have seen in an earlier chapter the seminal importance of Watergate which revealed in part that politicians doing scandalous stuff is old news. Nixon, recall, was acutely aware that both Johnson and Kennedy had bugged their opponents, and so was particularly angry that it was he who was going down for it. Or we can think of the Clinton Whitewater scandal (which we only ever so briefly touched on; if you want more information, you can google), or, just a few pages ago, a scandal which arguably dwarfs any that Trump, unpleasant though he is, has (yet) managed, namely the misleading the public about the justification for the war in Iraq.

And if we think of the president's many (alleged) sex crimes (a strange sentence to type), then the reader of this book will now think of Monica Lewinsky, and a reader of another book might recall Kennedy's aside, to (the shock of) then British prime minister Harold MacMillan that if he—Kennedy—didn't have sex every day, he got horrible migraines.

In short, some of what seems to be distinctive of Trump, and thus of our era, arguably is just the latest iteration in how postwar presidents seem to behave. Here again, our perspective helps, as does some of the more theoretical material we introduced in earlier chapters. For example, in our chapter on postmodernism, we noted that Baudrillard argued that a definitive feature of postmodern culture was a certain privileging of representation over reality. It can seem all too obvious to draw the connection to Trump, who is, after all, someone who was the boss in a TV show and somehow made the leap to being boss of the country. Again, the political world of *The Simpsons*—which, as has been pointed out, predicted Trump's presidency in a throwaway gag—in which on Homer's screen presidential debates vie with ridiculous Mexican cartoons, seems to fit bizarrely well with our president's threatening of world leaders in our Twitter feed alongside the meme du jour. Or yet again, our Black feminist theorists who tell us that we live in a world of prevailing white epistemologies that suppress other perspectives might seem particularly apt in a world in which bona fide white supremacists are part of the political scene. All that could lead a reader to think that Trump is merely the working out of themes already latent in postmodern philosophy, race theory, and TV.

But that—apart from the race theory bit—sounds wrong. America is a very big country, full of very many different types of people the vast majority of whom don't care about animated comedies that have been weak for decades and 99.9 percent of whom haven't even heard of Baudrillard. If we want to explain Trump, we must do better.

Can any of the three epochal events help explain him? Can either 9/11 and the war on Iraq, the iPhone, or the crash explain Trump, and thereby help explain our Zeitgeist?

I think in each case the answer is partially yes, but in noteworthily different ways. Consider first the iPhone (Web 2.0). We will see this in greater detail later, but one of the things I'll argue is that the sense of ironic detachment that tends to get associated with the 90s has migrated onto the internet. Moreover, it is well recognized that the alt-right among Trump's fanbase traffic in irony. To take but a couple of examples from recent popular books on the topic, in Mike Wendling's *Alt-Right: From 4chan to the White House*, he notes:

12. And Then ... 9/11, the Financial Crisis, the iPhone, Trump

> The alt-right's oft-noted internet-age "playfulness" has spawned everything from electronic dance music remixes of Trump speeches to memes of Jewish people Photoshopped into gas chambers. The sense of irony acts as a weapon and a shield. They may make jokes about Nazis, but if anyone accurses an activist of actually being a Nazi, they can turn around and mock the opponent for their lack of a sense of humour [p. 75].

Or consider this very open explanation of how the alt-right works from the founder of an influential alt-right website:

> A movement which meets all of the SPLC's definitions of a Neo-Nazi White Supremacism using a cartoon frog to represent itself takes on a subversive power to bypass historical stereotypes of such movements, and thus present the ideas themselves in a fun way without the baggage of Schindler's List [quoted in David Neiwert's 2017 *Alt-America*].

And with this in mind, recall our earlier discussion of how *The Simpsons* managed to portray American political history in a light way, but how they also did so in a cynical, distanced way. Or think about David Foster Wallace's diatribe against the deadening effects of irony. With this in mind, one way to understand this particular part of contemporary nationalism is as making use of rhetorical styles of the 90s to bad political ends. The alt-right is *The Simpsons* but evil; or they show quite how deadening the ironist can be, because, as Wallace tells us, they can never be pinned down.

All of this suggests that the home for irony that the internet provides must play some part in our explanation of Trump, but that at the same time we can only understand why 2010s America would be a fertile ground for such a prima facie bizarre mode of political discourse by attending to 90s pop culture. This is one of the important results we should take from this study.

Similarly, "economic anxiety" is frequently trumpeted—often in an exculpatory tone—as explaining Trump support. Certainly, there's bound to be something in that—namely, that the depression which replaced the false bounce of the pre-2008 economy choked the life out of already struggling postindustrial America, a story made salient by the seemingly daily *New York Times* profiles of rust-belt Trump supporters or books such as the well-received 2016 memoir *Hillbilly Elegy* by J.D. Vance or Irish journalist Catríona Perry's 2017 *In America: Tales from Trump Country*. But it's unclear that this can be the whole story. The data, which we'll see presently, doesn't seem to suggest poverty was a big factor in Trump's win, simply because many non-poor people voted for him.

Nineties to Now

What about terrorism? Here, I think we are arguably getting closer. We can note Trump's attempted Muslim ban relatively early in his presidency, in light of the fact that it didn't really make any sense, can be seen as a sign to his supporters about his stance on non–Americans and/or those perceived to be non–Americans.

And while not directed at terrorism per se, we can note that immigration is a big thing for Trump. We might think that Trump is speaking for a nation that feels itself uniquely threatened from abroad when he began his campaign on June 16, 2015, with the truly shocking (from someone seeking political office) diatribe against Mexican immigrants:

> When Mexico sends its people, they're not sending their best. They're sending people that have lots of problems, and they're bringing those problems with us [sic]. They're bringing drugs, they're bringing crime, they're rapists. And some, I assume, are good people.[4]

On this story: it's foreign policy that done it, and in particular the need for America to reassert itself in the face of foreign enemies, be they religious or economic.

As I said, I'm not the person to answer these very difficult and interesting questions. However, I want to present one answer from a recent book that, if nothing else, deserves much more attention, especially from the sort of person who reads monographs on pop culture. As ever, I present it both for the inherent interest it has but also because I think it can help tie together some of the arguments I have presented.

Eric Kaufmann's *Whiteshift* (2018) presents a range of interesting theory, data, and history, concerning racism, anti-racism, and nationalism and cosmopolitanism in the U.S. and Europe, suggesting a picture of the world quite different from what people left of center (or even in the center) seem to assume.

The take-home message is that Trump has to do with *immigration*—as he claims data to reveal—and that it's the anti-racist, pro-immigrant populace (among whom I count both myself and the readers of this book) that deserve some of the blame for making a political environment in which Trump could succeed on his hateful and lie-based platform.

Here's the story Kaufmann tells, necessarily condensed. The first thing to note is that he takes it that data shows that immigration is the most crucial predictor of Trump support. His reasoning is worth consideration if, in my view, ultimately not irrefragable. Note that in fact, per the polling, the best predictor of Trump support is *education*.

12. And Then ... 9/11, the Financial Crisis, the iPhone, Trump

Education, he argues, does not neatly correlate with money—there are many well-educated poor people (your author, for one), and many not well-educated rich people. Moreover, he thinks that it's not what people learn at university that makes them not vote for Trump. The important thing about university, he thinks, is that people with a certain set of values, favoring openness, select into university (p. 119). So what education is really marking is the distinction between two sets of values, one favoring openness and one closedness.

There's a certain hegemony among at least a decent-sized subset of liberals today that favors what we can call, for want of a better word, identity politics. According to identity politics, in Kaufmann's gloss, the key features are that the white nationality or tradition is looked down upon and viewed as something that can't be the object of pride whereas many other marginalized identities are to be cherished, a view that bears at least a passing resemblance to some of the feminist theory we looked at in a previous chapter. He remarks that whereas formerly the liberal position was that many different nationalities, creeds, and conceptions of the good are *possible* in society, now, with the crucial exception of white people, they are necessary.

He presents interesting history here, and I encourage the interested reader to consult his book (Chapter 7) for the whole story. On his reading, the civil rights movement, which formed a sort of lynchpin of this book, was the beginning of a crucial cultural change that has just recently fully flowered. The civil rights movement produced, if not to the extent that we should be satisfied with, various improvements for the lives of people previously unfairly oppressed. But those achievements—which he is univocally supportive of—led to a sort of overreach, whereby the dominant attitude toward, say, Black people, was not that they should be able to live lives as free as white people, but that their lives and voices are *more* deserving in some sense. This rhetorical switch, he points out, echoes that of an earlier period in American race-relations before roughly the 1920s, when a group of people called the Young Intellectuals valorized other groups at the expense of WASP-y (white Anglo-Saxon Protestant) types.

On his story, this move toward valorization of marginalized identities spread with the development of the internet, which thus does have an explanatory role to play. Some of the statistics are revealing: asked about how much discrimination against African Americans there was, 20 percent of white liberals in 2009 said "a lot" or "a little"; this increased to 40 percent in 2012 and almost 80 percent in 2016. Similarly, this demographic developed cooler feelings for whites and more support for affirmative action.

The left-modernist position, as he calls it, was the main position for parties left and right for at least the latter half of the 20th century. Anti-racism became a great taboo that neither side could speak against, for fear of being labeled racist.

The problem is, and this, I take it, is the second takeaway from the book, many people do not like left-modernism, and in particular many people don't like the idea that WASP-y traditions are the only ones that should be eradicated. There is, after all, another set of values, one that favors traditions and is less big on openness.

He has several important pieces of data in support of this claim that non-openness is a sort of personality type, not a hateful anomaly to be suppressed. He first is that he claims to find in the data that fondness toward one's race doesn't imply antipathy toward others; it is not the case, he wants to say, that liking white people is a hateful attitude as, I think it's fair to say, a lot of liberals would argue. He writes:

> Warmth towards whites is correlated with warmth towards both blacks and Latinos. A positive feeling towards whites, much more than negative feelings towards minorities, predicts whether a white person voted for Trump or wants less immigration [p. 120].

On his view, a fondness for white people among whites, or even among other minorities, is a perfectly respectable viewpoint that deserves attention, not an irrational prejudice. Indeed, he thinks it's precisely this fact—that people fail to realize it's reasonable to like one's race even if one is white—that causes so many problems. It is this, he thinks, that causes politicians to lie that immigrants are sources of crime or use of resources (neither of which bear scrutiny). He claims that politicians have to say this because the anti-racism/anti-pro-whiteness position is so hegemonic.

Now, I don't expect the reader to accept all this. For one, you should check out the book and its sources. And it's of course extremely puzzling why, if the above story—that Trump supporters merely were warm toward whites—Trump himself and many of his supporters would be such hateful racists. More importantly, as I write this final draft of the book, in summer 2020, Black Lives Matter protests are taking place all across America, protesting against the murder of Black people by the police. It is very tempting to think that the above analysis is dated, or tone deaf: that what these protests are pointing to is something very

12. And Then ... 9/11, the Financial Crisis, the iPhone, Trump

deeply wrong at the heart of American society, and that to mistake what certainly seems like hate for love (love of the people like oneself) is glib and perhaps even offensive.

I don't have anything conclusive to say about this. Maybe it is glib and offensive, maybe Kaufmann is just straight wrong, and maybe even entertaining his view to the extent that I have done is also wrong. That might be. I don't know.[5]

What I do take myself to know, though, is the lessons his book has for mine. A view according to which the ideas of the 80s feminist theorists seem to have borne fruit in the last decade or so, just as the very opposing position became a platform on which one could win the presidency, seems to some extent to be supported by the data Kaufmann assembles.

The point of all this for our book is several. If he is right, then social media has a bit to do with Trump and all the absurdities that come in his train, but the real culprit is immigration and attitudes to racism that have been developing since the 60s–70s. Just as, on my reading, a backlash to that movement explains the nostalgia of 90s art, so a more pronounced backlash explains our current situation, and more generally suggests that racism or at least fear of the non-white-male is one of the key explanatory concepts for understanding 20th-century culture.

To expand briefly on a point just made: Kaufman suggests that a sort of conservatism might be not a matter of stupidity or evilness, but just a certain cast of mind. That could help explain why the creators of the 90s so longingly looked back to the 50s—they were of that cast of mind, despite occupying the traditional liberal societal role of artist. Lynch, Tarantino, *The Simpsons* writers—all these people might be, if this account is correct, psychologically conservative, a new and interesting theory of art. And with that mention of art, let's turn to see how things have changed as we approach the third decade of the 21st century.

13

Pop Culture Today

We seem to be in a decidedly different era, at the end of the second decade of the 2000s, than Americans were at the start or even at the end of the 90s. At the start, history ended; at the end, the dot-com bubble notwithstanding, the economy was roaring, and America was unchallenged on the world stage.

Now, though, things are different. The U.S. is not secure, it is—per its very president, at his inauguration!—a "land of abandoned factories, economic angst, rising crime," an era of "carnage." Capitalism has seen its biggest failing since the 1930s, and our whole way of life, on a day-to-day level, has been overhauled by technological innovation. The central question becomes: what has that done to us, to how we think of the world and represent it in art?

In the previous chapter, we looked at how things evolved in the non-cultural world. We showed how branding and dephysicalization have continued apace, how the much talked about epidemic of loneliness and mental ill health are arguably continuations of trends already clearly present in the 90s. We saw, too, that our bitterly divided political scene, with identity-political left and the nationalist right and Trump, also have their antecedents in the disputes of a previous era.

That is to say, it seems that an overall take home here is *continuity*. Certain broad socio-politico-economic trends seemed to continue to work themselves out. Of course, events, the stuff of history, have impacted how these trends get expressed, perhaps serving as gasoline on the fire to ramp up what has happened. To create ever more casualization and dephysicalization; to widen the gulf between Left and Right in social media echo chambers; to activate a fear of outsiders that was perhaps a latent psychological feature of many. But if I'm right, in the extra-artistic realm, continuity is greater than difference.

But recall this book takes a two-pronged approach. In addition to events, to politics and economics, we are interested in culture: TV,

13. Pop Culture Today

movies, literature. In this chapter, I want to consider how that has changed, both for its intrinsic interest (how does culture evolve, and is its evolution determined by intelligible factors?) and because I think it can help shed light on the ideology of the day. I will begin with drama, before considering comedy and novels.

Recall my thesis about 90s drama: that was it postmodern, marked by a turning away from reality toward a mythical pseudo-50s, before OPEC, Watergate, and the civil rights movement. I suggested that this was partly because that's when things were good (for middle-class whites), and partly because that's when things were bad (for women and ethnic minorities, in a way that was good, or at least nonthreatening) for many. But at the same time, I also argued, and maybe slightly paradoxically, that this postmodern style led to forms of art apt to capture late 20th-century life. I argued that Lynch's surrealism is actually in service of a realistic portrayal of life. Similarly, I argued that *The Simpsons*, in its choppy, digressive style, was actually an apt representation of the mind of someone who consumed a lot of television. So, on my reading, the formal playfulness of these 90s shows plays a handful of roles, some good, and some bad.

Now here is an interesting question: does postmodern nostalgia still reign? I submit that the answer to this is—when it comes to TV, movies, and novels—no.

What are the era-defining shows of the 2010s? Here's a partial list: *Game of Thrones, Mad Men, The Walking Dead, Westworld, Breaking Bad, Stranger Things, True Detective*.

Of these, I think the really interesting ones are shows like *Game of Thrones, The Walking Dead*, and *Westworld*. While one might quibble about the eventual cultural significance of *Westworld* and *The Walking Dead*, it is, I take it, more or less undeniable that any story of the 2010s will need to account for *Game of Thrones*.

And here is what is interesting about it: it presents a non-actual world, just as much as do our 90s favorites, but via a completely different means, the means of high fantasy (or sci-fi in the case of *Westworld* and post-apocalyptic [lite] horror in the case of *The Walking Dead*).

What should we make of this fact? Where do sci-fi and fantasy fit on the realism/anti-realism or postmodernism/non-postmodernism side? I think, though this is tentative, that one can make the case that such genres share more with realism, oddly enough, than with postmodernism. *Game of Thrones*, for example, is no *Twin Peaks*. In *Twin Peaks* absurdist comedy meets—to use a phrase I don't like—sexual horror;

it's a world where the strange trippy soundtrack intrudes into the reality of the show. It is weird, and playful, and unique. By contrast, *Game of Thrones* is primarily just a big, indeed an epic, story. It's unclear we ever cared much about characters of 90s TV (or, more accurately, care about the characters in the shows and movies I've discussed), but we did care when Jon Snow died, and many people cared when Dany broke bad right at the end. Even the eminently hummable epic theme tune puts us in a different stylistic world than does *Twin Peaks*'s trippy jazz.

I think this line can be expanded: shows like *House of Cards*, *True Detective*, and others are primarily straight shows, shows that play little with form and concentrate on telling interesting, compelling stories. Even the bona fide nostalgic shows, like *Mad Men* or *Stranger Things*, are nostalgic in a completely different way than 90s postmodern nostalgia. They don't attempt to meld together different eras. All of this suggests to me that the best interpretation of these many and varying shows is that they are primarily realistic or, perhaps better, post-postmodern.

Before going on, I want to notice an extremely interesting fact. Recall a central thesis of mine about nostalgia: part of its appeal to the creators of the time was that it enabled one to go back to a time before not only the economic vicissitudes of the 70s, but also before the gender and racial advances that decade saw. I argued that this nostalgia was a strategy to, for the most part, portray stereotypical gender roles and, perhaps especially, to keep questions of racial politics out of the picture.

Today? The sexual politics of much TV is, to put it mildly, not good. Even in many well-reputed shows you see rape or sexual abuse or sexual discomfort used as a plot device to no particular purpose other than, seemingly, titillation.[1]

But it's very interesting to note how the most popular and arguably best shows deal with this problem. Here, I take it, is a dilemma: many women and men will be put off by presentations of them as sex objects. That's just not how our society works, they'll want to say.

But, the creators—and perhaps the viewers—reply: we want those presentations! We remain fundamentally uncomfortable with female sexuality and empowerment. And so, they have a bright idea, somewhat similar to the bright idea the creators of the 90s had: they simply turn their eyes away from contemporary society.

Game of Thrones, perhaps, is the clearest case. It has a large female fanbase, and although it does have powerful female characters, it also has a lot of gratuitous nudity and—most notably of all—a loveable main character who can say lines like "You've forgotten the most important

13. Pop Culture Today

thing about whores. You don't buy them, you only rent them." Now just imagine a character—a main protagonist—in something set in the contemporary world either expressing that sentiment, or even using the word "whore" as opposed to "sex worker."

It can't be done. It would never happen; if it did, people would be very upset. And herein, I think, lies the trickery behind much contemporary (television) pop culture: it manages to sneak antiquated attitudes about women in through the back door, by any artistic means necessary.

Here are some other examples, again taken from shows that are both popular and critically acclaimed. The premise of *Westworld* is that it is a theme park containing androids, mechanical beings capable of behaving in every way like humans. It enables people to go and live out their fantasies of blood and sex in a sanitary environment. And so people do. There are many sex scenes, and it is presented in a sense as a utopia for a particular style of male sexuality: you get to have sex with attractive girls without considering them in any way, because they are inanimate, programmed creatures. Again, I think *Westworld* is a reflection of how what we can call misogyny prevails even in contemporary acclaimed pop culture. The female Westworld "host" is identical, in almost every respect, to an actual woman. But beneath her skin there is just robotics, and it is this invisible core that enables the viewers and writers to have their cake and eat it too: to portray women as sex objects without really doing so.

The third example is *Mad Men*. It is a slightly different case and can be treated of more quickly. Set around the start of the 60s, it presents the world of Madison Avenue advertising executives, boozy lunches and secretary harassing very much included. Although it, like the other shows, attempts to atone for this by having a central and powerful female lead, still my read on this show is that, seeing reality is no longer receptive to attitudes that many men yearn for, the creators simply ignored reality.

Before going on, I want to consider some counter responses to the line I've just suggested, before recapping a bit. I first argued that 90s art reflected a rejection of contemporary mores in favor of a mythical time, then that, in a different way, so does 2010s art. But you might think: that's not so! As I've mentioned, each of these shows have clear and strong female protagonists, and not only in an idealized perfect woman sense, but as having flaws and, well, character. Peggy, Cersei, Theresa Cullen—are all strong interesting female characters. And below we'll see some other female-centric shows.

Nineties to Now

Or consider—as we haven't yet—race. One of the most noteworthy differences between contemporary (televised) pop culture and that which preceded it is the presence of people of color. This is clearest in the case of sitcoms, where it is now ubiquitous that main characters of American sitcoms at least roughly correspond to the actual demographic facts of a country in which about 40 percent of people are Latino/a or Black.

You might think that these two facts are reflective of the fact that art today has internalized the lessons of the 70s in a way that art of the 90s hadn't (you can count the number of people of color in *Seinfeld*, *The Simpsons*, and *Twin Peaks*, literally, on one hand, and they are all at very best peripheral characters). Indeed, recalling the interest in the notion of "representation," something that was seen as an important feature of the 90s culture wars, one might think that it's mission accomplished.

It will be helpful to consider an example. Watching a sitcom today—say *Brooklyn Nine-Nine* (debuting in 2013)—you might not notice, unless it was pointed out to you, that most of the cast isn't white (although tellingly, the protagonist is). In the slightly later (2015) *Superstore*, the protagonist is in fact a Latina.

Faced with this, we might think real progress has been made. But it's worth noting that it's a peculiar sort of progress. In our discussions of race and gender, we saw the importance of a plurality of perspectives, each of which can contribute something to the production of knowledge or culture. But it's important to note that there are different, more or less good, ways of having that plurality. In the essay of Patricia Hill Collins we discussed which introduces the notion of standpoint, she writes:

> Although designed to represent and protect the interests of powerful White men, neither schools, government, the media and other social institutions that house these processes nor the actual epistemologies that they promote need be managed by White men themselves. *White women, African-American men and women, and other people of color may be enlisted to enforce these connections between power relations and what counts as truth* [p. 253, my italics].

In light of this, we should be open to the unhappy possibility that the diversification we see on our TV screens is not reflective of a deep underlying change in attitudes (a fact supported by the continuing misogynistic portrayals of women I have presented), but rather something like a sop thrown to people to satisfy them while not enacting real change.

I think this is a possibility that needs to be seriously considered. Take the protagonist of *Superstore*, Amy Sosa. Arguably, her Latina

13. Pop Culture Today

roots and her being a woman (indeed, a single mom) in a position of power don't get reflected too much in the plots of the sitcom. We don't see her really struggling with daycare or with preschool, with Trump-supporting customers or, perhaps, Trump-supporting extended family.

And it's notable, as a quick check on Wikipedia will confirm, that almost all the episodes were written by white men. For Collins, these two points might seem to go together: there is an absence of a strong Latina presence behind Amy because she is being written by white men who don't have access to her standpoint.

The point extends, indeed almost grotesquely, when we consider *Brooklyn Nine-Nine*. Its cast is almost all people of color, the boss is a Black man, but ... they are *police*. It doesn't require being particularly far left to be aware of the ghoulishness of the United States' prison-industrial complex, which locks up and thus disenfranchises—for profit—huge numbers of Black people. Captain Holt being Black can't make up for that.

On this—pessimistic but perhaps realistic—line, the 2010s, superficial diversity, and the occasional socially relevant plot notwithstanding, it is still a white male production, even if it appears more diversified.

Ultimately, I'm not sure what conclusion to draw from this. It certainly seems not great that it's predominantly white men who do the writing, and who thus create the art. And if you buy the line I've just given, that the mere presence of diversity does not imply that the real diversity of standpoint found in the world is reflected in art, then we are compelled to say that the 2010s and the 90s are of a piece in this important respect, reflecting as they do white male perspectives.

Not completely, of course. One of the standout shows of the 2010s was HBO's *Girls*, which told the story of young women and young women's problems. On the other side of the Atlantic, Phoebe Waller Bridge's *Fleabag* did something similar also to very wide and well-deserved acclaim. And perhaps the defining show of the last third or so of the millennium has been the adaptation of Margaret Atwood's *The Handmaid's Tale*, which is straightforwardly about misogyny and male control of sex. Even with these shows, I think there is a sense, to some at least, that they are primarily *aimed at woman*. By contrast, when a show is aimed at, or supports the worldview of men, like the shows we have discussed, it gets called universal.

To recap the rather sinuous argument of this section, I first argued that dramatic art underwent notable *stylistic* changes, as we moved toward less playful, less postmodern dramatic forms. But I also argued, somewhat more tentatively toward the end, that there was an interesting *thematic* commonality between these two notable bodies of work, and that was that both have not taken on board the progressive lessons of the 70s. Pop culture in the 2010s was still in opposition, albeit perhaps not quite so conscious and intentional opposition, and with some fighting against the tide, to developments in society.

Let me turn now to televised comedy, on which I spent a lot of time, because I think it represented some of the best work available. How do things stand with sitcoms in 2021?

It will be helpful to answer this question to consider, all in one go, the sitcoms going back to the 2000s. I think a more or less canonical list would be the following: *Brooklyn Nine-Nine, Superstore, Parks and Recreation, The Office, 30 Rock, Arrested Development*. Are there any interesting themes or pattern we can discern in these works?

I think there clearly are. In order to see this, recall that I argued that *The Simpsons* was paradigmatically postmodern television. It will be helpful to pinpoint four features of postmodernism that are particularly relevant: (i) a mixing of high and low culture, (ii) a playfulness about form and recognition of itself as fictive, (iii) a tendency toward presenting a lot of factual information about the world, and (iv) a mixing of the personal with events of social or world historical momentousness. (Confusingly, postmodernism in this sense is a bit different from the postmodernism of Baudrillard, Lyotard, and Foucault, who are more, one might think, straightforwardly philosophical. We could call this cultural postmodernism, if a label helps.)

Thomas Pynchon's 1974 *Gravity's Rainbow* is paradigm (cultural) postmodernism: it's a story about the Second World War where psychological and mathematical theories appear alongside vaudeville and scatological humor (i), a story so meticulously researched that you can acquire a lot of information about war-torn London (about the German weaponry used on it, about what songs were playing on what radio station on what day at what hour, about much else) from reading it (iii), a story in which the fate of the Allies is tied up with the erections of its sillily named protagonist Tyrone Slothrop (i, iv). Other paradigm works which exhibit postmodernism's playfulness and awareness of itself as fictive (i.e., [ii]) include Paul Auster's *New York Trilogy* (with its protagonist called Paul Auster), David Foster Wallace's *The Pale King* (a central character in which is called David Wallace), and John Barth's *Lost in*

13. Pop Culture Today

the Funhouse, which is a collection of short stories about what it is to be a short story.

With that in mind, consider *Brooklyn Nine-Nine* (which, as mentioned, first aired in 2013). Does it have any of these features? I suggest that the answer to this is no. *Brooklyn Nine-Nine* is good simply because it's a good sitcom. It relies on no playfulness, it doesn't concern itself much with grand sociopolitical events, its tone is even, it doesn't wink to the camera and break the fourth wall to let the reader know that it is a sitcom. It wouldn't—apart from the fact that people of color occupy most of its main roles and it's otherwise much more socially progressive—be out of place in the 1980s.

So what, you might think. Why expect TV sitcoms to be postmodern? Well, because they were. To see this, rewind a bit.

What came before *Brooklyn*? Well, for one, the U.S. version of *The Office*. Now let's again ask: does it have any postmodern features? Not really, apart from one thing: it's a mockumentary. This is a very important feature (a feature shared by the in other respects similar *Parks and Recreation*, which I view as of a piece with *The Office*). The reason for this is that it lets the writers break the fourth wall and thus the show can convey an awareness of itself as a fiction (thus exhibiting the paradigm postmodern feature [ii]) while giving us, in other respects, a straight sitcom. It essentially does this by cleverly bringing the fourth wall into the show, so it can break it while still remaining in its own self-contained fictional universe. Jim can look at the camera when Dwight does something ridiculous and we can feel that he's looking out at us, that it's an in-joke. This lets the viewer have their postmodern distanced comfort, but it doesn't serve quite the alienating effect that traditional fourth-wall breaks have. Jim breaks the fourth wall without really doing so because the fourth wall is part of the show itself, and this allows the writers to maintain a tone of sincerity. In the same vein, I think it's extremely pertinent that many of the most emotionally charged scenes in *The Office* adopt a particular and interesting strategy: silence.

Thus think about when Michael leaves the office (season 22 episode 7); he doesn't get the chance to say goodbye to Pam. Although their relationship has had its ups and downs, there is real love there. She goes to the airport to say goodbye to him, and then—we don't hear what she says. The camera is too far away. They speak, they hug, and he leaves. What is so good about this moment, in my understanding, is that it manages to find a way around the Umberto Eco quotation about how it is impossible to verbalize love in postmodern times because corny movies and pop songs have exhausted the significance of the word. *The Office* gets around this by simply not letting us hear the words, which would anyway, for Ecovian reasons, possibly fall flat or sound mawkish.[2]

My read of this is that in 2005, when the show started, a straight-up sitcom would have felt off to viewers. They were used—as we'll see in a second—to their comedy being more self-aware, more playful with form. A straight-up portrayal of people working, living, and loving at a paper office wouldn't have flown. The mockumentary format, I propose, was used to wean viewers away from postmodernism.

To see this, consider what comes before *The Office*. *Arrested Development* (beginning in 2003) is arguably the standout early postmillennial sitcom.[3] And with it we are in postmodern territory. It plays with form (ii). It has a narrator who is not an impartial observer and recorder of events: he interjects his own opinions, corrects people when they get his name wrong, and so on (it's a bit pretentious to say so, but what is really going on here is that the show is challenging the idea that there is one canonical, official story to be told about some event—it is anti-metanarrative). It is endlessly self-referential: many jokes (about chicken dancing, cornballers, *Star Wars* reenacting) pop up again and again, referring back to themselves (what fancy theorists would call inter-, or rather intra-, textuality). It has the Pynchonian mixture of the personal and the political (iv), as when petty crook George Bluth finds himself involved in the Iraq War. It is crammed with (albeit fictional) information (iii), presented in a documentary format—websites, news reports, ads for old products, and so on. It even has silly Pynchonian names (GOB, Maeby, etc.)!

If you weren't convinced before, I hope you're now coming round to the thought that postmodernism has been a part of recent sitcoms.

What was before *Arrested Development*? Now we're in the 90s, and we have *The Simpsons* and *Seinfeld*. Playing with form (ii) is almost compulsive: from *Seinfeld*'s show within a show about nothing to Bart whistling *The Simpsons* theme while sliding down the banister. The personal and the political are completely flattened in *The Simpsons* (iv). In it, you can watch an episode the premise of which was that Homer squabbles with a former president who is also his neighbor, for example. And it contains a lot of factual information (iii): your present author's first exposure to the course of American postwar history came from watching the show. Finally, it blends high and low culture (i): it's the sort of show you literally need annotations for, but a lot of its humor is just: Homer falls down or hurts himself. It has all the features of the

13. Pop Culture Today

postmodern, I claim. Arguably, in fact, *The Simpsons* is the most postmodern work in any medium there has yet been.

What's the point of this reverse chronology? Well, played forward, this is what it suggests: U.S. sitcoms have gradually been depostmodernizing themselves. The reason for this, plausibly, is just that *The Simpsons* did postmodernism so well that people had to try something else, but at the same time they couldn't move away from the postmodern model too quickly because it would jar with audiences. So, instead, we witnessed it gradually happen: gradually postmodern features got taken out of the best sitcoms, and so today we watch Andre Braugher as Ray Holt helming a precinct which—diversity notwithstanding—wouldn't be out of place in pre–Simpsonian times. TV sitcoms have gone past the postmodern and have looped back around: they are, let's say, post-postmodern.

Another way to see this is by concentrating on plot and character, as opposed to merely stylistic elements like (i)-(iv). Here again there is a gradual but marked change. In particular, there is a gradual move away from absurd, unrealistic characters and from absurd plots, to more realistic people and plots.

Thus *The Simpsons* is peopled with zany characters and plots. Homer himself is absurdly stupid; Bart occasionally bursts into 18th-century cockney argot, and so on. Moreover, the plots and themes of *The Simpsons* are, the first few seasons notwithstanding, absurd. *Arrested Development* is the same: GOB is a highly ridiculous character, as is Buster, although it does have straight characters.

Especially noteworthy is the absence of love in these 90s/early millennium sitcoms. Michael from *Arrested Development* (not to speak of his parents), Liz from *30 Rock*—for the most part, the course of true love doesn't run smooth there, and the real relationships (Michael and George Michael, Liz and Jack) are non-romantic and thus less intense. By contrast, from *The Office* to *Parks and Recreation* to *Superstore*, depictions of realistic romantic relationships become more common. Pam and Jim, Lesley and Ben, Jake and Amy are, for some, #relationship-goals, things in which you can recognize yourself or find something to aspire to. They speak to us in a different way from their more superficial forebears from a previous era. Michael Scott is, I think, one of the great fictional creations of recent decades; even smaller characters like Jan or Ryan are drawn so perfectly well that they almost seem like friends (enemies) of yours.

What this suggests to me is that we are in an era, when it comes to sitcoms, of realism. Although of course primarily aimed at making us laugh, to a large extent they also attempt to tap into other feelings we have.

I believe the point also stands when we turn to literature. In order to see this, I think it's useful to draw a comparison between the standout voice of the millennial generation, Sally Rooney, and that of Generation X, David Foster Wallace. The former excels in telling psychologically astute and relatable stories that, to a large extent, focus on relationships. Her style is spare and unfussy, with a keen ear for dialogue, and her plots are entirely realistic: boy meets girl, there's some issues, and so on. Her most famous book begins with a quotation from George Eliot and is the sort of thing that one could call a comedy of manners, of the perils of negotiating love across the institutions of contemporary youth—school, university, the first serious relationship.

David Foster Wallace ... does something else. I've already spoken about this some but just to reiterate, he favors, to a large extent, wacky plots. As his friend Jonathan Franzen noted, his novels are empty of love. Dialogue, as critics have pointed out, is not his strong suit, with many of his characters ending up sounding kind of like the narrator voice (also the voice to be found in his nonfiction).

So here's a claim: Sally Rooney is to *Brooklyn Nine-Nine* as David Foster Wallace is to *The Simpsons*. And I want, although I must admit that my grounds for this claim seem weaker and are more open to the accusation of cherry picking, to suggest that something similar to the depostmodernizing effect we saw in the sitcom also holds for literary fiction.

That story would go something like this. We should view David Foster Wallace, with his claim to leave ironizing behind (seen in a previous chapter), as the end of literary postmodernism which began roughly with people like Pynchon, and just as the 2000s, in sitcoms, saw a gradual shift away from postmodernism, so did literary fiction.

So, for example, one could note that Jonathan Franzen's 2000 novel *The Corrections*, widely hailed as one of the best novels of the new millennium, has some postmodernist features but also shows a movement toward realism (indeed, Franzen explicitly said that he was trying to move away from Pynchon-esque postmodernism).

It's worth talking about it a bit. Here are some elements of the book that might lead one to brand it as "postmodern." One of the main characters, for a while, teaches near the "newly rechristened Viacom arboretum"; the same teacher analyses a set of advertisements which had been

13. Pop Culture Today

given, like a normal television show, a Nielsen rating indicating how many people watched it; yet the same character, in something not out of place among the perversions of Pynchon or especially Roth, fucks a chair before—this being somewhat of a low point—going into business with a Lithuanian politician from the party VIPPAKJRIINPN17, i.e., the One True Party Unswervingly Dedicated to the Revanchist Ideals of Kazimieras Jaramaitis and the "Independent" Plebiscite of April 17, one of whose aims is to privatize the country, whose utilities were privatized and sold to a hedge-fundie in the way that (when squinted at, at least) happened to newly uncommunist countries in the mid- to late 90s.

From that synopsis (which only covers the roughly first-quarter of the book I reread in preparation for the above paragraph) you might think we are still in high postmodern mode: the absurdist humor, the world-political intrigue, the obsession with the media, and so on.

But this isn't so. For the most part it's a compelling and movingly told story that focuses, with a deep and serious attention, on the truly profound: aging, sickness, and death, and growing up in the U.S. at the end of the century. It does so with great sensitivity and insight; when one reads about (or indeed experiences firsthand) how novels have the power to change one emotionally, this is the sort of novel they mean.

Indeed, so successful was it at this that—notoriously—it was chosen as an Oprah's Book Club pick which Franzen—bizarrely—was unhappy about. The details are available online for those who care about gossip, but it's a very clear case of someone serving the twin masters of compelling literary realism while weaning himself off postmodernism which I take to be typical of the era.

From around the same time, Jonathan Safran Foer's novel *Extremely Loud and Incredibly Close* is about 9/11 and is very formally inventive: its pages contain pictures and illustrations of various sorts. But these postmodern features, arguably, are balanced by a sadness at heart and a compelling narrative voice. Again, I'd want to say we have here half-in, half-out postmodernism. The third novel that I think arguably illustrates this is Junot Díaz's 2007 *The Brief Wondrous Life of Oscar Wao*. It has many postmodern features—it's literary fiction about a guy obsessed with pop culture, it plays with form by having footnotes, in which it presents factual information. But at the same time, and as with *Extremely Loud*, much of its charm is in the characterization and plotting, and it is much less clearly postmodern.

Now, I don't want to rest too much weight on any of this. These are after all but three novels, and indeed three novels by men. And there are many, so many novels that were popular and successful but which don't, as far as I can tell, fit my narrative: Cormac McCarthy's *The Road*, Barbara Kingsolver's *The Poisonwood Bible*, Jennifer Egan's *A Visit from the Goon Squad*, for three examples off the top of my head are both extremely popular and influential and neither clearly nor clearly not postmodern (although Wikipedia tells me that the latter has a section formatted like a PowerPoint slide, something I must have missed when listening to the audiobook). Here, perhaps more than anywhere, there's a risk that I've cherry-picked the works I talk about to serve my overall narrative, so caveat lector.

In sum, then, I think we can say that there's *some case* for saying that the 2000s in literary fiction, to a large extent, followed the same evolutionary path as sitcoms did.

Taking Stock

Before going on, I want to take a quick break and consider the findings so far. I have made the case that in sitcoms, literature, and drama, there has been a depostmodernizing effect, and a turn toward realism, at least as far as possible. Gone is the zany and maximalist, and it has been replaced by more or less stylistically straight programs.

The first thing to note is that this trend toward difference is somewhat different from the trend we saw in various other domains: in business and in the spectacle of politics, for example, the 90s can be seen to be continuous with the 2010s, with that latter decade making more explicit, perhaps prompted by the urging of events, trends that have been in place. Here, in pop culture, although we can spot the same gradual unfolding, the place we end up at, straightforward realism, seems markedly different from the postmodern surrealism where we started.

What explains this fact? This is an interesting and tricky question both intrinsically and also because of the structure of the overall argument so far. Because note that when I discussed the pop culture of the 90s, I attempted to explain features of it by appeal to features of the wider world in which its creators grew up, and in particular I made the case, at length, that the pop culture of the 90s should be seen as a reaction to the events of the 70s, and thereby as implicitly in dialogue with the postwar period.

Now, if that explanation is to be anything other than ad hoc, one might think that it should apply here too. We would turn the clock back

13. Pop Culture Today

to, in fact, the period we have been studying, the 90s (which is 20 years before the 2010s, as 1970 is 20 years before 1990), and try to find features of the political/social/economic situation that could serve to explain the pivot to realism.

Ultimately, that's *not* going to be the approach I will want to take. But there is a potentially interesting answer along these lines, that I want to sketch just for the sake of it. It turns on some thoughts the Hungarian Marxist literary theorist György Lukács had about realism and non-realism (such as modernism) in art. I quote from literary critic Terry Eagleton:

> The great realist writers arise from a history which is visibly in the making; the historical novel, for example, appears as a genre at a point of revolutionary turbulence in the early nineteenth century, where it was possible for writers to grasp their own present as history—or, to put it in Lukács's phrase, to see past history as "the pre-history of the present." Shakespeare, Scott, Balzac and Tolstoy can produce major realist art because they are present at the tumultuous birth of an historical epoch [*Marxism and Literary Criticism*, p. 14].

There is something new for them to see and capture—the world as it is is topic enough. But not everyone is lucky to be placed at a time when a new epoch is coming, and when one is not so lucky, when "history is already an inert object, an externally given fact no longer imaginable as men's dynamic product," less realist forms replace them. For the Marxist Lukács, the failure of the 1848 revolution marks one turning point that somehow made history stale. I must confess to not quite getting the historical point, but I don't think that matters. Per Eagleton, Lukács thinks that if one is working in an era that is not the tumultuous birth of a historical epoch, one will be forced into irrealism, something he thinks typifies the movement known as modernism:

> In the alienated words of Kafka, Musil, Joyce, Beckett, Camus, man is stripped of his history and has no reality beyond the self; character is dissolved to mental states, objective reality reduced to unintelligible chaos ... both individual and society consequently emptied of meaning. Individuals are gripped by despair and angst, robbed of social relations and so of authentic selfhood [p. 29].

Now, one might argue that the worlds of the 90s are alienated in something like this sense—in the bombarding of pastiche image upon image, in *The Simpsons* and Tarantino, for example. We can recall Jameson's point that postmodernism is defined by an attitude toward history, an inability to present either the present or the past as fully itself and the creation of a sort of in-between style. Following that line, we would have it the artists of that era came of age at an ahistorical era and that was the cause of their non-realist styles.

Does that make sense? Arguably, yes. After all, as we have seen a couple of times already, the 90s were famously known as the era of the end of history, the time marked by the victory of capitalism and the demise of socialism. One could then try to argue that the retreat to formal playfulness in these works is a reflection of the fact that history is over but hasn't ended well. And then the birth of realism would be marked with the rebeginning of history, something we could perhaps date to September 11, and that would explain the increasing straightness of pop culture over the past two decades.

I think this is a kind of neat and interesting theory, and definitely worth some consideration. But I'm not sure if I can help myself to it. After all, a key thesis of this book is that the 70s were precisely the birth of a new historical epoch, and so, one might think creators who came of age then should be alive to it and should seek realistic portrayals of the new feminist multicultural descending middle-class, post-stagflation American people. Moreover, because I've been making the case that, when properly placed in its historical context, the seemingly radically different times we're living in are actually the working out of earlier trends, it isn't right to say we're in a Lukácsian period of history in the making. So, ultimately, while intriguing, this theory is not the one I will go for.

Instead, I think the natural thing to say is that continuity rather than difference is important, and a better understanding of contemporary culture is arrived at by considering it not as a new response to a new world, but as a continuation.

So, the move toward realism we witness in the 21st century is a reflex of intra-artistic logic, just as the move toward platform capitalism is a reflex of intra-brand logic. And I think David Foster Wallace hit the nail on the head: the postmodernism, the cynicism, the irony that he and other creators of the 90s used was good for some purposes, for making sense of an alienated world, but bad for others, such as capturing genuine human feeling. This flaw in postmodernism led to its overcoming in the post-millennium. This happened slowly, because people are reticent to move to new artistic paradigms too quickly. Again, I think sitcoms are the clearest example of this slow gradual process, as they *gradually* removed those features of themselves that made them postmodern, gradually shedding those features until they become more or

13. Pop Culture Today

less straight. On this view of viewing things, art evolves gradually in its own terms from one phase to another.

Continuity, accordingly, is a central theme, both in artistic and in extra-artistic life, and many of the things we might take to be uniquely definitive of our era are well understood as things that have gradually come to be over the past couple of decades.

But difference is also important. After all, I've just extensively made the case that we've moved from a postmodern to a post-postmodern era in art. By contrast, it's arguable that both the Starbucks of the 90s and contemporary platform capitalisms are well understood in the same terms, as two different points along the same dimension. Uber, you might think, is a brand on steroids, selling nothing but information, whereas there is a great difference between *Game of Thrones* and *Twin Peaks*, or between Rooney and Wallace. Sometimes the gradual process leads to what appear to be discontinuities, other times not. I take this to be a central finding of this study: that the present is best understood as a development of ideas latent in the past, even when—as in the case of art—there seems to be a big difference.

Another central finding concerns realism. I argued that work like *The Simpsons* is best understood, despite what it seems on the surface, as being in the service of a realistic portrayal of the world—its choppy, surreal, digressive style expresses what it was like to live in an era of ubiquitous television. I made the same case for the hyper-referential Tarantino and the surrealist Lynch. Overall, my assessment of 90s art was that it was good at portraying end-of-the-century life, that to be a realist then was to be a postmodernist.

But times have changed, I just said. We've moved on from postmodernism. And so a question naturally arises: if we have moved on from postmodernism, and postmodernism gives us the tools to understand a media-saturated life, have we deprived ourselves of the tools needed to represent and so understand life today, which, in the age of always on internet and social media has, if anything, just become more media saturated?

I don't think we have, and attending to this leads to a fascinating perspective on contemporary (pop) culture. I want to end this book by making the case that the postmodern aesthetic so apt for portraying the glued-to-screens lives we lived in the 90s and do so even more now has not, despite what we have just seen, disappeared. No: it's migrated to the internet, where social media is a domain of pop culture of its own where these attitudes persist. The result is a fascinating and entirely novel bifurcation of pop culture: we have the traditional media, TV and film, which has diverged from by building on 90s postmodernism, and the new media, which has stayed the course. I will finish this chapter by making, at some length, this point.

Social Media as Pop Culture

We see, then, in the domains we considered—dramatic TV, comedic TV, novels—contemporary pop culture has various and distinct relations to its past as manifest in the works from the 1990s we have chosen. We have seen background ideas—such as feminism or postmodernism—get worked out in different ways, as creators attempt to integrate them into artistic popular media.

A premise of this whole study was that by inspecting pop culture we could inspect what I called the spirit of the times—we could get a window into what people felt by looking at what they most liked to consume. This indirect method was both desirable and required—desirable because one might think that artists in a sense are better placed to express what we feel, and required because there is no clear other way to access this culture (at least, for one with my skillset, interests, and spatiotemporal location).

But things have changed. If 2010s culture shows many continuities with 90s culture, as I hope to have convinced the reader at this point, one thing is clearly brand new: social media. And in an era when world politics are carried out on the president's Twitter, any account of life today must take it into account.

So let's ask: where does social media fit into the theory presented here? How we can use it to tell us about what it's like to live today, in a way that is consonant with the style and methods of this book?

Various possible answers are available. One might think that the serious study of social media is undesirable, at least for a book concerned with culture. Even if one is on board with pop culture as an object of serious study, social media, you might think, is too lowbrow or irrelevant. Another possibility is that you might think social media is useful as giving us, without intermediation, the Zeitgeist, that rather than having to take the detour through what artists tell us, we can now in this democratized age use social media as a means of hearing everyday people talk. On this view, social media would be like a meeting place the Zeitgeist-seeker could hang about in. If this were the case, and

13. Pop Culture Today

interesting results would come from examining social media, this study would be notably bipolar. Starting with art, it would end with opinion.

My own take on this is that we should view social media not as an irrelevance, but neither as a marketplace. Rather, we should think of social media as the newest iteration of pop culture, and, as a piece of popular culture, as one that is extremely revelatory of the spirit of the time. As we will see, social media today exhibits all in one place many of the features of the 90s Zeitgeist.

Let me begin by defending the claim that social media should be deemed as a piece of pop culture. You might deny this. If you're open to the claim that it's possible that people can congregate online—just hang out, spend time together—then you might think that that is the purpose of social media. Social media doesn't appear to be an art form in any interesting sense: it doesn't have plots and characters and themes like any of the works we have considered. It is, you might think, a fundamentally different type of thing.

I think this line of reasoning can be shown to be false. Here's a quick and dirty argument for the conclusion, that is not in any way original to me. Social media is pop culture Uberized. Uber replaced what is seemingly the central parts of the transportation business—cars and drivers—with gig economy workers who supply their own vehicles and who bear themselves the costs of their illnesses and holidays. Pop culture, at least televised pop culture, is that form of art that sells content for attention-to-ads. Since social media sells attention-to-ads, it must provide content, and the Uberizer of pop culture will try to get by with just providing a platform for others' content (as Uber gets by with providing a platform for others' driving and automotive property). But providing a platform for the content of others is what social media does, and so if we accept that pop culture makers are Uberizing, as other businesses are, we should conclude that their platforms are Uberized pop culture.

That's the first bit of my argument. It's meant to raise your credence in the claim that social media is today's pop culture. It is not, I fully grant, a knockdown argument. After all, newspapers have been in the business of exchanging attention to advertisers for content for a while. So it could be that social media is something like a free, user-generated newspaper.

Here are some other reasons to maintain the (slightly weaker) claim that social media plays the same role in our lives as televised pop culture did in the 90s. Firstly, data bears out the claim that our attention has switched from the former to the latter; second, and more anecdotally, social media plays, in our day-to-day lives, the role of the latter. In the 90s we had water-cooler TV. As to the first, googling will give you an array of figures for how long we spend online, according to some of which it's up to six hours a day. It is natural to think that doing so has, for many, replaced watching TV. As to the second, get a group of young people around today (or even look at a WhatsApp thread) and you will see much silent passing of links to memes. Around the modern-day equivalents of the water cooler, there's more internet talk and less TV talk.

Recall another concept that I suggested was important for understanding the 90s, namely the spectacularization of politics, the idea of treating it as an entertainment. I traced this idea from the epochal Watergate hearings, when many people's first exposure to the corridors of power was via the televised hearings in which they were disgusted by the seamy, incompetent, and all-too-human aspects of their representatives. This continued into the 90s, of course, with Clinton, semen-stained dresses and blowjobs in the West Wing, and it spread into the pop culture, as I took pains to show: at the heart of *The Simpsons*, and its omnipresent TV, was a blurring of the distance between the political and personal, as we could jump from reference to reference from recent American political history. In a similar vein, there are things like Fox News—if *The Simpsons* is entertainment with a political focus, Fox News is politics with an entertainment focus.

One might think that politics was spectacularized in the most profound way possible when the president decided Twitter was the platform from which he would speak. An argument from this observation would go: whatever medium is used to spectacularize politics is a pop cultural medium; Twitter is used to spectacularize politics; so Twitter is a pop cultural medium. It's a weak argument, but not entirely, I think, devoid of force. We should pay proper attention to how strange it is that so many of us spend so much time engaging with politics online, when there is apparently little upside to it.

Let me consider finally some slightly more philosophical ideas. Recall what we saw when discussing the work on postmodernism on Jameson, and the films of Lynch and Tarantino, as well as *The Simpsons*. We discussed there a certain style of art, according to which elements of that art—music, character, cinematography—pointed to or referred back to previous works. This was the idea of postmodern pastiche, whereby because we struggle to bring the present adequately into view, we fall back on distorted figures from others' work to make our point.

13. Pop Culture Today

We lack an original vocabulary to make sense of our times, according to the postmodernist. But the crucial idea I wanted to present was that *maybe this was a good thing*. It was good, I think, that *The Simpsons* had the style it did, because it adequately represented the fundamentally weird nature of a life lived in front of the television.

As we have seen, this sense of aesthetic postmodernism waned in the more obviously pop cultural productions of the new millennium. We saw a move, albeit not a complete one, toward straight art; or sometimes we saw a move toward straight-up fantasy in a way that isn't postmodern. But then here's a reason to think that postmillennial pop culture has been lacking: internet culture shares many of the features of television culture, and so by abjuring postmodern style, contemporary culture becomes unable to present a realistic account of what it's like to live today, because what it is like to live today is interestingly continuous with what it was like to live in the 90s.

Now here's my suggestion: aesthetic postmodernism didn't die, it simply migrated to social media. Merely to scroll one's internet feed is a paradigmatic postmodern affair. Now you see friends' joys or sorrows, now dumb jokes, now anger and fighting, now the president. It's a weird mishmash of tones and voices, from the world-historical to the most ephemeral, and it fills our mind every day. The truly interesting thing is that this content is made by *we ourselves*, not by some fancy Hollywood scriptwriters or some Brooklyn MFA novelist. On social media, we are both the product and the consumer, and we are postmodern about it.

Let me try to substantiate this point a bit by considering some examples. It's an immediately and obviously noteworthy feature of social media communication that, to a large extent, it goes by the medium of memes. A meme is a paradigm example of aesthetic postmodernism. It is pastiche in its purest form, in the sense that—recalling Jameson—it somehow quotes without quoting someone. The original context of a meme—say, the distracted boyfriend meme—doesn't matter. When we use it, we are not referring back, quoting someone's previous use. We use it as we use any piece of language, to express our own meaning, forgetting about its context and history. Yet it still bears its context and history with it, as it bears the ever-increasing chain of others doing the same as us with it, expressing *their* own meaning.

Here's another sort of example, one which shows how social media mixes matters of importance with low-cultural nonsense. This is, I take it, completely obvious, but anyway for the sake of example. If I open my feed, I see first a video of a lawyer presenting the case for impeaching

Trump; then a retweet about an "AI for Good Global Summit"; then a cartoon (frame one: person looking at medicine bottle which says "keep away from children," asking themselves "wait, the pills, or...," frame two: same person in foreground with children behind, finishing the thought "in general?"). Finally, a tweet saying "Happy 189th Birthday, Emily Dickinson," with a picture of her.

Now, let's just note: this is *weird*. It's incredibly weird that these juxtapositions make up much of the media we consume, as our attention flits in all possible directions and our mood changes (we laugh at the cartoon, recall reading Dickinson in school, think about impeachment). To the extent that art should capture the interesting features of our life, it should capture this. And so, on my story, it does, because there is no sensible line to be drawn between this part of pop culture and life. To live online is to participate in pop culture.

And here's another example that I came upon when I first started thinking about these things that is, hopefully, helpful. A clickbaiting Libertarian decided to play devil's advocate and argue that even if the Grenfell tragedy of 2017, in which hundreds of people in a London tower block burned to death because of inadequate fireproofing, would have been avoidable by installing sprinklers, it wasn't necessarily the right thing to do. It's overly coercive, she claimed, to force people to install such things as they infringe upon one's liberty to get burned to death and spend money on other things.

How can one respond to such an enormity? Well, here's how people did respond. Among many others, a quick Twitter search revealed one person replied with a gif of *The Thick of It*'s Malcolm Tucker looking upset, and another with a screengrab from *The Simpsons*, of Homer, the caption reading, "Sure, it'll save a few lives, but millions will be late." This is highly typical: treating a highly political matter with bathetic humor which references old TV. Apart from its savagery—it's unlikely even Montgomery Burns would suggest such a thing—this is something that one could easily imagine happening in *The Simpsons*.

And finally, a simple one: the use of silly names. It's a somewhat bizarre feature of erstwhile avant-garde American literature that it is peppered with Oedipus and Vs, with Madame Psychoses and The Moms; and it's a bizarre feature of *Arrested Development* that its protagonists include someone called GOB (pronounced Job, as in the Biblical sufferer) and Maeby (whose fictitious cousin is called Shirley). And so it's noteworthy that even this weird and seemingly inconsequential detail about literature finds its way onto Twitter, where people regularly

13. Pop Culture Today

change their display name to something topical and un-name-like. Opening up my feed, I see someone with a display name "McKinsey Foucault" a conjunction of the consulting company with the French theorist of power.

This is what I think happened: the 90s were marked by a particular aesthetic trend across some of the most popular pop culture. That trend fell by the wayside in a way that we have just been exploring, but it didn't die. It *moved*, and in particular it moved to the internet. Like the spirit of a person reincarnated in a different body, the spirit of the age of the 90s in whose pursuit we've been has been reincarnated in contemporary internet culture.

And it did so in a particularly interesting way: because internetified pop culture is something we consume, but also something we produce, it reflects our interests and perspectives in a clear way, because it *is* our interests and perspectives. Social media is a pop culture that gives us directly what it's like to live in an age.

So, what about our big concepts, how do they appear on social media? An interesting example here is debates concerning representation, race, and privilege. I was somewhat equivocal in my assessment in the role such considerations played in televised pop culture: on the one hand, casts have undeniably gotten more diverse, but on the other, there's a risk that this is really an unacceptably bare minimum, and the feminist theorists we surveyed might respond that works such as *Superstore*, with its Latina single-mom lead, doesn't do enough to highlight the experience of single-mom Latinas. Televised pop culture, you might think, is kind of centrist on these issues. More liberal than some, more conservative than others.

What about social media? It wouldn't be easy to argue that it is too centrist. When these issues arise, at least in my extended corner of the social media world (which consists of primarily liberal/leftist people but also the people they dislike, and computer science and economics people), opinions are very heated. It's very hard to speak about in a way that doesn't caricaturize the idea, but at the time of writing many people expend a lot of time worried about what is called "woke" politics, identity politics, trans rights, freedom of speech, the value of science, the prevalence of racism, and so on. And social media is not a medium prone to mild sentiment.

Indeed, it has been thought to be a paradigm means of furthering what is called *group polarization*. Group polarization, according to Cass Sunstein, in an influential article entitled "The Law of Group

Polarization," is the apparently empirically supported regularity according to which if you get a group of people with similar views about a topic, the result of any discussion they might have will be that they will move toward a more extreme version of the view they previously each held. Put a group of people leaning pro-choice together and they'll come out more pro-choice, and the same for the anti-choice people.

Twitter seems intuitively a cauldron for group polarization. And indeed studies seem to suggest it—per the abstract of one, "Replies between like-minded individuals strengthen group identity whereas replies between different-minded individuals reinforce ingroup and outgroup affiliation. Our results show that people are exposed to broader viewpoints than they were before, but are limited in their ability to engage in meaningful discussion."[4]

The significance of this is as so. There is much discussion on Twitter these days about postmodernism, feminism, sexism, and so on. To take simply the example literally du jour (the jour on which I'm writing this paragraph). A Black woman physicist wrote an article entitled "Making Black Women Scientists under White Empiricism: The Racialization of Epistemology in Physics," in which she argues, among other things, that a failure to pay attention to women's voices while always being happy to listen to men leads to poor science. People are happy to fund research into string theory, for example, despite it being, in a sense, being inconsistent with empiricism as there is no way to test its claims (at present). By contrast, the scientific community is less likely to take into account Black people's perspectives about how science should be done, even though there is some intuitive sense to the idea that differing perspectives could yield different insights.

The actual argument isn't so important. But the style is: this is not an uncommon sort of thing to hear, and for such a niche topic, it has provoked a lot of attention: when first tweeted by the author, it got 180 or so retweets and 625 likes. Today, a few weeks later, it has provoked attention from various corners of the intellectual dark web, one of whom did a thread takedown of it, which has got 214 retweets and about 800 likes. In turn, a reply to that guy by a popular philosopher on Twitter got 236 retweets and 1.4k likes. This counts, it's fair to say, as pretty viral in the small world of physics-cum-Black-feminist-theory. People care about this stuff: some are wildly against it, some wildly for it. And every day, for at least the last few years, if you cared to, you could see people tweeting about related topics, retweeting the ones they like and snarkily quote-tweeting the ones they don't like. Whereas mainstream pop

13. Pop Culture Today

culture is tepid and uncertain (presumably because it's trying to reach as wide an audience as possible), internet pop culture is polarized and vicious (presumably because that's what gets the retweets and the likes and the follows users of the various platforms seek).

There's a very big worry that Twitter isn't representative, of course, and certainly one must admit that the vast majority of the population are not wildly interested in whether it's bad practice to study string theory while avoiding standpoint theory. But it's nevertheless clearly the case, I think, that a lot of people *are* interested in these topics, and not only philosophers and academics but more general onlookers.[5] People have opinions about these things, strong opinions, and opinions which hearken back to the Black feminist work we saw.

Moving on, consider cynicism and disaffection or irony. This, again, prima facie appears to be something that has been moved on from: much of our pop culture is straight. But one could argue that the vicious, meme-filled world of Twitter, where people get canceled and called out, quote-tweeted and ratioed with absurd memetic humor, is that of a culture that is angry and looking for a fight. A lot of this aggression (but not all of it) is across political lines, but one might think that the modern Twitter warrior is the heir to the unfeeling world of *Seinfeld* or the anger of *Fight Club*.

In order to bolster this case, I want to look at one example in some depth: the case of the political podcast, the most salient example of which is *Chapo Trap House*.[6] I think it is worth doing so both because the *Chapo* hosts are representative of how a lot of people think and because they are interestingly related to their 90s forebears.

Recall that I have argued that a defining feature of the 90s mood is disaffected irony, a sort of distanced attitude. The *Chapo* gang explicitly brand themselves as ironic. In the first few pages of their tie-in (but worth reading) book (*The Chapo Guide to Revolution*, 2018), for example, they present their "fully ironic ideology," some terms of which are:

1. Three-day workweek, four-hour workday
2. Health care, childcare, education, housing, and food are free and paid for by turning all existing billionaires into thousandaires and/or Soylent
3. The use of logic, facts, and reason is outlawed
4. Feelings become fiat currency [etc.] (p. 7)

In general, the book and podcast are motivated by a sort of disgust: disgust for the pusillanimous liberal, whom they portray as spineless and jerked ever-rightward by an increasingly malevolent GOP, whom one almost gets the sense they admire for their commitment to evil. Their discussion of the Left is peppered with words like "tepid," "void," "dainty," "wimp out," while their discussion of the Right begins, "We're openly, 100 percent evil," and the chapter ends with Lovecraftian gurglings. The GOP, they think, is straight evil.

This rhetorical strategy is by no means unique to the *Chapo* gang: there is a tendency in social media when faced with the latest Republican enormity not to respond with the reasoned assessment of why that is bad qua policy and for the country (which, the line would go, is pointless because the GOP isn't in the business of doing good or enacting sensible policy), but with scatological nonsense.

Consider this passage from the book, which is extremely typical of their style of humor, or of the style of weird Twitter:

> Endless and aimless struggle against evil is ... a great way to keep military budgets and their pleated trousers swole. The War on Terror is the bathtub our empire lies in, surveying a sunset over a wheat field in the Cialis commercial that is our twenty-first-century international statecraft [p. 35].

Or, take this tweet from (at the time of writing) six hours ago by one of the podcast's hosts and which has received 1.7k likes:

> Pete Buttigieg Murdering His Dog After Placing 4th In Iowa ASMR

This perhaps needs a slight bit of unpacking: the person mentioned (again at the time of writing) is a candidate for Democratic nomination for 2020; Iowa is an all-important primary state; ASMR is a new form of ... something that is popular on YouTube, whereby people read things in a particular hushed tone that is meant to evoke a physical reaction of pleasure. And "murdering his dog," well, it's dog murdering.

This, I would argue, has all the hallmarks of the *Chapo* sensibility, a sensibility shared by many on social media: a sort of weirdness that combines somewhat recondite pop culture references, political opinion, and violent or disturbing imagery.

But return to the quotation from the book. We have a seriously meant complaint about American imperialism mixed up with dick jokes. And now consider this passage from the stand-up comedian Bill Hicks, from the early 90s:

> See, everyone got boners over the technology, and it was pretty incredible. Watching missiles fly down air vents, pretty unbelievable. But couldn't we feasibly use that same technology to shoot food at hungry people? Know what I mean? Fly over Ethiopia, "There's a guy that needs a banana!" BOOM!

13. Pop Culture Today

> The Stealth Banana. Smart fruit! I don't know. Once again, I was watching the f'ing news, and it really threw me off. It depressed everyone, it's so scary watching the news, how they built it all out of proportion, like Iraq was ever, or could ever possibly, under any stretch of the imagination be a threat to us-wwwwhatsoever [Hicks and Lahr, p. 79–80].

In another routine, he says he saw on the news:

> There's a quote from Saddam Hussein going we have nothing against America we just want to see George Bush beheaded and his head kicked down the road like a soccer ball I'm thinking that's what I want to see [Hicks and Lahr, p. 173].

The tone is very similar. Similarly, although tonally different from *The Simpsons*, it is fair to say that *The Simpsons* incorporates the same distanced, noncommittal attitude, not to mention the callousness of the *Seinfeld* gang. There has been an ongoing response to the modern, especially political world that throws its arms up in disgust.

As I suggested with *The Simpsons*, it's unclear how much this disgust is helpful. Is it helpful to be told that the GOP is 100 percent evil? One could argue that that is just a lie, and a lie that misleadingly draws one further from political reality, that having one's rhetorical playbook be so constrained by irony prevents one from making the sort of genuine commentary needed.

That is to say, it could be that political satire in the 2010s, because it hasn't moved on from the irony and cynicism of the 1990s, has in fact had a harmful effect on political discourse.

Of course, it could also be that the opposite is true. After all, we are in the middle of an era in which socialism, which the *Chapo* boys favor, is viewed well by young Americans, and more generally we're in an era in which there is, from *Teen Vogue* to MarketWatch, from the scions of big business to the chattering classes' reading,[7] a much greater eagerness for the existing order to change, and a realization that there must be something better than neoliberal small-state capitalism. Maybe the tone in which that message needs to be conveyed, for the modern audience, is in terms of scatological tweets and podcasts, in roughly the same way that the GOP needs to mobilize its base by lying on Fox.

Against that, though, it's worth pointing out that the great white hopes (and, it's not incidental that they were white) of Anglo-American politics, namely Jeremy Corbyn in the UK and Bernie Sanders in the U.S., fell down, in their respective campaigns in 2019, pretty decisively, and against weak opponents. It might be that, words aside, things aren't really changing, and that might be because of the ironic fatalism that permeates the culture. It's disappointing, of course, that I can't offer a compelling case either way, but hopefully at least this book has framed the problem somewhat uniquely, and it's better to be true to an ambiguous reality than to force facts to fit your narrative.

But there remains a question to be answered. Why has the tone and attitude not changed in the intervening era? One answer would be that the political satire is responsive to political reality, and if political reality hasn't changed, then neither should satire. U.S. imperialism was already mightily apparent to Hicks in the First Persian Gulf War and the Iran-Contra affair; not much has changed as we fast-forward through the still-ongoing fighting in the same part of the world.

***

Let's sum up. If I wanted to present a neat narrative of the findings of this book, it would go as so. The 1970s happened, and they were epochal, seeing changes in economics, politics, and society more generally, some of which were good and some bad. The 1990s are best understood as a society responding to that, trying to make sense of what it was like to live in such an era. The retro-postmodernism, on my reading, played a twin role: it enabled artists to look back to a time which they took to be better, but, by eschewing realism, it paradoxically gave itself the room to adequately depict turn-of-the-century life. From then, continuity is important. Contrary to what we might by reflex think, we are better off understanding our present culture and society as working out themes already present in the 90s, with the very notable difference that postmodern culture left TV and the novel and migrated to the internet.

I think this is a neat story, and deserving of consideration. But equally important to note is the messiness of all this. There is no grand unified theory once you move to a finer grain: differences abound. Branding and business are largely well understood as continuous from the 90s to now, just being worked out in different ways as technology has made different tools available. The 90s' postmodern realism has gradually been sloughed off in contemporary TV and literature, but has done so in an interesting gradual way. The case of minorities has seen ambiguous progress: on the one hand, we now have diverse casts and writers, but at the same time, it seems that there has merely arisen a new set of misogynistic strategies, new ways of escaping from the real post–*Roe v. Wade* world. Some, but not all, of the lessons of the epochal

13. Pop Culture Today

70s have been taken on board. The internet, and the migration of the 90s Zeitgeist to it, permits no ready explication (at least, I haven't found one). More generally, we see some cultures which are responsive to historical events (the 90s responding to the 70s), and some cultures developing from previous cultures: two distinct styles of cultural evolution, that, at least as far as this study is concerned, must be considered brute facts not permitting an explanation.

Just as children inherit now eye color, now accent, now fondness for football from their parents by very different and often interacting mechanisms, so the mechanisms by which we inherit our culture are manifold and complicated, but in lots of cases, if the arguments of this book are right, we today are indeed children of the 90s.

Chapter Notes

Chapter 1

1. "The spectre of Vietnam has been buried forever in the desert sands of the Arabian Peninsula," George Bush candidly said (quoted in Howard Zinn, *A People's History of the United States*, p. 600); for the same sentiment in the media, see the *Christian Science Monitor*, March 14, 1991, https://www.csmonitor.com/1991/0314/astand.html.

2. https://www.nytimes.com/1995/06/18/style/the-short-shelf-life-of-generation-x.html.

3. For this somewhat annoying buzzphrase among the contemporary online left, see Aaron Bastani, *Fully Automated Luxury Communism* (Verso Books, 2019). A better book on similar lines is Paul Mason's 2015 *Postcapitalism*.

4. For the unradicality, consider this quotation from Noam Chomsky: "Bernie Sanders is ... considered radical and extremist, which is a pretty interesting characterization, because he's basically a mainstream New Deal Democrat. His positions would not have surprised President Eisenhower, who said, in fact, that anyone who does not accept New Deal programs doesn't belong in the American political system. That's now considered very radical." Or again, see books like Jacobin editor Bhaskar Sunkara's *The Socialist Manifesto*, which spends a lot of time arguing in favour of unions and codetermination, mainstays of post-war social democracy.

Chapter 2

1. https://ourworldindata.org/extreme-history-methods.

2. Or, indeed, as is sometimes overlooked, by cutting taxes for the rich with the goal of incentivising them to invest, a course of action proposed by Democrat Kennedy and later enacted by Democrat Johnson in 1964. See Wapshott, *Keynes Hayek*, p. 239 for this in particular, but also for an accessible account of post–World War II presidents' attitudes toward these big economic questions.

3. Introductory presentations of the Keynesian theory abound; in addition to the works already cited, a reader might like to consult Paul Krugman's accessible history of economics in the post–70s period, *Peddling Prosperity* (W.W. Norton, 1994), chapter 1; for more background to the rise and (partial) fall of neoclassical economics, *The Assumptions People Make*; for vastly more history than I have given, J. Bradford DeLong's online freely available economic history of the 20th century is also worth consulting. For more technical detail, pretty much any introductory economics textbook will do; the ones consulted here are Begg, Fischer, and Dornbusch, *Economics*, sixth edition (McGraw Hill, 2000), and Mischkin, *The Economics of Money, Banking, and Financial Markets* (Pearson, 2003).

Chapter 3

1. In case you don't want to mess up your search history, here's a discussion from mainstream media: https://www.cosmopolitan.com/sex-love/news/a39382/whats-up-with-the-rise-of-incest-porn/.

2. It's hard to pull a neat quotation

Chapter Notes

from Lynch on this, but the reader of *Lynch on Lynch* comes away thinking that Lynch himself isn't really in control of what he produces.

3. http://wiki.tarantino.info/index.php/Pulp_Fiction_Movie_References_Guide.

4. A reader for this press, in response to this, points out that pastiche is in no way a new artistic style that sprung into existence near the end of the 20th century. So we shouldn't say that this sort of style is (even close to) uniquely definitive of the 90s. However, I hope the weaker point that, compared with other eras, it is more prevalent is on firmer, although again not irrefragable, ground.

Chapter 4

1. When mathematician Alan Sokal, in the mid–90s, strung together a lot of postmodern jargon and got the resulting word salad published in an academic journal. It's worth noting that a similar thing happened in 2017, in the so-called Sokal Squared hoax, in which three provocateurs managed to get nonsense published in a number of journals, supposedly to call into question postmodern theory. We'll see a bit more of the continuity between the culture wars then and now, although it won't be a main theme. Wikipedia is a good resource both for the original and the updated hoax.

2. https://www.sciencenews.org/blog/scicurious/popularity-twitter-partisanship-pays.

Chapter 7

1. The relevant papers are a google away; here is a popular account in which you can find the references: https://www.vox.com/the-highlight/2019/5/20/18542843/intersectionality-conservatism-law-race-gender-discrimination.

2. One example: https://www.politico.com/story/2016/11/bernie-sanders-democrats-identity-politics-231710. Others are easily findable by googling.

3. Of course, Black people *are* disproportionately convicted of crimes, but most of us would want to say that instead suggests the representation of the police and criminal justice system as biased.

4. https://www.opendemocracy.net/en/opendemocracyuk/exiting-vampire-castle/.

Interlude

1. http://fair.org/extra/gulf-war-coverage/.

2. http://abcnews.go.com/Archives/video/march-1991-rodney-king-videotape-9758031?cid=share_addthis_widget. Needless to say, it's disturbing.

3. https://www.cbpp.org/research/family-income-support/chart-book-tanf-at-20.

4. https://www.gpo.gov/fdsys/pkg/GPO-CDOC-105hdoc311/pdf/GPO-CDOC-105hdoc311-3.pdf.

5. For the speed at which this history has unfolded while I've written this book, see https://twitter.com/MarkusforDC/status/1312247548082614272, posted the day before I submitted the final draft.

Chapter 8

1. At least there wasn't until the 591st episode, when Smithers came out. I thank an anonymous reader for reminding me of this fact.

2. Well, maybe. A boring biographical fact is that I wrote this book and then rewrote it two years later, and in those two years I have come to have much more sympathy for bothsidesism.

Chapter 9

1. From Oval Office recordings (for which see below), available at http://www.csdp.org/research/nixonpot.txt.

Chapter 10

1. There are of course works from the Latinate atrabiliousness of Robert Burton's *The Anatomy of Melancholy* to the neurotics and compulsives in Dostoevsky or *The Waste Land* or Baudelaire to the addicts of *Naked Lunch* that

discuss distress and addiction and are at least somewhat canonical, and this list could probably be expanded were I more erudite.

Chapter 11

1. http://www.dannydorling.org/wp-content/files/dannydorling_publication_id0901.pdf; https://www.theguardian.com/society/2017/jun/29/nhs-prescribed-record-number-of-antidepressants-last-year.

Chapter 12

1. See the references in http://www.oecd.org/officialdocuments/publicdisplaydocumentpdf/?cote=SDD/DOC(2019)1&docLanguage=En.
2. https://www.insidehighered.com/news/2018/10/12/about-three-quarters-all-faculty-positions-are-tenure-track-according-new-aaup.
3. https://www.youtube.com/watch?v=97NYPR-DABs.
4. https://time.com/3923128/donald-trump-announcement-speech/.
5. These sorts of issues—of whether there has been a "backlash" against the progressive advances—were stirred up by another book of the same era, Angela Nagle's *Kill All Normies*, which critics took to be arguing that calls for things like respect for gender identity and trigger warnings on campuses led to the alt-right. These debates seem to be ongoing, with much dull talk of "cancel culture" and "wokeness" on social media.

Chapter 13

1. For example (and this is literally just off the top of my head, from things I've seen recently): *The Americans, American Gods, The Ozarks, Start Up* all feature, very early on, sex scenes that serve no purpose other than discomfort (or titillation, if discomfort titillates you).
2. I owe the observation noted in this paragraph to Datri Bean. Of course, it doesn't apply across the board: there are many voiced sincere scenes that, at least to this watcher, also succeed despite falling foul of Eco's point.
3. Much of the points made here hold for the very slightly later *30 Rock*.
4. https://www.danah.org/papers/2010/BSTS-TwitterPolarization.pdf.
5. I write the day after the first Biden vs. Trump presidential debate in September 2020, where critical race theory, improbably, was one of the topics discussed.
6. Other examples include *Cum Town*, *Red Scare*, and many, many more. The names alone give a pretty good sense of the aesthetic.
7. For *Teen Vogue*, see https://jacobinmag.com/2019/10/teen-vogue-samhita-mukhopadhyay-interview/. For the much more surprising case of MarketWatch, see https://www.marketwatch.com/story/taking-the-racism-out-of-capitalism-isnt-good-enough-11598555456. For CEOs' changing conception of their aims, see https://www.nytimes.com/2019/08/19/business/business-roundtable-ceos-corporations.html, and for the point about the chattering classes, think again about the popularity, or at least renown, of people like Thomas Piketty or the magazine *Jacobin*.

Bibliography

Atwood, Margaret. *The Handmaid's Tale*. Houghton Mifflin, 1986.
Auster, Paul. *The New York Trilogy*. Penguin Books, 1990.
Barth, John. *Lost in the Funhouse*. Bantam Books, 1978.
Bastani, Aaron. *Fully Automated Luxury Communism: A Manifesto*. Verso, 2019.
Best, Steven, and Douglas Kellner. *Postmodern Theory*. Macmillan Education UK, 1991.
Bloom, Allan. *The Closing of the Western Mind*. Simon & Schuster, 1987.
Bloom, Harold. *The Western Canon: The Books and School of the Ages*. Harcourt Brace, 1994.
Brokaw, Tom. *The Greatest Generation Speaks: Letters and Reflections*. Easton Press, 1999.
Collins, Patricia Hill. *Black Feminist Thought: Knowledge, Consciousness, and the Politics of Empowerment*. Revised 10th anniversary ed. Routledge, 2000.
Coupland, Douglas. *Generation X: Tales for an Accelerated Culture*. Abacus, 2013. First published 1991 by St. Martin's Press.
Cowan, Tyler. *Big Business*. St. Martin's Press, 2019.
Davidson, Telly. *Culture War*. McFarland, 2016.
Díaz, Junot. *The Brief Wondrous Life of Oscar Wao*. Riverhead Books, 2007.
Eagleton, Terry. *Marxism and Literary Criticism*. University of California Press, 1976.
Ehrenreich, Barbara. *Nickel and Dimed: On (Not) Getting by in America*. Metropolitan Books, 2001.
Faludi, Susan. *Backlash: The Undeclared War against American Women*. 15th anniversary ed. Three Rivers Press, 2006.
Fisher, Mark. *Capitalist Realism*. Zero Books, 2009.
Fishman, Charles. *The Wal-Mart Effect: How the World's Most Powerful Company Really Works—and How It's Transforming the American Economy*. Penguin Press, 2006.
Foer, Jonathan Safran. *Extremely Loud & Incredibly Close*. Mariner Books, 2005.
Franzen, Jonathan. *The Corrections*. Farrar, Straus, and Giroux, 2001.
Friedman, Milton, and Rose D. Friedman. *Free to Choose: A Personal Statement*. Harcourt Brace Jovanovich, 1980.
Frum, David. *How We Got Here: The 70's, the Decade That Brought You Modern Life (for Better or Worse)*. Basic Books, 2000.
Gordon, Robert J. *The Rise and Fall of American Growth: The U.S. Standard of Living Since the Civil War*. Princeton University Press, 2016.
Harrison, Colin. *American Culture in the 1990s*. Edinburgh University Press, 2010.

Bibliography

Herman, Edward S., and Noam Chomsky. *Manufacturing Consent: The Political Economy of the Mass Media*. Pantheon Books, 1988.
Hicks, Bill, and John Lahr. *Love All the People: Letters, Lyrics, Routines*. Constable & Robinson, 2004.
hooks, bell. *Feminist Theory from Margin to Center*. South End Press, 1984.
Kaufmann, Eric. *Whiteshift: Populism, Immigration and the Future of White Majorities*. Allen Lane, 2018.
Kaysen, Susanna. *Girl, Interrupted*. Vintage Books, 1994.
Kirsch, Irving. *The Emperor's New Drugs: Exploding the Antidepressant Myth*. Basic Books, 2010.
Klein, Naomi. *No Logo: Taking Aim at the Brand Bullies*. Picador, 2000.
Krugman, Paul R. *Peddling Prosperity: Economic Sense and Nonsense in the Age of Diminished Expectations*. W.W. Norton, 1994.
Leitch, Vincent B., editor. *The Norton Anthology of Theory and Criticism*. Norton, 2001.
Lewis, Michael. *The Big Short*. W.W. Norton, 2011.
Livingstone, James. *The World Turned Inside Out: American Thought and Culture at the End of the 20th Century*. Rowman and Littlefield, 2011.
Mallaby, Sebastian. *The Man Who Knew: The Life and Times of Alan Greenspan*. Penguin Press, 2016.
Mason, Paul. *PostCapitalism: A Guide to Our Future*. Allen Lane, 2015.
Mitchell, E. Siobhan. *Antidepressants (Drugs: The Straight Facts)*. Chelsea House, 2003.
Palahniuk, Chuck. *Fight Club*. Norton, 2005.
Patterson, James T. *Restless Giant: The United States from Watergate to Bush v. Gore*. Oxford University Press, 2005.
Perlstein, Rick. *The Invisible Bridge: The Fall of Nixon and the Rise of Reagan*. Simon & Schuster, 2014.
Piketty, Thomas, and Arthur Goldhammer. *Capital in the Twenty-First Century*. Belknap Press, 2014.
Putnam, Robert D. *Bowling Alone*. Simon & Schuster, 2014.
Pynchon, Thomas. *Gravity's Rainbow*. Penguin Books, 2006.
Rodley, Chris, editor. *Lynch on Lynch*. Faber & Faber, 1997.
Roth, Philip. *American Pastoral*. Vintage Books, 1998.
Said, Edward W. *Orientalism*. Pantheon Books, 1978.
Schlefer, Jonathan. *The Assumptions Economists Make*. Belknap Press, 2012.
Schlosser, Eric. *Fast Food Nation: The Dark Side of the All-American Meal*. Houghton Mifflin, 2001.
Sirota, David. *Back to Our Future: How the 1980s Explain the World We Live in Now—Our Culture, Our Politics, Our Everything*. Ballantine Books, 2011.
Sorkin, Andrew Ross. *Too Big to Fail: The Inside Story of How Wall Street and Washington Fought to Save the Financial System from Crisis—and Themselves*. Viking, 2009.
Stiglitz, Joseph E. *The Roaring Nineties: A New History of the World's Most Prosperous Decade*. W.W. Norton, 2003.
Strauss, William, and Neil Howe. *Generations: The History of America's Future, 1584 to 2069*. Quill, 1991.
Turner, Chris. *Planet Simpson: How a Cartoon Masterpiece Defined a Generation*. Da Capo Press, 2004.
Twenge, Jean. *iGen*. Atria Books, 2017.

Bibliography

Valley, Eli, and Jon White, editors. *The Chapo Guide to Revolution: A Manifesto Against Logic, Facts, and Reason*. Touchstone, 2018.
Vance, J.D. *Hillybilly Elegy*. Harper, 2016.
Wallace, David Foster. *Consider the Lobster and Other Essays*. Little, Brown, 2005.
_____. *The David Foster Wallace Reader*. Little, Brown, 2014.
_____. *Infinite Jest*. Little, Brown, 1996.
_____. *The Pale King: An Unfinished Novel*. Hamish Hamilton, 2011.
Wapshott, Nicholas. *Keynes Hayek: The Clash That Defined Modern Economics*. W.W. Norton, 2012.
Wheelin, Charles. *Naked Economics: Undressing the Dismal Science*. W.W. Norton, 2002.
Whitaker, Robert. *Anatomy of an Epidemic: Magic Bullets, Psychiatric Drugs, and the Astonishing Rise of Mental Illness in America*. Crown Publishers, 2010.
Woodward, Bob. *Plan of Attack*. Simon & Schuster, 2004.
Wright, Lawrence. *The Looming Tower: Al-Qaeda and the Road to 9/11*. Knopf, 2006.
Wurtzel, Elizabeth. *Prozac Nation: Young and Depressed in America*. Riverhead Books, 1995.
Zinn, Howard. *A People's History of the United States: 1492–Present*. New ed. HarperCollins, 2003.

Index

Airbnb 8, 68, 72, 147
Areo (publication) 80
Aristotle 128
Atwood, Margaret 163
Auschwitz 51

Balzac, Honoré 171
Barth, John 164
Bastani, Aaron 14
Baudrillard, Jean 47–50, 52, 57, 63, 152
Beckett, Samuel 171
Bernstein, Carl 109
Bloom, Allan 84–5
Boom, Howard 84–5
branding 10, 68–73; in contemporary capitalism 147–8, 172–3; in *Generation X* 65–6; in *Infinite Jest* 126; in 90s art 66; in *Seinfeld* 65; in *The Simpsons* 66
Breaking Bad 31, 159
Brooklyn Nine-Nine 2, 10, 32, 74, 162–5, 168
Burroughs, William 46
Bush, George Herbert Walker 91, 108, 183, 187n1
Bush, George Walker 141–3

Camus, Albert 17, 171
capitalism: contemporary attitudes to 146–8, 150; in Generation X 15–6; in the post-war period 19–30; *see also* branding
Carlson, Tucker 107
Chapo Trap House 2, 87, 181–3
Cheney, Dick 142
Chomsky, Noam 119–22, 143, 148, 187n4
Clinton, Bill 6, 28, 91, 94–6, 108, 122, 141, 151, 176
Clinton, Hilary 84, 87
Coates, Ta-Nahesi 75
Collins, Patricia Hill 80–81, 84–5, 89, 162–3
Coupland, Doug 11–19, 40, 66, 116
COVID-19 95, 146
Crenshaw, Kimberlé 82–4
culture wars 75, 86–87, 162, 188

Dante, Alighieri 100
Darwin, Charles 50–2
Dickinson, Emily 178
Disneyland 48–9
Doom 96

economy 19–30; *see also* branding; capitalism
Ehrenreich, Barbara 72, 94
Ehrlichman, John 116–7
Engels, Friedrich 51
equality: for gay people 78; for people of color 79; in post-war period 20–1, 22–5; for women 75–8

Facebook 73
Faludi, Susan 76
Federer, Roger 124, 129
feminist theory 80–5
financial crisis (2008) 144–6
Fisher, Mark 52, 57, 86–7, 93, 146
Fleabag 163
Foer, Jonathan Safran 169
Foucault, Michel 55–7
Franzen, Jonathan 168–9
Frege, Gottlob 48
Friedman, Milton 26–7, 79
Frum, David 27, 77–8, 81
Fukuyama, Francis 92

Game of Thrones 31, 99, 159–61, 173
Gay, Roxanne 75, 89
gay people 21, 78–9, 81, 93, 98, 114
Generations (Strauss and Howe) 11
Gödel, Kurt 52
Gordon, Robert 20–1, 76, 149
Gulf War 11, 91–2, 101, 122

Haldeman, H.R. 116–7
Herman, Edward S. 120–1
Hicks, Bill 2, 182–4
hooks, bell 83, 84
House of Cards 160
Hussein, Saddam 11, 91–2, 119, 142, 183

Index

irony 5–6; among online Trump supporters 152–3; in David Foster Wallace 124–5, 130–1; in *Generation X* 17; in internet culture 181–4; in *The Simpsons* 101–2; *see also* postmodernism; realism; sincerity
It's Always Sunny In Philadelphia 61

Jameson, Fredric 31, 54, 176–7
Johnson, Lyndon 22, 120
Joyce, James 53, 98–111, 171

Kaufmann, Eric 154–6
Kellner, Douglas 49
Kennedy, John F. 49, 108, 110, 151–2
Kennedy, Ted 106
Keynes, John Maynard 22–8
King, Martin Luther, Jr. 79
King, Rodney 92–3
Klein, Naomi 68–73, 86–7, 94, 138, 148
Krugman, Paul 26, 144, 187

Laden, Osama Bin 140, 142
Lehman Brothers 145–6
Lewinsky, Monica 99, 152
Lukács, György 171
Lynch, David 3, 19, 31–41, 43, 54, 58, 89, 101, 130, 157, 173, 176, 188
Lyotard, Jean-Francois 50–2, 85, 113, 164

Mad Men 69, 76, 159, 160–1
Mailer, Norman 16
Marx, Karl 50–2, 80, 84
mental illness 9, 123–4, 132–8
monetarism *see* Friedman, Milton
Moore, Michael 94
Musil, Robert 171

Nirvana 93
Nixon, Richard 22, 49, 76, 108, 110, 114–9, 151, 188
nostalgia 7, 54, 59, 67, 82, 84, 89, 157, 159–60; in *Generation X* 13–8

The Office 32, 74, 164–7

Parks and Recreation 32, 74, 164, 165, 167
Patterson, James 77, 141
Paulson, Hank 145
people of color: changing socio-economic fortunes of 79; in contemporary political life 154–7; lack of representation 33, 54, 74–90; representation in contemporary media 162–3; *see also* Collins, Patricia Hill; Krenshaw, Kimberlé
Perlstein, Rick 27, 114–5
Piketty, Thomas 147, 189
Plath, Sylvia 126
pornography 38–9, 48, 58, 117, 150, 187
postmodernism 2–3, 31, 32, 34–6, 46–58; in contemporary culture 159–61, 164–70, 172–2, 176–8, 184; *see also* irony; realism; sincerity
Powell, Collin 142–3
Putnam, Robert 104–5, 150
Pynchon, Thomas 164, 166, 168, 169

Quilette (publication) 80

Reagan, Ronald 6, 14, 28, 49, 91, 100
realism: in contemporary art 159–73; in Lynch 34–40; in *The Simpsons* 101–4; *see also* irony; postmodernism; sincerity
Roe vs. Wade 39, 77, 81, 84
Rooney, Sally 2, 75, 168, 173
Roth, Phillip 16, 117, 169

Said, Edward 83–5
Sanders, Bernie 14, 84, 87, 148, 183, 187
Seinfeld 3, 6, 9–10, 17, 59–68, 71, 74, 112, 116, 123, 130, 162, 166, 181, 183
September 11th (9/11) 139–41
Shakespeare, William 85
sincerity: in contemporary art 164–70; in David Foster Wallace 125, 130–1; in David Lynch 34–6; in Generation X 16–8; *see also* irony; postmodernism; realism
sitcoms 162–3, 165–8
social media 56–7, 149, 157, 174–184
standpoint theory 80–83
Starbucks 70, 72–3, 173
Stranger Things 41, 74, 159–60, 167, 179
Superstore 162–3, 164

Tarantino, Quentin 17, 40–45, 110, 157, 171, 173, 176
30 Rock 32, 74, 164, 167
Tolstoy, Leo 171
Truman, Harry 49
Trump, Donald 50, 58, 88, 93, 95, 100, 110, 115, 122, 148, 151–7
Twenge, Jean 150
Twitter 174, 176, 178, 180, 182, 188–9

Uber 8, 51, 68, 72–3, 147, 173, 175
Ulysses 53, 98, 100, 106, 111
Updike, John 16

Vance, J.D. 153
Vietnam war 22, 92, 102, 119–22

Wallace, David Foster 41, 75, 116, 123–31, 153, 164, 168, 172
Walmart 69, 72
Watergate 6, 14, 48–9, 54, 63, 76–7, 95, 109, 114–8, 122, 143, 151, 159, 176
Westworld 31, 159, 161
Wittgenstein, Ludwig 51–2
Wurtzel, Elizabeth 124